PREFACE.

My object, in the preparation of the following work, has been to present the theistic argument, and the replies to the prominent modern skeptical theories, in such a shape as the best to impress the American mind of the present day. I have sought to reach this object in three ways:—*First*, by selecting from the vast material before me such main topics as seem most likely to affect those whom I address; *second*, by relying almost exclusively on this country as the basis for induction and illustration; and, *third*, by reducing the argument to such an analysis as will best subserve the purposes of students.

F. W.

Gambier, Ohio, *April*, 1859.

A

TREATISE ON THEISM,

AND ON THE

MODERN SKEPTICAL THEORIES.

BY

FRANCIS WHARTON,

AUTHOR OF "A TREATISE ON AMERICAN CRIMINAL LAW;" "A TREATISE ON THE AMERICAN LAW OF HOMICIDE;" "A TREATISE ON MEDICAL JURISPRUDENCE;" "STATE TRIALS OF THE UNITED STATES," ETC.; AND PROFESSOR IN KENYON COLLEGE, OHIO.

PHILADELPHIA:
J. B. LIPPINCOTT & CO.
TRÜBNER & CO., LONDON.
1859.

ANALYTICAL TABLE.

BOOK I.

EVIDENCE OF THE EXISTENCE AND CHARACTER OF GOD.

CHAPTER I.

FROM CONSCIENCE.

1*

CHAPTER II.

FROM MIND.

CHAPTER III.

FROM THE EXISTENCE OF LAW IN THE UNIVERSE.

CHAPTER IV.

FROM MATTER.

CHAPTER V.

FROM DESIGN IN NATURE.

CHAPTER VI.

FROM THE PROGRESS OF SOCIETY.

CHAPTER VII.

FROM GEOLOGY.

CHAPTER VIII.

THE RELATIONS OF GOD AND MAN AS DETERMINED BY NATURAL THEOLOGY.

BOOK II.

SKEPTICAL THEORIES.

CHAPTER I.

"AN IMPERFECT CREATOR."

CHAPTER II.

POSITIVISM.

CHAPTER III.

FATALISM.

CHAPTER IV.

PANTHEISM.

CHAPTER V.

DEVELOPMENT.

BOOK FIRST.

EVIDENCE OF THE EXISTENCE AND CHARACTER OF GOD.

CHAPTER I.

CONSCIENCE.

a. THE EXISTENCE OF GOD AS A LAWGIVER INFERRED FROM THE EXISTENCE OF CONSCIENCE.

§ 1. *a*[1]. *From conscience as to self.*

Let us suppose a stranger from some distant land to be dropped down at dusk on the suburbs of one of our great cities. On the unfenced commons where he alights he observes pathways, at first slight and ungraded, gradually expanding into paved and leveled streets, and lights, beginning with the old-fashioned and dim lamp, and brightening, as the city limits open, into the frequent and brilliant gas. He sees many places of danger, it is true, but he finds a corresponding number of guards. At one point he hears the snort of a locomotive dashing across the horizon, but precisely as there is a danger to human life from its approach, are precautions taken to make that danger less. By the country road a sign-post is planted. As the road draws nearer to the city, a sentry-box is placed at the juncture, by which a watchman is stationed to give warning whenever a train is due. So it is with respect to other dangers. In the fields or in the remote and sparse suburbs, a few constables are enough to keep the peace. But in the midst of the dense population which crowd toward the centre, the number of gilt stars and printed badges show that the precautions are multiplied as the dangers increase. That quiet, unofficial-looking man, who may be lounging listlessly at one moment in the lobby, or at another looking intently at the stage, is a special policeman, commissioned to be ready to spring forward at the first alarm to extinguish those sparks which the inflammable material collected at a theatre are so apt to kindle into a conflagration. Guards are stationed at the outside of a mock-auction store, cautioning the unwary against imposition. Others are seen, whose directions are to place a rope around a house on fire, so as to keep from it the curious or idle, who may be crushed by the falling walls. Others stand at depots or landings, watching the pickpocket, who is himself watching his intended prey. And all unite in proclaiming the one truth, which the traveler will not be long in discovering—the existence of a city on the one side, which is beset with many temptations and difficulties, and the existence of a municipal government on the other, whose office it is to resist these temptations and obviate these difficulties. The *police* prove both the *government* and the *temptations of that which is governed.*

§ 2. The same proof is afforded by conscience. The self-examiner is hardly able to take a turn in the recesses of his own heart without meeting one or more of the deputies of this indefatigable police magistrate. Wherever there is moral danger, a watchman is posted. Sin may advance through its subtlest approaches, but the watchful monitor is, nevertheless, ready to give warning. The stormiest gusts of passion or of lust are preceded by their own special cautions. Nor are these inward guardians lax in the discharge of their duties. It requires a long course of maltreatment to drive them from their posts. The experience of each one of us will testify to this. We can all look back to the time when we entered upon any particular course of sin to whose influence we may have ultimately succumbed. We recollect how vehement were the remonstrances of conscience, and how those remonstrances continued to be uttered in tones the most piercing until the watchman was either expelled or our ears became so hardened as to be unable to perceive his cries.

§ 3. b^1. *From conscience as to others.*

The police jurisdiction exercised by us over the conduct and motives of others, affords the same presumption as that exercised over ourselves. St. Paul incidentally draws an argument for the existence of conscience from this very quality. "Therefore thou art inexcusable, O man, whosoever thou art that judgest: *for wherein thou judgest another, thou condemnest thyself.*" In other words, the faculty of judgment as to others implies a correspondent supreme governing power. Must not the Chief Magistrate, who constitutes and directs all this mechanism, be Himself necessarily a judge?

§ 4. c^1. *From conscience as to abstract right and wrong.* So it is with the opinions we are constantly forming as to right and wrong. No man would take up a digest of decisions without saying, as he opened it, and, as he observed proposition after proposition laid down as the principles of determinations in the past and the precedents for adjudications in the future, without recognizing the existence of a law-promulging authority in the same way that the decisions themselves prove the existence of one that is law-applying.

b. THE EXISTENCE OF GOD AS AN UNCONDITIONED EXECUTIVE, PUNISHING THE VIOLATORS OF HIS LAW, INFERRED FROM THE QUALITIES OF CONSCIENCE.

a^1. From its action.

a^2. Incessant.

b^2. Unconditioned by time.

c^2. Unconditioned by matter.

§ 5. a^2. *Conscience is incessant in its action.*

We may be only conscious of that action at particular moments, but, whenever the curtain which covers it is lifted, we see its machinery, as we see that of a steamer when the engine door is unclosed, moving with an activity none the less incessant, from the fact that it had been unobserved. The agencies by which this spectacle is uncovered, and proof thus given of the incessant activity of conscience, will be examined under a subsequent head. It is sufficient here to advert to the effect of discovery of guilt by others as recalling the consciousness of remorse in its pristine vigor in the criminal himself, as well as to the similar effect produced by coming suddenly upon the spot where a crime was committed, or by having any of the implements or incidents of that crime recalled. Conscience, observed or unobserved, proceeds unceasingly in its task of pronouncing and registering a decree of approval or condemnation on each particular act. This process of registry is in nowise affected by its escaping our notice.

It is here that we find one of the chief retributive elements of conscience. It places the soul under recognizances to keep the peace; and, on each violation, judgment is entered for a specific penalty. We may not be conscious of this, but the judgment is, nevertheless, entered, and proceeds to accumulate interest until the period of execution arrives.

§ 6. That this process of judgment goes on even in reference to acts of mere carelessness, (and *a fortiori* to acts of positive guilt,) a slight observation will show. A lock-tender omits to fasten at night the gates of the lock. The next morning he finds that through an additional and unexpected force of water, the gate has been burst open, and the boats lying in the basin injured. A switch-tender on a railway, in like manner, neglects his duty, and still more serious consequences ensue. A servant forgets to lock a hall-door, and that very night thieves find their way in. Now in each of these cases the offender may be entirely unconscious at the time of the wrongfulness of the negligence. The fact of conscience condemning it entirely escapes him. But it is otherwise when the evil result follows. This lifts the covering off the registry, and shows him that the act received its specific judgment. Its moral condemnation was the result of its own inherent culpability, not of its consequences. It was the consequences that unfolded the condemnation. They did not create it.

§ 7. *b^2. From conscience as unconditioned by time.*

What I propose now to show is, that time has no effect in abating even the retrospective powers of conscience, but that the sentence of condemnation, recorded on us by ourselves, although frequently lost sight of, continues in full vigor, ready, whenever our attention to it is renewed, to be recalled in sometimes increased distinctness. We turn suddenly upon the spot where a crime was committed, and the judgment of conscience, condemning that crime, is revived in its early terror. The inanimate creation, in fact, bears an important part in furnishing the attesting witnesses to each decree of condemnation. In one of the most splendid rhetorical passages that literature affords, St. Paul depicts all creation waiting for the manifestation of the sons of God, and, like some huge, and yet exquisitely and most sensitively constructed animal, straining itself on tip-toe, so as to catch the first rays of that glory which is to release it from its own bondage:—

"THE EARNEST EXPECTATION OF THE CREATURE WAITETH FOR THE MANIFESTATION OF THE SONS OF GOD. FOR THE CREATURE WAS MADE SUBJECT TO VANITY, NOT WILLINGLY, BUT BY REASON OF HIM WHO HATH SUBJECTED THE SAME IN HOPE."

And, as creation will respond to and be united in the future deliverance, so it bears witness to the present penalties for guilt. It may be years since we visited the spot of a former crime, and that crime may have been long since apparently forgotten, but the scenery will at once reopen the old remorse. Nor is the witnessing of nature purely mechanical. It is not necessary to do more than refer to Mr. Babbage's theory of a future state, by which he makes one of the chief agencies in the misery of the lost, in that awful condition, to be the constant presence of an atmosphere which combines, in an acute and eternal pressure, every idle word spoken during this life of probation. For, as he shows us, the palpitation of the air, produced by the slightest of sounds, though it may be, in the dullness of our present senses, apparently lost, yet continues to swell and expand in continually increasing circles, until that momentous period when, by the infinitely sensitive perceptions, even infinitely attenuated utterances are appreciable.

§ 8. But these witnesses speak for the present as well as for the future. A very remarkable homicide trial, in one of our Southwestern States, may illustrate my meaning in this respect. A young man was riding a blooded mare, on his way to a distant county, where he hoped to establish himself and his newly-married wife. He was waylaid, and assassinated on the road, and his body so buried under a pile of leaves that no traces of its sepulture were visible. It so happened that suspicion was turned to the real assassin, from the fact that he was found in possession of the mare the deceased had ridden. The arrest was made, and the accused, under charge of the sheriff, was carried to prison over the very road near which the homicide was committed. As they reached the spot, the mare, which was ridden by one of the officers, began to display unmistakable evidences of terror, which increased or diminished as she approached or receded from a given centre. The attention of the party was arrested, and an examination was commenced, which led to the discovery of the remains in the grave where they had been deposited. The attesting witnesses of creation, both animate and inanimate, called forth into vehement and responsive activity the direct evidence of conscience within the breast of the prisoner himself. He quailed and shivered, and blood and muscle, if not voice, confessed. The invisible detective police of nature were called into action to enforce the decrees of the great Chief Magistrate who presides over the heart.

Even where direct association, such as that just described, fails to recall the consciousness and the pangs of guilt, imagination creates the wanting link. Göethe touches upon this with his usual delicate accuracy, in that famous scene where Faust and Mephistopheles visit the Hartz Mountain :—

FAUST.

Seest thou not a pale,
Fair girl, standing alone, far, far away?
She drags herself now forward with slow steps,
And seems as if she moved with shackled feet:
I cannot overcome the thought that she
Is like poor Margaret.

MEPHISTOPHELES.

Let it be;—pass on:
No good can come of it,—it is not well
To meet it; it is an enchanted phantom,
A lifeless idol; with its numbing look
It freezes up the blood of man; and they
Who meet its ghastly stare are turned to stone,
Like those who saw Medusa.

FAUST.

Oh, too true!
Her eyes are like the eyes of a fresh corpse
Which no beloved hand has closed: alas!
That is the breast which Margaret yielded to me,
Those are the lovely limbs I once possessed!

MEPHISTOPHELES.

It is all magic, poor deluded fool!
She looks to every one like his first love.

§ 9. We find, therefore, that our temporary unconsciousness of the action of conscience does not affect the permanency of its record. It may be, that at the time of committing a guilty act, we may, either through levity or intoxication, not have paused to consider its quality. That quality, however, exists, and if the act produces consequences, they will ultimately arouse us to the judgment pronounced on it. Nor is this peculiarity of conscience different from that of our other attributes. Dugald Stewart tells us that in reading aloud there is a distinct act of volition for every syllable, though probably if we had stopped to observe this volition, the process would have been suspended. This is no more than we are led, by our ordinary experience, to presume concerning conscience, whose action, accusing or excusing, proceeds with equal certainty when observed or unobserved.*

The action of memory gives us an additional analogy to the same purpose. Coleridge mentions a servant-girl,

---

* *Ante*, § 5.

who, in an attack of fever, recalled and uttered several pages of Latin, which she had heard her master, a clergyman, read aloud when she was cleaning his study.

Dr. Adam Clarke tells us that, when near drowning, his memory recalled, in a moment, all the scenes of past guilt.* Like phenomena are often observed in dying, among which, we may mention the case of Mr. Benton, whose eye, at that final moment, turned back to the scene of his Tennessee boyhood :—

Cœlumque
Adspicit, et dulces moriens reminiscitur Argos.

§ 10. Similar to this, are the cases Dr. Rush mentions of old Swedes, whom he attended at the Pennsylvania Hospital during their last sickness, and who spoke Swedish when dying, though, perhaps, they had not heard the language for fifty or sixty years. So it was that Dr. Johnson, in his last hours, passed from the sonorous cadences of those Latin chants, in which his mighty spirit had so much delighted, and was heard, by his attendants, muttering a child's hymn which had been sung to him by his mother when in his cradle.

A still more striking phenomenon is given in Wasianski's account of the death-bed of Kant. That profound philosopher, as we are told by the narrator, was afflicted most painfully, as his last hours approached, by the ringing, in his ears, of melodies which, in his earliest youth, he had heard in the streets of Königsberg. "These," Mr. Wasianski went on to say, "kept him awake to un-

* See Dendy's Philosophy of Mystery, p. 390.

seasonable hours; and often when, after long watching, he had fallen asleep, however deep his sleep might be, it was suddenly broken by terrific dreams, which alarmed him beyond description."

Mr. Rogers, in one of his Greyson Letters, touches, with great felicity, on the effect of association in recalling affections which had apparently long since been extinguished. A locket of hair, for instance, belonging to one whom we may have loved and lost, will have the power, if suddenly hit upon, of letting in once more upon the soul, in overwhelming power, the waters of grief. We may suppose that the affections which are thus resuscitated are now so torpid and numb as to be incapable of any acute sensations. We may even feel that we have reduced ourselves to a state of stoical contentment; all at once comes the lock of hair, accidentally discovered, perhaps in opening a secretary, and we feel ourselves overwhelmed with the bitterest grief.

Mr. Webster, we are told, for some years kept near his heart a little red-worsted sock, which he had taken from the foot of a child he had lost in early infancy. Perhaps this showed how deep and tender were the home affections which glowed under that iron breast. Suppose, however, after a long series of years had passed, that little sock had once again crossed the eye of the great statesman, would it not have told him a leading truth, namely, that memories may be buried, but do not die; that affections and impulses, though they be temporarily deadened, have yet immortal attributes, and that, with the soul, of which they are a part, they continue to live forever, either as elements of peace or of sorrow?

We have a kindred illustration of the same truths in a phenomenon which often accompanies the discovery of hidden guilt. A man may for years have concealed a crime, until at last he may have ceased to be conscious of its enormity. Suddenly it is discovered. All at once his old sensation of misery and remorse return. It is not merely shame at the discovery by his fellow-men, or fear of punishment; he may feel these abundantly, and yet there will be, besides them, an appreciable remorse; his old sense of guilt will revive, perhaps with all its former acuteness; he will then learn the great truth that remorse as well as memory has a substantive existence apart from the habits of thought and volition.

§ 11. The nature of remorse itself, as it is more fully discussed under a coming head, involves the idea of perpetuity. There can be no life-estate in remorse. It has been urged, as an objection to imprisonment for life as a punishment for murder, that it will be no check to the worst kind of offenders, since they will go on murdering, *ad infinitum*, the maximum of punishment being already reached, and there being no additional penalty. This position applies, with infinitely increased power, to a life limitation of remorse, as a moral discipline. The punishment can be avoided by doubling the crime; the murderer may so ossify his heart by drink, as to be incapable of even remembering his guilt. The worldly and ambitious may go on, in round after round of gayety or guilt, until remorse is choked by the very excess of occasion for it. The necessities of remorse, as a penal discipline, involve its continuance beyond the limits of time.

§ 12. c^2. *Conscience unconditioned by matter.*

There is a great deal in our intellectual structure to establish, and nothing to dispute, the proposition that THERE EXIST IN THE SOUL ELEMENTS, DERIVING THEIR TONE, IT IS TRUE, FROM THE COURSE OF PROBATION, BUT CONTINUING INDEPENDENTLY OF CORPOREAL CONDITIONS AND OF THE SANCTION OF THE WILL.

§ 13. The proof of this proposition may be considered as follows :—

a^3. *From the nature of conscience itself.*

The sense of guilt, as has been observed, is arbitrarily recalled to the mind in full force by involuntary circumstances, *e.g.* discovery, hitting upon the indices or scenes of crime, etc. As was shown in the last division, conscience, in its general sense, is incessant and unlimited by time. It acts with equal energy under circumstances of bodily ease and strength, and of bodily wretchedness and debility; in the first conceptions of childhood, and in the last consciousness of old age. It is said to be a proof of the immortality of the mind that the body can be cut away, piece by piece, while the intellectual powers remain. But even when the mind is destroyed the moral sense continues to operate.

b^3. *From analogy.*

§ 14. a^4. *Recalled impressions.* No thought, as may be inferred from the phenomena stated above, is ever lost. The recollection of the servant-girl just mentioned, those of dying persons, those of drowning persons, serve to show, to adopt the language of President Hitchcock, that thought "may seem to ourselves to be gone, since we have no power to recall it. But numerous facts show that it needs only some change in our physical or intellectual condition to restore the long-lost impression."*

§ 15. b^4. *Dreaming* presents similar phenomena. An important Scotch lawsuit was depending upon the recovery of papers which had been in existence fifty years back, but the genuineness of which was disputed. The trial was about to be abandoned, when a very aged man dreamed that they would be found in an out-of-the-way parcel, which had entirely escaped notice. There they were discovered. There was no divination in this. Fifty years back, when a child, the old man had seen these papers packed away in this parcel. No *voluntary* action on his part could recall the impression. It existed, however, to be brought to light by a power outside of himself. It existed, to adopt an illustration already given, in the same way as the machinery of a boat exists in which we may be gliding over the waters. We lose the consciousness of the incessant, though quiet action of the works by our side until, on passing the engine door, it is opened, and we see the clean and smooth limbs of the pistons gliding up and down in their giant base.

The demolition of space and time by dreams is a phenomenon with which we are all familiar. Dr. Abercrombie tells us of a gentleman who dreamed that he had enlisted as a soldier; that he had joined his regiment; that he had deserted; was apprehended, and carried back to his regiment; was tried by a court-martial, condemned to be shot, and led out for execution; at the moment of the completion of these ceremonies, the guns of the platoon were fired,

* Hitchcock's Lectures, p. 136.

and, at the report, he awoke. It was clear that a loud noise in the adjoining room had both produced the dream, and, almost at the moment, awoke the dreamer.

Lavalette, in his memoirs, mentions a procession that was five hours in passing before his dreaming vision, accompanied with such a precise, though horrible measurement of time, as to make its registry on the dreamer's mind indelible. It so happened that he was able to time the dream by his watch to be within ten minutes.*

---

* The evidence to be drawn from these phenomena of the immateriality of the soul has not been overlooked either by classical or Christian antiquity. In the *Phædo*, Plato tells us that "the body is the prison of the soul; that the soul, when it came from God, knew all, but inclosed in the body, it forgets, and learns anew." Seneca tells us, "Corpus hoc animi pondus est." "I remember," says Dendy, in his *Philosophy of Mystery*, from which the points, under this head, are drawn, "in Fulgosius, a legend told by Saint Austin to Enodius. There was a physician of Carthage, who was a skeptic regarding the soul's immortality and the soul's separate existence. It chanced one night that Genadius dreamed of a beautiful city. On the second night, the youth who had been his guide reappeared, and asked if Genadius remembered him; he answered yes, and also his dream. 'And where,' said the apparition, 'were you then lying?' 'In my bed, sleeping.' 'And, if your mind's eye, Genadius, surveyed a city, even while your body slept, may not this pure and active spirit still live, and observe, and remember, even though the body may be shapeless or decayed within its sepulchre?'"

The same thought—the spiritual independence of the soul—is thus beautifully given by Longfellow:—

His lifeless body lay
A worn-out fetter, that the soul
Had broken and cast away.

§ 16. c^4. *Insanity.* Of the detachment of the mind from corporeal conditions when in this state, we have an illustration, taken from a statement of Robert Hall, after his first attack of mania,—"All my imagination has been overstretched. You, with the rest of my friends, tell me that I was only seven *weeks* in confinement, and the date of the year corresponds, so that I am bound to believe you, but they have appeared to me like seven years. My mind was so excited, and my imagination so lively and active, *that more ideas passed through my mind than in any seven years in my life. Whatever I had attained from reading or reflection was present to me.*"

The exemption of insane persons from many epidemic diseases, and their insensibility to heat and cold, arise from their attention being drawn from bodily suffering and external influences. "And shall not a cultivated, well-directed volition," agues, from this, Feuchtersleben, from his skeptical stand-point, "have as much, nay, greater power, than furious anger or the horrible energy of the insane?" But may not the inference be more correctly stated to consist in the proposition, that the control of the body over the soul is neither absolute nor perpetual?

§ 17. d^4. *Comatose state.* On this point we have the following statement from Sir Benjamin Brodie:—

"The mind may be in operation, although the suspension of the sensibility of the nervous system, and of the influence of volition over the muscles, destroys its connection with the external world and prevents all communication with the mind of others. It is indeed difficult to say when the external senses are completely and absolutely closed. I might refer to numerous facts, which have fallen under my observation, as illustrating this subject, but the following will be sufficient:—An elderly lady had a stroke of apoplexy; she lay motionless, and in what is called a state of stupor, and no one doubted that she was dying; but, after the lapse of three or four days, there were signs of amendment, and she ultimately recovered. After her recovery, she explained that she did not believe that she had been unconscious, or even insensible, during any part of the attack. She knew her situation, and heard much of what was said by those around her. Especially she recollected observations intimating that she would very soon be no more, but, at the same time, she had felt satisfied that she would recover; that she had no power of expressing what she felt, but that, nevertheless, her feelings, instead of being painful, or in any way distressing, had been agreeable rather than otherwise. She described them as very peculiar; as if she were constantly mounting upward, and as something very different from what she had before experienced."

"I have been curious to watch the state of dying persons in this respect, and I am satisfied that, where an ordinary observer would not for an instant doubt that the individual is in a state of complete stupor, the mind is often active even at the moment of death. A friend of mine, who had been for many years the excellent chaplain of a large hospital, informed me that his still larger experience had led him to the same conclusion."

§ 18. Sir Benjamin records the case of Dr. Wollaston, which is a remarkable instance of this.

"His death was occasioned by a tumor of the brain, which, after having attained a certain size, encroached on the cavities (or, as they are technically termed, the ventricles) of the brain, and caused an effusion of the fluid into them, producing paralysis of one side of the body; and it is worthy of notice, that certain symptoms which he had himself noted, and as to the cause of which he had been in the habit of speculating, proved that this organic disease must have existed from a very early period of his life, without interfering with those scientific investigations which made him one of the most eminent philosophers, and one of the greatest ornaments of the age in which he lived. During his last illness his mental faculties were perfect, so that he dictated an account of some scientific observations, which would have been lost to the world otherwise. Some time before his life was finally extinguished, he was seen pale, as if there were scarcely any circulation of blood going on, motionless, and, to all appearance, in a state of complete insensibility; being in this condition, his friends, who were watching around him, observed some motions of the hand which was not affected by the paralysis. After some time it occurred to them that he wished to have a pencil and paper; these having been supplied, he contrived to write some figures in arithmetical progression, which, however imperfectly scrawled, were yet sufficiently legible. It was supposed that he had overheard some remarks respecting the state in which he was, and that his object was to show that he possessed his sensibility and consciousness. Something like this occurred some hours afterwards, and immediately before he died, but the scrawl of these last moments was not to be deciphered."

To the same effect is a narrative of the Rev. Adam Clarke.*

§ 19. The Rev. Wm. Tennent, a Presbyterian minister of great eminence, and of the highest character for truth and simplicity, was attacked, when in his nineteenth year, by a lung fever, of whose effects he apparently died. "His body," to adopt his own narration, as given to us by one of those to whom he communicated it himself,† "was laid out in the usual manner, in the back part of a room in one of the old-fashioned Dutch houses. On Monday morning, when they went to put him in the coffin, a man by the name of Duncan, who was assisting, called out to the others to lay him down, for he felt his heart beat, and was sure there was life in him. His brother Gilbert derided the assertion of Duncan, and, indeed, there was everything to induce a belief that he was dead. The length of time that he had been sick, his emaciated body, his black lips, his sunken eye,—all appearances were against remaining life. But, after this declaration of Duncan, it would not do to bury him, and the funeral was postponed till Tuesday, when the people assembled for the burial. In the mean time, all means had been used to restore life. They were again about to put the body into the coffin, when again Duncan called out 'Lay him down, for I am sure there is life in him.' No other person believed there was life, and yet, so long as *he* retained this opinion, they would not allow the funeral-service to proceed.

---

* *Post*, § 169.

† See Letter from General Cumming, 2 Sprague's Annals Am. Pulp., p. 55.

The funeral was again postponed until Wednesday, and the means of restoring life meanwhile applied with the utmost diligence and vigor. At the time appointed, the people again assembled, and the doctor was sitting on the bedside, with a looking-glass in one hand and a feather in the other, trying them alternately at his mouth and his nose. At the very last moment, to the unspeakable surprise of all, he opened his eyes, gazed at them, and swooned away for about two hours."

Mr. Tennent lived to the age of seventy-two, and led a life remarkable for its integrity and purity. During the whole of this life he maintained that, while in this state of apparent suspended animation, his spirit was in a condition of vivid and beatified consciousness.*

§ 20. We may be permitted to add a well-authenticated American case. A gentleman, in a state of suspended animation, was given over by his family as dead, and was subjected to the usual preparations for burial. He fortunately was restored to active conciousness, and, as soon as he could express himself, detailed the acute horror with which he had watched, without the power of resistance, the successive arrangements made for his sepulture.

To the same point is the following statement, made by one of the companions of the late Dr. Kane :—"The soul can lift the body out of its boots, sir. When our captain was dying,—I say dying, I have seen scurvy enough to know,—every old scar in his body was a running ulcer. If conscience

---

* See, for a full narration, Dr. Sprague's Annals, etc. vol. ii. p. 52.

festers under its wounds correspondingly, hell is not hard to understand. I never saw a case so bad that either lived or died. Men die of it usually long before they are so ill as he was. There was trouble aboard; there might be mutiny. So soon as the breath was out of his body, we might be at each other's throats. I felt that he owed even the repose of dying to the service. I went down to his bunk, and shouted in his ear, 'Mutiny, captain, mutiny!' He shook off the cadaveric stupor. 'Let me up,' he said, 'and order these fellows before me.' He heard the complaint, ordered punishment, and, from that hour, convalesced. Keep that man awake with danger, and he wouldn't die of anything until his duty was done."

§ 21. e^4. *Lust.* A very striking case, which may fall under this head, is reported as having lately occurred in a Paris hospital. A man, notorious as a miser, was announced by the nurse in attendance as dead. In the next cot lay a pickpocket, who had been quietly waiting for the moment when he could crawl up to his intended prey and empty his gorged pockets. It was midnight, and the ward was deserted of its attendants, when suddenly an unearthly shriek was heard. The nurses rushed to the spot, and found the dead man, with his long-nailed fingers fixed through the thief's neck. The miser, apparently insensible, had felt the thief approach. The ruling passion of avarice was still raging, with unabated fury, within his almost lifeless frame. Outside of that frame it was about to rage through all eternity, torturing and tortured. But now, by one of those violent nervous efforts which prove so remarkably the ascendency of mind over body, the deserted frame was once more convulsed by the return of this unearthly lust. It was but for a moment, and then the miser and the thief fell lifeless to the ground.*

Colonel Chartres may be taken as a type of that class of cases in which lust survives the bodily mechanism through which it worked, and in which it was incased. Of immense wealth and of aristocratic connection every effort was turned to the gratification of animal passion. Even in his old age, his body burned to a cinder, the fire of passion continued unabated. Utterly impotent in body, he pursued the shadow of the same lusts with the same energy with which he had once pursued their substance. At last, a scheme was laid to entrap him, which resulted in his prosecution for rape. He was tried, convicted, and executed, though it afterwards appeared that there was perjury as to the overt act. Swift's epitaph is well worthy of study, not only for its fierce eloquence but for its psychological truth :—

HERE continueth to rot
the body of
FRANCIS CHARTRES,
Who, with an INFLEXIBLE CONSTANCY and
INIMITABLE UNIFORMITY of life, PERSISTED, in spite of
AGE and INFIRMITIES, in the practice of EVERY HUMAN VICE,
Excepting PRODIGALITY and HYPOCRISY :
His insatiable AVARICE exempted him from the first,
His matchless IMPUDENCE from the second.
Nor was he more singular in the undeviating *pravity of his manners*,
Than successful in *accumulating* WEALTH : for, without

* See an article in the Episcopal Review for July, 1858, by the present writer, from which a portion of the remarks in the text are drawn.

TRADE or PROFESSION, without trust of
PUBLIC MONEY, and without
BRIBE-WORTHY SERVICE, he acquired,
Or more properly created, a
MINISTERIAL ESTATE.

He was the only person of his time who could CHEAT without
The mask of HONESTY, retain his primeval MEANNESS
When possessed of *ten thousand* a year;
And, having daily deserved the
GIBBET for what he *did*,
Was at last condemned to it for what he *could* not *do*.

O indignant reader!
Think not his life useless to mankind!
PROVIDENCE connived at his execrable designs,
To give to after-ages a conspicuous
PROOF and EXAMPLE
Of how small estimation is EXORBITANT
WEALTH in the sight of GOD, by
His bestowing it on the most UNWORTHY of
ALL MORTALS.

§ 22. b^1. *The existence of God as an eternal executive, punishing violators of His law, inferred from the spiritual consequences of a violation of conscience.*

Under this head it will be sufficient to mention *remorse.* Poets have rivaled psychologists in depicting the punitive power of this passion, but neither have been able to equal truth. Shakspeare's keenness of perception and energy of expression have come near to it, in the passage where the death of Cardinal Beaufort is described:—

SCENE—*Cardinal's Bed-chamber*

Enter KING HENRY, SALISBURY, and WARWICK.

K. Hen. How fares my lord? Speak, Beaufort, to thy sovereign.

Car. If thou be'st death, I'll give thee England's treasure,
Enough to purchase such another island,
So thou wilt let me live, and feel no pain.

K. Hen. Ah, what a sign it is of evil life,
When death's approach is seen so terrible!

War. Beaufort, it is thy sovereign speaks to thee.

Car. Bring me unto my trial when you will.
Died he not in his bed? where should he die?—
Can I make men live, whe'r they will or no?—
O! torture me no more; I will confess.—
Alive again? Then show me where he is;
I'll give a thousand pound to look upon him.—
He hath no eyes; the dust hath blinded them.—
Comb down his hair; look! look! it stands upright,
Like lime-twigs set to catch my winged soul!
Give me some drink; and bid the apothecary
Bring the strong poison that I bought of him.

K. Hen. O, thou eternal Mover of the heavens,
Look with a gentle eye upon this wretch!
O, beat away the busy, meddling fiend,
That lays strong siege unto this wretch's soul,
And from his bosom purge this black despair!

War. See, how the pangs of death do make him grin!

Sal. Disturb him not; let him pass peaceably.

K. Hen. Peace to his soul, if God's good pleasure be!
Lord Cardinal, if thou think'st on heaven's bliss,
Hold up thy hand, make signal of thy hope.—
He dies, and makes no sign. O, God, forgive him!

War. So bad a death argues a monstrous life.

K. Hen. Forbear to judge, for we are sinners all.—
Close up his eyes, and draw the curtain close;
And let us all to meditation.

Dr. Beecher, some years back, gave a sketch of a remarkable visit paid by him to the Pennsylvania Hospital for the Insane. He observed a man, then advancing in years, standing before him, frozen apparently to the ground. "I asked who that was, so fixed, the image of despair. It was the son of Dr. Rush, (of revolutionary memory,) and, in the dreadful hour of revenge and pride, he had killed a fellow-man in a duel. There he stood, like a pillar. Sometimes he would apparently wake up to recollection; he would pace off the distance, and give the word, 'fire!' Then he would cry out, 'he is dead! he is dead!'" It may be added, that the quarrel was one between two friends, then scarcely past their boyhood; that the difficulty was about a mere trifle, but was carried on, and consummated in hot blood; and that, from that period to a gray old age, the survivor continued to react, with all the sincerity of despair, the awful scene of the duel.*

§ 23. Nor do these retributions confine themselves to what are commonly called *crimes*. Remorse may follow levity as well as overt guilt; neglect as well as positive wrong. Nowhere, not even in the pages of Puritan theology, is this more vividly and splendidly illustrated than in the following lines of a poet, than whom no one is more distinguished for the denunciation and ridicule of what he called religious cant. A lady, who lived in luxurious ease and inaction, thus speaks of the vision of a dream:—

---

* As to the illimitable attributes of mind, see *post*, § 29.

For the blind and the cripple were there, and the babe that pined
for bread;
And the houseless man, and the widow poor, who begged—to bury
the dead!
The naked, alas! that I might have clad, the famished I might have
fed!

Each pleading look, that long ago I scanned with a heedless eye,
Each face was gazing as plainly then as when I passed it by;
Woe, woe for me, if the past should be thus present when I die!

No need of sulphurous lake, no need of fiery coal,
But only that crowd of human kind, that wanted pity and dole—
In everlasting retrospect—will wring my sinful soul!

Alas! I have walked through life, too heedless where I trod;
Nay, helping to trample my fellow-worm, and fill the burial sod,
Forgetting that even the sparrow falls not unmarked of God!

I drank the richest draughts, and ate whatever was good—
Fish, and flesh, and fowl, and fruit, supplied my hungry mood;
But I never remembered the wretched ones that starve for want of
food!

I dressed as the noble dress, in cloth of silver and gold,
With silk, and satin, and costly furs, in many an ample fold;
But I never remembered the naked limbs that froze with winter's
cold;

The wounds I might have healed! the human sorrow and smart!
And yet it never was in my soul to play so ill a part;
But evil is wrought by want of thought, as well as want of heart!

§ 24. Schürmayer, not the least accurate of recent German writers on Forensic Medicine,* thus speaks: "Remorse

---

* Schürmayer, Gericht. Med., § 519.

often affects the mind so powerfully as to approach the appearance of insanity. The smothered self-reproach of the criminal sometimes expresses itself in the shape of deep dejection, and sometimes in that of petulance and irritability. Almost every defendant who is guilty will be seen to lapse, at least periodically, into a deep reverie, with the eyes staring in vacancy. The most consummate villains alone are exempt from such feelings. Criminals generally endeavor to suppress the voice of conscience because they fear to be betrayed by it. But this very action is perfectly legible in their faces, gestures, and general bodily condition. Under these circumstances the qualms of conscience frequently assume the appearance of disease. The accused, particularly if in confinement, does not sleep at night for weeks, and consequently looks pale and haggard, loses his appetite, and speaks with hesitation, and sometimes with trembling. When this condition reaches a point of great intensity, the guilty is visited by visions and hallucinations; avenging angels appear to him, or evil spirits, phantoms, or the shades of the dead and injured."

§ 25. What is called irritability, rising as it sometimes does to *oikeiomania* or domestic insanity,* may fall under this head. "I would much rather," says a keen observer, "expect a kind office from one who has previously done me a kindness than from one to whom such a kindness has been done." In other words, the very act of beneficence generates an evenness of temper, which, while it smooths the way for a continued flow of the same impulses, gives additional composure

* See Wharton and Stillé, Med. Jur. § 204.

and peace to the mind itself. In this view irritation is the retribution of petty social wrongs, approaching insanity as those wrongs amount to crimes. Psychological researches in recent days show that it is on the *perpetrator*, much more than upon the *victim* of great domestic wrongs, that the shock resulting from their commission falls. It is true that hearths are often desolated by the approach of that crime which makes innocence the cherished prey of lust. It is true that in cases, both far more numerous and far more subtle in their consequences, the unsubdued passions, or the perverse and perverting temper of a father or mother, a husband or a wife, may make a home wretched, may hurry the funeral to the door to carry to her first resting-place one who had been crushed by a system of wearying oppression or tantalizing wrong; or may drive into desperation those whom it would have required but a few kind words to have kept around the fireside in peace and sobriety. It is true, also, that the affections are often engaged by a system of attentions which the world may call innocent, but which, whether the result of design or levity, succeed in making desolate a heart which otherwise might have ripened into that full matronly beauty,—a beauty which nothing in nature can equal, —which the golden harvest of a loved and cherished womanhood presents. All these are common words in the world's mouth. So familiar are they, that when the ear hears or the eye catches the first word or two bearing upon them, it at once flits away, conscious that it knows all that is going to be said already, and rests upon some more congenial topic of meditation. But there is a counterpart to this, which is less known. It is, that it is the wrong-doer who receives, in his own person, in double virulence, the poison which he injects into the system of others. The vitals of the oppressor are consumed by a torture which, being slower, is more exquisite than that which is inflicted on the oppressed. We have a very pregnant illustration of this in a late statement by one of the most eminent and experienced of the present London psychological physicians. "Marital unkindness," says Dr. Mayo, "is subversive of soundness of mind in the person on whom it is exercised; and exercised it is in a thousand ways in this country without violence being had recourse to. 'The state of the law,' as Mr. Dickens well observes, and terrifically proves, 'is unprotective of wives.' But the mischief is not unavenged; and here the case of the husband's retribution commences. Many men are living in a state of continuous and exhausting remorse, under the consciousness that this system of torture is being carried on by them. For when once the habit is formed, they can neither shake it off nor bear their self-consciousness under it.

Culpam pœna premit comes.

"I need not speak of their retrospects, if they should outlive the object of their tyranny."

It is here, as recent developments have enabled us to determine, is to be found the secret of that phrensied remorse which marked the last days of Jonathan Swift. Others have been pointed out as the victims of the heartlessness which led him to trifle with the affections which he had won. But the most conspicuous victim was himself. Alternating between howling mania and paralyzing despair, the desolate close of his life is a fitting memorial of the truth that there is a retribution attached as much to wrongs done to the affections of others, as to wrongs done to their persons or property.

I may be permitted to close this topic with the following passage from a sketch given by the late Dr. Parrish, of Philadelphia—a very reliable witness—of the last hours of John Randolph:—

"A napkin was called for, and placed by John over his breast. For a short time he lay perfectly quiet, with his eyes closed. He suddenly roused up and exclaimed—'Remorse! Remorse!' It was thrice repeated—the last time at the top of his voice, with great agitation. He cried out—'Let me see the word. Get a dictionary; let me see the word.' 'There is none in the room, sir.' 'Write it down then—let me see the word.' The doctor picked up one of his cards, 'Randolph of Roanoke.' 'Shall I write it on this card?' 'Yes, nothing more proper.' The word *remorse* was then written in pencil. He took the card in a hurried manner, and fastened his eyes on it with great intensity. 'Write it on the back,' he exclaimed. It was so done and handed him again. He was extremely agitated—'Remorse! you have no idea what it is; you can form no idea of it whatever; it has contributed to bring me to my present situation. But I have looked to the Lord Jesus Christ, and hope I have obtained pardon. Now, let John take your pencil and draw a line under the word;' which was accordingly done. 'What am I to do with the card?' inquired the doctor. 'Put it in your pocket—take care of it—when I am dead look at it.'"*

§ 26. c^1. *The existence of God as an eternal executive,*

* Garland's Life of Randolph, p. 373.

punishing the violators of His law, inferred from the physical consequences of a violation of conscience.

Let us go, for instance, to Augustus the Strong, of Saxony, and observe in him in early life the "maximum of physical strength: can break horseshoes, nay, halfcrowns, with finger and thumb;"* of superb beauty, and possessor of two crowns. Meet him again when in the prime of manhood, and you see him bloated and putrid. A life of eminent dissipation has broken a constitution of eminent strength. So it is everywhere. We are placed, in fact, under recognizances to obey the decrees of conscience, and our bodies become our bail. If the bond is broken, the bail is seized upon and made to pay the forfeit. Nor is it bodily strength alone that is thus taken in execution. Nervous power, intellectual integrity, simplicity of heart, even lustre of genius, all these are in like manner sacrificed as penalties. Byron, Burns, Mirabeau—themselves desolating and desolated—lead us, in the agonized confession of their early though self-destroyed manhood, to the same truth of the organic connection between spiritual and physical demoralization.

Nor does the penalty stop here. The finer and more generous capacities of the heart become in like manner involved. The susceptibility for innocent joys—of all susceptibilities the finest—is lost. Burns speaks with a sad truth on this point:—

I waive the quantum of the sin,
The hazard of concealing,
But oh! it hardens all within
And petrifies the feeling.

---

* Carlyle, Fred. II. vol. 1, p. 148.

Take also that adaptation of society by which (1) approval and respect, utterly distinct from that subserviency which waits upon fortune, are paid to integrity even when in chains and penury, while, (2) as part of the same system, distrust and dislike attend selfishness. Here we have an additional evidence of the extent to which Providence presses and shores up by auxiliary sanctions this main pillar of conscience; and consequently here we find an additional proof of the contrivance exhibited in this great moral engine. "The upright man is trusted, and has a thousand means of advancing his interest denied to the cunning and deceitful. The friendly man receives friendship, which the selfish man can never obtain, or enjoy though it were granted to him."*

§ 27. Taking these phenomena in connection with those mentioned in a former section, they give the materials for an induction by no means incomplete, in reference to the character of the divine agent by whom this complicated machine is constructed and kept in motion. It is as if we saw sentinels posted on the parapets of a besieged fort to repel invaders, to preserve discipline and repress mutinies among the besieged, and to repair works which have crumbled by time or broken under assault. Comparative anatomists, we are told, are able to complete, from a single bone, the entire structure of what may be an extinct animal. The work before us is not so difficult. We have far more abundant materials to complete the structure than those which human sagacity considers sufficient to solve a temporal problem. It is well for us, therefore, to pause and contemplate the temple

* McCosh on Div. Govt., p. 326.

and its God, as they stand thus developed before our eyes. For human nature is a ruined temple, though a temple still. The greatness of its capacity, and the splendor of its architecture, show how divine is the hand that made it, and how important its purposes. That it is in ruins proves that some great disturbing force has swept over it and shaken it to its foundations. But the guards that have been placed around it show that even over the ruins there presides a wise and merciful God, ready not only to meet and correct the evils which this shock may produce, but to make it, by turning it into a means of probation, conduce to the moral and spiritual elevation of His people.

§ 28. Recapitulating the points taken in this chapter, we have—

a. The existence of a Supreme Lawgiver, inferred from the existence of conscience as a law.

b. The existence of a Supreme Judge, inferred from the existence of conscience as a judicial tribunal.

c. The existence of a Supreme Spiritual Executive, rewarding and punishing in life and after life, inferred from the retributive attributes of conscience, themselves incessant and unconditioned by time or matter, and aided by a complicated apparatus of physical and social sanctions.

We have the same species of proof for these propositions that we have for similar propositions connected with human society. From a code, we infer a law-making power; from a court, a judicial; from the enforcement of the decrees of such court, an executive. If, in addition to such data, we find that within certain limits the freedom of the subject is maintained, we infer that the government is one which, for purposes of its own, finds it wiser to preserve individual liberty and to impose individual responsibility, even though at the risk of occasional disorders, than to attempt to destroy these agencies, by making all action to depend upon a direct and resistless governmental impulse. And our conception of the power and prevision of such a government rises in proportion to the energy, the splendor, and the compass of the instrumentalities it brings to bear to carry out its polity. Applying this same reasoning to the facts before us, we have the spectacle of a God, Creator, Judge, and Avenger, establishing and vindicating a moral law by sanctions unconditioned by time and matter.

CHAPTER II.

FROM MIND.

a. THE NATURE OF MIND.

§ 29. The consciousness of each of us attests the existence of a distinct individuality, peculiar to ourselves, capable of choosing or rejecting; of comparing, judging, and classifying; of reasoning and of imagining. This individuality, viewing it in its intellectual relations, has no bounds. It is able to bring together instantaneously and often unconsciously—so flexible and rapid are its movements—the desert rock, on which the shipwrecked mariner may stand, and the hamlet four thousand miles off, in which lies his home. It spans myriads of years with its sudden arch. It stands on the observatory, and measures the height and determines the weight of stars, whose very light cannot reach us under a million of years. Nor is its dominion limited to things real. It creates as well as recalls; it convokes imaginary assemblages as well as reproduces those which have been dissolved by time. Blinded in front by an impenetrable veil it certainly is, for it can foretell not the events that are to come; but its sight backward and upward and downward is unobstructed, and the closing to it of the future is only another proof of that contrivance which gives enough light to illuminate, but not enough to destroy probation.

b. THE CAUSE OF MIND.

§ 30. What must have been that workshop in which agencies such as these were constructed? He that formeth the ear, does He not hear? He that makes the mind, guarded as it is, so as to subserve the purposes of probation, and yet unlimited for all else beside, does He not think?

This, however, may be illustrated still further. We stand, for instance, on the sea-shore, and see a vessel tossed in the waves—no human power, it would seem, can save it. A rope, however, is projected from the shore, by which the crew are ferried over and saved. In this we recognize the action of human intelligence and beneficence. Turn, then, for a moment, to another scene. Buildings are seen crowded with the sick and dying:—

The wounded from the battle plain
In dreary hospitals of pain,
The cheerless corridors,
The cold and stony floors:

Lo! in that house of misery
A lady with a lamp I see
Pass through the glimmering gloom,
And flit from room to room.

And slow, as in a dream of bliss,
The speechless sufferer turns to kiss
Her shadow as it falls
Upon the darkening walls.

We see human design in the rope cast to the foundering ship: shall we not see a divine purpose in an agency like this flung out among the sick and dying? Or can we refuse to see the same designing power, acting upon the same subject-matter of a fallen nature, when we view such a mission as that of Dorothy Dix to the insane of our own land?

§ 31. Let us take, however, one or two more illustrations. An Englishman is seen casting stones, apparently idly, into the Niger, and watching the bubbles as they slowly rise from the mud below. The women and children gaze almost in sympathy at one whose objects in life are apparently so much like their own. It is Mungo Park, calculating, from the length of time the bubbles take to rise, what is the depth of the mysterious river whose sources he is about to explore. A boy sits by a chimney-fire in Lancashire, curiously scanning the lid of the tea-kettle as it flaps up and down under the pressure of the steam arising from the boiling water beneath. The housewife scolds him for his idleness, but she need not. It is Watt, catching the first conception of the steam-engine. That subtle element of *mind*, residing within that boy's frame, is to project itself forward from the chimney-corner until it binds the world together with ligatures of iron,—until the steam-horse dashes over tressel-work and through tunnels, so as to equalize the markets and unite the sympathies of distant nations, and until the press so works as to supply every home with a library at the former cost of a tract.

Now how are we to account for the human mind otherwise than by the supposition of a spiritual creative power?

Mere matter might lead us no further than an elementary mechanism, soulless and discretionless, like the first cause of Schelling, or the inflexible and arbitrary germinative principle of La Place. But mind, in its multiform and flexible adaptations to life,—mind, conscious of its own independent volitions,—leads us above the prison-house wherein resides a Deity in chains. Mind, voluntary, free-acting, involves a free Creator. "He that made the eye, can He not see?" He that made the mind, is He miudless?

CHAPTER III.

FROM THE EXISTENCE OF LAW IN THE UNIVERSE.

§ 32. THIS topic will be considered under the following heads:—

a. UNITY AND HARMONY OF PATTERN.

Here we find a singular evidence of the *unity* of the Divine Machinist. The *trade-mark*, if we may use the expression, is always the same. "I know such a pattern," declares the expert who is examined before a committee of the House of Commons, as to the extent to which certain goods have penetrated in distant territories, "and the moment I saw it, though in central Africa, I recognized in it the stamp used by our firm in Manchester for a particular style of goods." So in traversing the regions divided by one of our trunk railways, as we observe the line of station-houses erected by the company, we say, "these we know at once—the castellated walls, or the old English roofs, show where the management of a particular road begins and ends." So we trace back one style of architecture to one period, and another style to another period. So in a particular combination of color with effect, we discover one old master of painting; in another combination, another old master.

Now if this is the case among the changing fashions of human society, how much more must it be so when this similarity of patterns runs over hundreds of thousands of years in time, and the whole universe in space. Forever, everywhere, as far as we can observe, are the same patterns applied, the same fundamental principles of structure observed. We pierce the pyramids, and discover in the funereal recesses of those vast mausoleums, urns of a certain shape, with hieroglyphics, marking a specific dynasty of the Pharaohs. We discover similar memorials going back to a similar period on the Upper Nile, and we at once infer a common origin. We infer, in like manner, the existence and unity of a now extinct race of civilized Americans, from the sacrificial mounds scattered over North America. And thus when we find primal types, beginning with the earth itself, coming down to our day, and spreading over the whole earth, we infer the unity as well as the unlimited existence of the great Artificer of all.

§ 33. Now how is it in point of fact? Let us, in order to answer this, go back, under the guidance of geology, to survey the beginning of organic life. Here we may pause for a moment, to notice an error of the most fascinating and graphic of all the historians of the pre-Adamite earth—the late Hugh Miller.

Impressed, as was natural to his passionate and manly temperament, with a vehement sense of the falsity of the theory of the author of the "Vestiges of Creation," he seized upon an imperfect induction to give an additional blow to an hypothesis which he had already effectually demolished by arguments of unquestioned validity. He thought, and in this he has been followed by others seeking to strengthen a theological analogy which requires no such support, that after the first animal creation there was a fall in the creative type. The earlier fishes and reptiles he held to be of a more perfect order, and these, he maintained, were followed by a series of lower and more degraded creations. Such, however, as has been abundantly demonstrated by an able and recent observer in our own country, is not the case.* The *Ganoids* and *Placoids*, on which Mr. Miller relied as instances of the superiority of the earlier creations, united, indeed, features which placed them in a higher position than the typical fishes that succeeded them, for, as embryos, they exhibited capacities which, though undeveloped in themselves, were the insignia of far higher forms afterwards to succeed. They were, in fact, the obscure prophecies of subsequent productions, but as prophecies they were interpreted and dignified by the event, but did not anticipate and pre-establish it. During the paleozoic period they were the "sole representatives of the vertebrate type, combining in themselves the characters of all classes." "The *Sigillaria* and *Leipodendron* stood as the representatives of both *Cryptogram* and *Phœnogram*, until these two ideas were separately and more distinctly expressed by the subsequent introduction of the typical forms of these two classes. It is as if nature first sketched her work in general terms and

---

* See Professor Le Conte's Lecture on Coal, Smithsonian Institute, 1857, p. 167. Prof. Agassiz, as will be seen, incidentally adopts the same position, which is also maintained with great fullness by Dr. Harris in his Pre-Adamite Earth.

then elaborated each subordinate idea in separate families; all these families, taken together as an organic whole, still containing the original idea in a more completely developed form, as if the problem of organic nature was first expressed in a few simple but comprehensive symbols, and then differentiated."* But while there was in the beginning this creation, as it were, of an outline pattern, (just in the same way, to adopt an illustration from the writer just quoted, as we observe in the first organization of human society the grouping together in individuals of several social functions, each man being, however imperfectly, his own blacksmith, shoemaker, and farmer, while afterwards, as the race progresses, the trades divide, each performing its functions the more perfectly, because separately,) yet there was no subsequent automaton development of the future stages of life. "If there is anything," is the conclusion of the very interesting paper now before us, "which geology teaches with clearness, it is that the animal and vegetable kingdoms *did not commence as monads,* or vital points, but as organisms, so perfect that even the maddest Lamarckian must admit that they could not have been formed by agency of physical forces; that species *did not pass into one another by transmission,* but that each species was introduced in full perfection, remained unchanged during the term of their existence, and died in full perfection; that physical conditions cannot change one species into another, but that a species will rather give up its life than its specific character." "As far as the evidence of geology extends, each species was *intro-*

* Smithsonian Institute, 1857, p. 165.

duced by the direct miraculous interference of a personal intelligence. There has, indeed, been a constantly increasing series, but the connection between the terms of the series has not been physical or genetic, but intellectual; not founded in the laws of reproduction, but in the eternal counsels of the Almighty."

§ 34. Let us go back, however, to this principle of identity of pattern, each formation in due time mounting to successively higher species, not by transformation, but by specific divine direction.* Then, when we take into consideration the almost infinite series of years during which this progress has gone on; the unlimited cosmical field on which it operates; the equally unlimited command of resources which it displays; the magnificent sweep of purpose and the exquisite delicacy of detail it combines, and at the same time the calm precision and evenness of the gradually narrowing cycles by which it concentrates itself upon man—we may well concur in the truths of the following attributes as belonging to the Divine Creator and Ruler of all:—

I. Unity of agency.

II. Consistency of purpose.

III. Unlimited power.

VI. Patience and majestic endurance.

V. A capacity for the most sublime development of plan and the most exquisite discrimination of detail.

VI. A continuing special superintendence of the world.

VII. The recognition of man, as occupying a post of final

---

* See Agassiz's Report on the Fossil Fishes of the Devonian System, Twelfth Report British Association, p. 85.

importance in this grand series of development, with behind him an almost unlimited past, instinct, with its lessons of humility, of dependence on the divine purpose, and yet, at the same time, of responsibility, showing us that man is the great moral centre of this immense educational as well as economical engine.*

VIII. The recognition also of the truth, that the defects and evils of this stage of spiritual existence are but ancillary to, and preparatory for, a higher order, in the same way that the defects and evils in the earlier stages of physical development are incident to the latter. These defects and evils are, therefore, inherent in an intermediate stage, in a series of advances, from chaos to final perfection.†

b. Union of harmony in general laws, with special adaptation of details.‡

§ 35. Under this head I cannot do more than adopt the following summary, in which Professor Agassiz, with a delicacy and exactness of analysis only excelled by the synthetical completeness of the material on which it rests, sums up the theistic inferences to be collected from the first volume of the great work which he has now under publication:—

"In recapitulating the preceding statements we may present the following conclusions:—

1st. The connection of all these known features of nature into one system exhibits thought, the most comprehensive thought, in limits transcending the highest wonted powers of man.

---

* See *post*, § 100. † See *post*, § 173. ‡ See *post*, § 229.

2d. The simultaneous existence of the most diversified types under identical circumstances exhibits thought, the ability to adapt a great variety of structures to the most uniform conditions.

3d. The repetition of similar types, under the most diversified circumstances, shows an immaterial connection between them; it exhibits thought, proving directly how completely the creative mind is independent of the influence of a material world.

4th. The unity of plan in otherwise highly diversified types of animals, exhibits thought; it exhibits more immediately premeditation, for no plan could embrace such a diversity of beings, called into existence at such long intervals of time, unless it had been framed in the beginning with immediate reference to the end.

§ 36. 5th. The correspondence, now generally known as special homologies, in the details of structure in animals otherwise entirely disconnected, down to the most minute peculiarities, exhibits thought, and more immediately the power of expressing a general proposition in an indefinite number of ways, equally complete in themselves, though differing in all their details.

6th. The various degrees and different kinds of relationship among animals which can have no genealogical connection, exhibit thought, the power of combining different categories into a permanent, harmonious whole, even though the material basis of this harmony be ever changing.

7th. The simultaneous existence, in the earliest geological periods in which animals existed at all, of representatives of all the great types of the animal kingdom, exhibits most especially thought, considerate thought, combining power, premeditation, prescience, omniscience.

8th. The gradation based upon complications of structure which may be traced among animals built upon the same plan, exhibits thought, and especially the power of distributing harmoniously unequal gifts.

9th. The distribution of some types over the most extensive range of the surface of the globe, while others are limited to particular geographical areas, and the various combinations of these types into zoological provinces of unequal extent, exhibit thought, a close control in the distribution of the earth's surface among its inhabitants.

10th. The identity of structure of these types, notwithstanding their wide geographical distribution, exhibits thought, that deep thought which, the more it is scrutinized, seems the less capable of being exhausted, though its meaning at the surface appears at once plain and intelligible to every one.

§ 37. 11th. The community of structure in certain respects of animals otherwise entirely different, but living within the same geographical area, exhibits thought, and more particularly the power of adapting most diversified types with peculiar structures to either identical or to different conditions of existence.

12th. The connection, by series, of special structures observed in animals widely scattered over the surface of the globe, exhibits thought, unlimited comprehension, and more directly omnipresence of mind, and also prescience, as far as such series extend through a succession of geological ages.

13th. The relation there is between the size of animals and their structure and form, exhibits thought; it shows that in nature the quantitative differences are as fixedly determined as the qualitative ones.

14th. The independence in the size of animals of the mediums in which they live, exhibits thought, in establishing such close connection between elements so influential in themselves and organized beings so little affected by the nature of these elements.

§ 38. 15th. The permanence of specific peculiarities under every variety of external influences, during each geological period, and under the present state of things upon earth, exhibits thought; it shows, also, that limitation in time is an essential element of all finite beings, while eternity is an attribute of the Deity only.

16th. The definite relations in which animals stand to the surrounding world, exhibit thought; for all animals living together stand respectively, on account of their very differences, in different relations to identical conditions of existence, in a manner which implies a considerate adaptation of their varied organization to these uniform conditions.

17th. The relations in which individuals of the same species stand to one another exhibit thought, and go far to prove the existence in all living beings of an immaterial imperishable principle, similar to that which is generally conceded to man only.

18th. The limitation of the range of changes which animals undergo during their growth, exhibits thought; it shows most strikingly the independence of these changes of external influences, and the necessity that they should be determined by a power superior to these influences.

19th. The unequal limitation in the average duration of the life of individuals in different species of animals, exhibits thought; for, however uniform or however diversified the conditions of existence may be under which animals live together, the average duration of life, in different species, is unequally limited. It points therefore at a knowledge of time and space, and of the value of time, since the phases of life of different animals are apportioned according to the part they have to perform upon the stage of the world.

20th. The return to a definite norm of animals which multiply in various ways, exhibits thought. It shows how wide a cycle of modulations may be included in the same conception, without yet departing from a norm expressed more directly in other combinations.

§ 39. 21st. The order of succession of the different types of animals and plants characteristic of the different geological epochs, exhibits thought. It shows that while the material world is identical in itself in all ages, ever different types of organized beings are called into existence in successive periods.

22d. The localization of some types of animals upon the same points of the surface of the globe, during several successive geological periods, exhibits thought, consecutive thought; the operations of a mind acting in conformity with a plan laid out beforehand and sustained for a long period.

23d. The limitation of closely allied species to different

geological periods, exhibits thought; it exhibits the power of sustaining nice distinctions, notwithstanding the interposition of great disturbances by physical revolutions.

24th. The parallelism between the order of succession of animals and plants in geological times, and the gradation among the living representatives, exhibit thought; consecutive thought, superintending the whole development of nature from beginning to end, and disclosing throughout a gradual progress, ending with the introduction of man at the head of the animal creation.

25th. The parallelism between the order of succession of animals in geological times, and the changes their living representatives undergo during their embryological growth, exhibits thought; the repetition of the same train of thoughts in the phases of growth of living animals and the successive appearance of their representatives in past ages.

26th. The combination, in many extinct types, of characters which, in later ages, appear disconnected in different types, exhibits thought, prophetic thought, foresight; combinations of thought preceding their manifestation in living forms.

27th. The parallelism between the gradation among animals and the changes they undergo during their growth, exhibits thought, as it discloses everywhere the most intimate connection between essential features of animals which have no necessary physical relation, and can, therefore, not be understood as otherwise than as established by a thinking being.

28th. The relations existing between these different series and the geographical distribution of animals, exhibit thought; they show the omnipresence of the Creator.

29th. The mutual dependence of the animal and vegetable kingdoms for their maintenance exhibits thought; it displays the care with which all conditions of existence, necessary to the maintenance of organized beings, have been balanced.

30th. The dependence of some animals upon others or upon plants for their existence, exhibits thought; it shows to what degree the most complicated combinations of structure and adaptation can be rendered independent of the physical conditions which surround them.

§ 40. We may sum up the results of this discussion, up to this point, in still fewer words:—

All organized beings exhibit in themselves all those categories of structure and of existence upon which a natural system may be founded, in such a manner that, in tracing it, the human mind is only translating into human language the divine thoughts expressed in nature in living realities.

All these beings do not exist in consequence of the continued agency of physical causes, but have made their successive appearance upon earth by the immediate intervention of the Creator. As proof, I may sum up my argument in the following manner:—

The products of what are commonly called physical agents are everywhere the same, (that is, upon the whole surface of the globe,) and have always been the same, (that is, during all geological periods;) while organized beings are everywhere different, and have differed in all ages. Between two such series of phenomena there can be no casual or genetic connection.

31st. The combination in time and space of all these

thoughtful conceptions exhibits not only thought; it shows also premeditation, power, wisdom, greatness, prescience, omniscience, providence.

In one word, all these facts in their natural connection proclaim aloud the one God, whom man may know, adore, and love; and natural history must, in good time, become the analysis of the thoughts of the Creator of the universe, as manifested in the animal and vegetable kingdoms."*

---

* Contributions to the Natural History of the United States of America, vol. i., part i., chap. i., sec. xxxii.

CHAPTER IV.

FROM MATTER.

a. UNIVERSAL BELIEF IN SOME ETERNAL EXISTENCE.

§ 41. The atheist concurs with the theist in holding that *something* must have existed from eternity, and that this something must have been unoriginated. If we examine the several schools of atheism we will find them all converge to this. He who holds that the earth is itself eternal; he who believes in an original fire-mist out of which all subsequent matter was evolved; he who holds to a chance creation,—each goes back to some primary existence, be it earth, or fire-mist, or random-atoms, which preceded this great universe.

b. THE ATHEIST'S ETERNITY EQUALLY OBJECTIONABLE WITH THE THEIST'S.

§ 42. The atheist, therefore, holds to a positive belief that is infected with all the objections that are raised against theism. For,

Atheism, as well as theism, necessitates a belief in something that is independent of the conditions of time and space.

Atheism, as well as theism, holds to self-existence and eternity.

c. INCOMPREHENSIBILITY OF ETERNITY NOT CONCLUSIVE.

§ 43. There is, however, a general objection, which may here be noticed. Eternity and self-existence are themes too mysterious to be contemplated; and, as mysteries, they should, therefore, be rejected. To this the answer is twofold.

a^1. To assert incomprehensibility is begging the question. How can eternity be mysterious unless it exists? Nor is an inability to comprehend a thing a valid ground for skepticism as to its existence. "There is a mystery about a plenum, and a mystery about a vacuum," to paraphrase one of Dr. Johnson's remarks, "but one must be true." There is a mystery about soul and about body, and yet we must believe in one, if not both.

b^1. Experience tells us that it is *limit* which is artificial, not *infinitude*. Infinitude is nothing more than limit untied. Take, for instance, the effect of the magnetic telegraph, which operates by destroying the obstructions by which the senses are impeded. Let us suppose, then, artificial obstructions to be removed, and we fall back at once upon eternity as to time, and infinitude as to space.*

There is an anecdote told by Mr. Rogers, in his "Table-Talk," which strikingly illustrates the unconscious confession by the human mind of this great truth. He was visiting a picture of the Transfiguration, in an Italian convent, and observed an old Benedictine monk silently looking on the same great scene. Day after day the poet repeated the visit, and day after day the monk was found at his post, gazing with an eye which seemed to view not so much the

---

* See this more fully stated, *post*, § 129.

painting as the sublime fact behind it. At last Mr. Rogers made an excuse for asking him a question which might draw out his opinion of the picture's artistic merits. "Sir," was the reply, "for fifty years have I paced to and fro in this chapel,—nearly three generations of monks have I seen pass away, and sink under those stone flags; and, as I look up to that vision of our transfigured Lord, I begin to think that it is *we* who are the *pictures*, and that the *reality*." And is there any one who has watched the rapid course of human life, who has, in the record of nature, seen how even mountains and oceans have been marshaled at their posts and then dismissed at a divine command, but has felt that it is the *created* that is artificial, and the *Creator* alone that is real?

d. DESOLATENESS OF A GODLESS UNIVERSE.

§ 44. Nowhere is this more vividly portrayed than by Jean Paul, in a celebrated paper, of which we give part of a translation by Mr. Carlyle. The author supposes himself to fall into a dream, which he prefaces as follows :—

"The purpose of this fiction is the excuse of its boldness. Men deny the Divine existence with as little feeling as the most assert it. Even in our true systems we go on collecting mere words, playmarks and medals, as the misers do coins; and not till late do we transform the words into feelings, the coins into enjoyments. A man may, for twenty years, believe in the immortality of the soul; in the one-and-twentieth, in some great moment, he, for the first time, discovers, with amazement, the rich meaning of this belief and the warmth of this naphtha well.

"Of such sort, was my terror at the poisonous, stifling vapor which floats out around the heart of him who, for the first time, enters the school of atheism. I could, with less pain, deny immortality than Deity; there I should lose but a world covered with mists, here I should lose the present world, namely, the sun thereof; the whole spiritual universe is dashed asunder, by the hand of atheism, into numberless quicksilver points of *me's*, which glitter, run, waver, fly together or asunder, without unity or continuance. No one in creation is so alone as the denier of God; he mourns, with an orphaned heart that has lost its great Father, by the corpse of Nature, which no world-spirit moves and holds together, and which grows in its grave; and he mourns by that corpse till he himself crumbles off from it. The whole world lies before him like the Egyptian sphinx of stone, half-buried in the sand; and the All is the cold, iron mask of a formless eternity."

Of the remarkable dream that follows, itself the most brilliant production of a very brilliant writer, the following passage is all that can be at present extracted:—

"I was lying once, on a summer evening, in the sunshine, and I fell asleep. Methought I awoke in the churchyard. The down-rolling wheels of the steeple clock, which was striking eleven, had woke me. In the emptied night-heaven I looked for the sun; for I thought an eclipse was veiling him with the moon. All the graves were open, and the iron doors of the charnel-houses were swinging to and fro by invisible hands. On the walls flitted shadows which proceeded from no one, and other shadows stretched upward in the pale air. In the open coffins none now lay sleeping but the children. Over the whole heaven hung, in large folds, a gray, sultry mist, which a giant shadow like vapor was drawing down nearer, closer, and hotter. Above me I heard the distant fall of avalanches; under me the first step of a boundless earthquake. The church wavered up and down with two interminable dissonances, which struggled with each other in it, endeavoring in vain to mingle in unison. At times a gray glimmer hovered along the windows, and under it the lead and iron fell down molten. The net of the mist and the tottering earth brought me into that hideous temple, at the door of which, in two poison bushes, two glittering basalisks lay brooding. I passed through unknown shadows, on whom ancient centuries were impressed. All the shadows were standing around the empty altar; and in all, not the heart, but the breast quivered and pulsed. One dead man only, who had just been buried there, still lay in his coffin without quivering breast; and on his smiling countenance stood a happy dream; but, at the entrance of one living, he awoke, and smiled no longer; he lifted his heavy eyelids, but within was no eye; and in his beating breast there lay, instead of a heart, a wound. He held up his hands and folded them to pray, but the arms lengthened out and dissolved; and the hands, still folded together, fell away. Above, on the church dome, stood the dial-plate of *Eternity*, whereon no number appeared, and which was its own index; but a black finger pointed thereon, and the dead sought to see by it."

CHAPTER V.

FROM DESIGN IN NATURE.

§ 45. In a fragment of Aristotle, preserved by Cicero, in his treatise *De Naturâ Deorum*, we find the following striking passage:—

"If there were beings who lived in the depths of the earth, in dwellings adorned with statues and paintings, and everything which is possessed in rich abundance by those whom we esteem fortunate; and if these beings could receive tidings of the power and might of the gods, and could then emerge from their hidden dwellings through the open fissures of the earth to the places we inhabit; if they could suddenly behold the earth, and the sea, and the vault of heaven; could recognize the expanse of the cloudy firmament, and the might of the winds of heaven, and admire the sun in its majestic beauty and radiant effulgence; and lastly, when night veiled the earth in darkness, they could behold the starry heavens, the changing moon, and the stars rising and setting in their unvarying course, ordained from eternity, they would surely exclaim, 'there are gods, and such great things must be the work of their hands!'"

From this stand-point, to which our very familiarity with these great spectacles requires that we should elevate ourselves in order to understand them, let us view, *a.* THE OCEAN.—Let us observe in this connection,

a[1]. *The sea-breeze.*

§ 46. To render a tropical country habitable, or at least to preserve in it health and comfort, what design would we, *a priori*, consider better than the periodical introduction of a breeze whose coolness and whose strength would relieve the heat of noon? Now this is what the sea-breeze does. The more tropical the climate, the more regular its approach and the more steady its continuance. "Usually," says Mr. Gosse, when speaking of the tropics, "about the hour of ten in the forenoon, when the heat of the sun begins to be oppressive, a breeze from the sea springs up, invigorating and refreshing the body by its delightful coolness, and continues to blow through the whole day, gradually dying away as the sun sinks to the horizon. Then about eight in the evening, an air blows off the land until near sunrise; but this is somewhat variable and irregular, always fainter than the sea-breeze, and dependent on the proximity of mountains. The application of what has been already said of the causes of wind in general will be readily made to these particular cases, the air on the surface of the water being cooler during the day, and that on the mountains during the night. Either is a grateful alleviation of the oppressive sultriness of the climate."* To this may be added the peculiarly refreshing qualities of the salt with which the sea-breeze is freighted.

b[1]. *The ocean salts.*

§ 47. Three things we would suppose necessary, *a priori*,

* Gosse, on the Ocean, p. 81.

in such a body as the ocean: *first*, such superior lightness as will make it a fit medium for the commerce of the world; *secondly*, such an amount of mobility and circulation as will afford highways for travel, as well as a preservative agency to the sea itself; *thirdly*, the material from which those numberless tribes by which the deep is thronged, may construct their homes. Now in view of such a design, what could be more effective than the salts by which the ocean is permeated? By them the specific gravity of the water is so far increased as to add materially to the buoyancy of whatever solids are placed in it. And the compensations by which this quality is maintained are no less worthy of notice. If a similar solution was placed in a vessel exposed to the sun, there would soon be little left besides a dry saline crust. But by a most delicate adjustment of the exquisite accuracy of which science can best judge by the results, the water evaporated by the sun is so far restored by the rivers as to retain throughout the vast volume the same specific gravity and the same saline admixture.

These salts contribute largely to that great system of oceanic circulation on which commerce so much depends. *Fresh* water is but feebly affected by the dynamical impulses set on foot by changes of temperature; *salt* water, through its peculiar contraction as its temperature lowers, is so agitated as to produce those great currents which form the ocean railways. From this we have a "surface current of saltish water from the poles toward the equator, and an under current of water salter and heavier from the equator to the poles. This under current supplies, in a great measure, the salt which the upper current, freighted with fresh water from the clouds and rivers, carries back. Thus it is to the salts of the seas that we owe that feature in the system of oceanic circulation which causes an under current to flow from the Mediterranean into the Atlantic, and another from the Red Sea into the Indian Ocean. Hence, too, we infer that the transportation of warm water from the equator toward the frozen regions of the poles, is facilitated; and consequently here, in the saltness of the sea, have we not an agent by which climates are mitigated—by which they are softened and rendered more salubrious than it would be possible for them to be were the waters of the ocean deprived of their property of saltness?"*

§ 48. To the salts, but more particularly to the solutions of lime which the fresh water streams pour into the ocean in such large amounts, we owe another very important element in the marine economy. It is here that the little builders of the ocean find the quarries from which their houses are constructed. Hence come the stone and the mortar which is worked into the creviceless dome which rises over the oyster's home. Hence come the minarets which form at once the guards and the ornaments of one species, and the peaked spear-heads which strengthen the armor of another. Here it is that the masons of the coral bank find their stone. When we recollect the myriads of creatures whose happiness is promoted and whose life secured by this process, we may well, as we look at the limestone rivulet that washes

* Maury, Phys. Geog. of the Sea, § 316, &c.

the mountain side, admire the wisdom and goodness by which its ingredients are composed and its course is directed. For it goes to aid in building innumerable cities to be inhabited by an active and useful population,—a population whose members not only subserve their immediate end as parts of the great chain of created beings, but perform an important office in maintaining that balance of life without which man himself would cease to exist.

For by them is no small part of the great work of the movement of the waters carried on. We all know in how short a time a comparatively small body of insects—the soldier-ant, for instance—is capable of undermining a solid wall. But here, in an element in a vast degree more susceptible to their subtle action, we have myriads upon myriads of artificers at work. Thither they proceed, these hod-men of the seas, carrying away from its ocean beds their countless little loads of mortar, of salts, and of solids. "How much solid matter," says the same intelligent observer whom we have just quoted, "does the whole host of marine plants and animals abstract from sea water daily? Is it a thousand pounds, or a thousand millions of tons? No one can say. But whatever be its weight, it is so much of the power of gravity applied to the dynamical forces of the ocean. And this power is derived from the salts of the sea, through the agency of sea-shells and other marine animals. Yet they have power to put the whole sea in motion, from the equator to the poles, and from top to bottom."

c^1. *The Gulf Stream.*

§ 49. Assuming, at the outset, the division of the earth

into zones, of such a character as to generate variety of produce and of character, and hereby to promote enterprise, both in commerce and in productive industry, it must follow, that large sections, unless some compensatory process be adopted, will be so far removed from the mean temperature as to be unsuitable for human habitation. Thus, without some such process, England, Norway, Sweden, and even the north of France, would be desolated on the one side by cold, and the islands of the Caribbean Sea, and the countries bordering on the Gulf of Mexico, by heat. What process would we suppose an intelligent and beneficent Creator to adopt to equalize these extremes, by drawing from the one to the other the excess of heat, and by throwing back the excess of cold?

Now, before we answer this question, let us suppose that we visit, in the dead of winter, one of the larger and more complete hot-houses, by which the vegetables and fruits of summer are brought to the market in early spring. There, where all the skill of recent experience is brought to bear, we will find, in a cellar under an out-house, a large boiler, in which water is heated. From this pipes are taken to a chamber, where they are so flared out as to raise to a high degree of heat a given body of air, which is afterwards taken by a hot air-pipe to the green-house. The water, being cooled, is collected again in a single pipe, and thus returned to the boiler to be re-heated. Again the circuit is commenced, and again completed, and so on until the desired temperature is reached. So it is, that, by a very simple and yet beautiful apparatus, the climate of summer is diffused, where otherwise the cold of winter would prevail, and a perennial verdure and fructification maintained.

Those who acquiesce in the contrivance displayed in such an apparatus as this, may be well taken to view a similar mechanism, though on an infinitely grander scale, in the Gulf Stream. It is, as Lieutenant Maury has shown us with great beauty, as if the Mexican Gulf and the Caribbean Sea were the cauldrons, the torrid zone the furnace, and the grand ocean sweep between the Grand Banks of Newfoundland and the shores of Europe the reservoir, into which the warm waters of the Gulf Stream, which is the pipe, are so played as to produce the maximum of effect. For, to use the striking language of this capable observer, "there is a river in the ocean. In the severest droughts it never fails, and in the mightiest floods it never overflows. Its banks and its bottom are of cold water, while its current is of warm. The Gulf of Mexico is its fountain, and its mouth is in the Arctic seas. It is the Gulf Stream. There is in the world no more majestic flow of waters. Its current is more rapid than the Mississippi or the Amazon."

Let us watch, then, in this view, the progress of this extraordinary river, as it proceeds on its mission of equalizing the heats of the countries which it touches. The burning Mexican plains, where the river begins, contribute the fuel. There, as we are told, "the quantity of specific heat daily carried off by the Gulf Stream from these regions and discharged over the Atlantic, is sufficient to raise mountains of iron from zero to the melting-point, and to keep in flow from them a molten stream of metal greater in volume than the waters daily discharged from the Mississippi River." From the Caribbean Sea the cooler water is supplied. It enters this vast basin through the southern line of the channel, which is guarded by Yucatan and Florida, and then, with a temperature, at the depth of four hundred and fifty fathoms, of but 43°, it increases, when it passes from the furnace, 40° in heat. Through its watery banks, which are so sharp and well marked, that a vessel may lie on the dividing-line and touch the two distinct strata on each side, it passes on, at a maximum temperature of 86°, until, after having traversed three thousand miles, it retains a summer warmth in the depth of winter. "With this temperature it crosses the fortieth degree of north latitude, and there, overflowing its liquid banks, it spreads itself out for thousands of square leagues over the cold waters around, and covers the ocean with a mantle of warmth that serves so much to mitigate in Europe the rigors of winter. Moving now more slowly, but dispensing its genial influences more freely, it finally meets the British Islands. By these it is divided, one part going into the Polar basin of Spitzbergen, the other entering into the Bay of Biscay, but each with a warmth considerably above the ocean temperature."

§ 50. Let us first view its effect on England. The port of Liverpool is never closed with ice; it is 2° farther north than that of St. Johns, Newfoundland, which, being frozen half the year, is of course incapable of sustaining commerce. Let us look, for a moment, at the consequences, had the same bands existed round the English coast. Cowper has well described the spectacle that now awaits the visitor to those shores:—

From side to side of her delightful isle
Is she not clothed with a perpetual smile,
Her fields a rich expanse of wavy corn,
Poured out from plenty's overflowing horn;
Her peaceful shores, where busy commerce waits
To pour his golden tide through all her gates?

This scene would be changed to one where ice-choked ports would be fed only by rivers, themselves frozen half the year, and where a mist, as constant as that of Labrador, would give through its fissures and breaks only sunlight enough to mature the coarsest grain. From such a climate commerce would be excluded, and agriculture would obtain but a scanty subsistence. The England of our fathers, and the England of our own days, would never have existed. It is one of the properties of that peculiar climate—the bracing winters, and the springs and summers, gradual, equal, and genial, as well as of the seafaring habits it produces—to generate a race, which, whether it remains at home or follows Raleigh and Davenport to American forests, or charges with Clive on the hosts at Arcot, always has maintained the same indomitable energy, the same sturdiness of moral character, the same indifference to the dramatic, but profound appreciation of the real, which led not only to the English reformation and to American colonization, not only to the revolution that made William of Orange King, and that which made George Washington President, but to the publication of Protestant doctrines and free principles throughout the globe. Our own land would not have remained undiscovered, but it would have been approached, not through the rugged rocks and scanty sea-board, but through the northern or southern entrances to the Mississippi valley. Those who visit that superb domain will concur in the remark, that had the valley of the Mississippi been known in time, the ravine-broken and stormy coast that lies east of the Alleghanies would never have been populated. The light and sociable French, or the indolent Spaniards, would not have hesitated. The magnificent tract which lies between the Rocky Mountains and the Alleghanies would have been their seat. There, cathedrals, like those of Mexico, would have arisen, to be thronged with a Creole race, in which the less worthy traits in each component element would have formed a servile union. No adventurous seamen would have thence sprung, to vex the remotest seas with their harpoons, and to exchange the produce of their native fields for the staples of foreign lands. The curling vapor over the salt-wells of the Kanawha; the heavy pall of smoke which now shrouds Pittsburg, and Zanesville, and Wheeling; the stern-wheel boat that, like a water-spider, and drawing hardly any more water, jerks up the shallow tributary, and the steam-hotel that traverses in state the mighty river; the snort of the locomotive, as, rather like a panther than a horse, it couches in the lair of the tunnel, and then springs onward to another tunnel over its air-line of tressel-work; the fierce glare of the furnace, as its blaze, stirred by the iron rod of the engineer, is seen along the river for miles through the midnight air,—these things would not have been noticed. In their place, it is true, a gay and contented peasantry, such as that we sometimes meet along the banks of the St. Lawrence, might have filled the prairies of the central Mississippi, and perhaps worked the sugar plantations of what was once New France. But in losing the stern discipline of a less propitious clime; in losing those hereditary traits of energy, of self-reliance, of personal inquiry, which a descent through a hardy and industrious ancestry produces; in losing the Protestant faith, —the colonies would have lost those elements which were to produce their ultimate national independence.

§ 51. What a difference to the world would have been worked by the reversal of this heat-equalizing agent it is not necessary here to discuss. It may be enough to say, that, if by this the Anglo-Saxon race had failed to acquire those energies which, by giving it the control of commerce, have given it the grand central distributing engine by which alone opinion is to be disseminated over the globe, the destinies of mankind in the future, as well as their liberties and faith in the past, would have been sadly altered. And when, as we may believe, to this island of England, so sea-tempered as to produce energy and virtue in their best human form, and to her empire-colonies of America—no less her colonies in lineage because no longer so in civil dependency—is to be assigned the great work of universally publishing evangelical faith and civil equality, we may well see something more than a mere economical purpose in that decree which turned the Gulf Stream from its Caribbean feeders into a canal, whose banks are themselves water, and directed it to flow through this same strange channel for three thousand miles, until it reach those shores which it is to temper.

b. CLIMATE.

§ 52. It is not proposed to consider here at large the influence of climate. One or two remarks, however, may be casually thrown out with regard to those discriminations, which seem at the first view inconsistent with an equal benevolence.

a[1]. *Its alternations as producing contentment and patriotism.*

The severe climates are not the subjects of depreciation by those who live in them. On the contrary, the sympathy of others with those who inhabit such climates, like that of the wealthy anarchist in Canning's admirable satire of the needy knife-grinder, is entirely uninvited by those on whom it is spent. Nowhere is there so strong and deep a love of country as that engendered in these same inhospitable climes. Nostalgia, or home-sickness, (heimweh,) is almost entirely confined to the inhabitants of mountainous and sterile soils. "It is remarkable," says Dr. Rush,* "that this disease is most common among the natives of countries that are least desirable for beauty, fertility, climate, or the luxuries of life." And Goldsmith thus touches on the same point,—

> The intrepid Swiss that guards a foreign shore,
> Condemned to climb his mountain-cliffs no more,
> If chance he hear the song, so sweetly wild,
> Which, on those cliffs, his infant hour beguiled,
> Melts at the long-lost scenes that round him rise,
> And sinks a martyr to repentant sighs.

---

* Rush, on the Mind, pp. 38, 39.

Those who have watched over a collection of boys, drawn, as is often the case in our own country, from a wide diversity of climates and soils, will recollect how it is that those homes are most pined after which, in a worldly point of view, are the least inviting. The cottage by the mountain-side, in which a rigid economy abridges even the few comforts which a hard soil and a narrow estate permit, plays in a sweet pathos before the sleeping vision of the boy, the dreams of whose next neighbor flit but lightly back to what the world would consider the infinitely superior charms of a luxurious city home.

b[1]. *As producing home virtues.*

§ 53. These climates are accompanied by home-enjoyments which are, in an eminent degree, bracing and comforting. Such a result, in fact, is incidental to the domestic life which a cold climate generates. Take, for instance, the inclement winter of England, which drives the family around the fireside, and compare it with the warmth of that genial French and Italian sky which draws them to the open field, or to the roadside where the village takes the place of the home. In the one scene, it is true, we see much that is plain and coarse. The rude and sometimes austere manner which, to strangers, will be absolutely harsh; the home-spun dress, cut in the most uncouth shape, arise, it cannot but be confessed, often from an entire want of perception of those graces and elegancies which give polite society one of its chief charms. But with these ruder qualities there is a deep and passionate domestic affection which pierces to the recesses of the hearts of those on whom it acts, and draws up from them the pure waters of a remunerative love. With this there is a practical, personal sense of responsibility to God, which is so apt to be lost where *home* is merged in *society*, and an equally conscientious, though perhaps reserved and undemonstrative sense of responsibility toward others. Such a picture as that which Burns gives us in his "Cotter's Saturday Night" could not be drawn in France, unless, perhaps, among those hills where the Huguenots found refuge. On the other hand, we shall be equally at a loss to discover, under the vicissitudes of even the most genial climates of our own land, and shall more so under the austere sky of England, scenes such as that where

> France displays her bright domain,
> Gay, sprightly land of mirth and social ease,
> Pleased with herself, whom all the world can please.

But grace is here dearly bought when the price is the surrender of home seclusion, and the merging of the real in the dramatic. If it should turn out that we are to make choice between the reserved earnestness of the domestic affections and the pictorial elegance of the social, we cannot but determine that the former is most conducive to a higher order of happiness. Tennyson tells us that

> 'Tis better to have loved and lost
> Than never to have loved at all;

and the practical experience of all is that none would part even with a grief, if with it is to go the memory of an earnest affection. There is still less ground for a comparison, if one must needs be made, between the home and the social affections when each is in successful play. For the difference is the old one between happiness and pleasure;

between the exercise of the healthy impulses of the heart in the view of conscience, and the display of its sensibilities in the eye of others; between a real and relied on reciprocation of affection, and a mere complimentary obeisance, paid out and received as such.

§ 54. To this it may be added, that a wide field of objects of enjoyment is not always accompanied by an increased capacity in enjoying. As the circuit of the instrument increases, its power of perception is weakened. The microscope may unfold the beauties of atom-worlds that lie in a butterfly's dust, but to do this it must be pointed to that dust alone. By increasing its range, we may see an hundredfold more objects superficially, but we will not see one entire. Thus it is that the frugal dweller by the hillside has often many more luxuries than the wealthy inhabitant of the city. For, as the latter's wealth increases, his luxuries diminish, until, when there is none which his wealth cannot purchase without self-denial, they cease to exist. All who have experienced an increase of wealth know how it is accompanied by a diminution of objects of real and innocent delight. What we called "treats," in more frugal days, have ceased to exist, just in the same way as there can be no holiday when all is vacation.*

* Charles Lamb has developed this thought with great beauty in the following passage from his letter on "Broken China":—"I wish the good old times would come again," she said, "when we were not quite so rich. I do not mean that I want to be poor; but there was a middle state,"—so she was pleased to ramble on,—"in which I am sure we were a great deal happier. A purchase is but a purchase, now that you have money

To these considerations it may be added, that human pleasure, so far from increasing, rather diminishes in the inverse ratio of its concentration.

> 'Tis pleasure to a certain bound,
> Beyond 'tis agony.

---

enough and to spare. Formerly it used to be a triumph. When we coveted a cheap luxury (and oh, how much ado I had to get you to consent in those times!) we were used to have a debate two or three days before, and to weigh the *for* and *against*, and think what we might spare it out of, and what saving we could hit upon that should be an equivalent. A thing was worth buying then when we felt the money that we paid for it.

"Do you remember the brown suit which you made to hang upon you till all your friends cried shame upon you, it grew so threadbare, and all because of that folio which you dragged home late at night from Barker's, in Covent Garden? Do you remember how we eyed it for weeks before we could make up our minds to the purchase, and had not come to a determination till it was nearly ten o'clock of the Saturday night, when you set off from Islington, fearing you should be too late? And when the old bookseller, with some grumbling, opened his shop, and, by the twinkling taper, (for he was setting bedwards,) lighted out the relic from his dusty treasures; and when you lugged it home, wishing it were twice as cumbersome; and when you presented it to me, and when we were exploring the perfectness of it, (*collating* you called it;) and while I was repairing some of the loose leaves with paste, which your impatience would not suffer to be left till daybreak,—was there no pleasure in being a poor man? or, can those neat, black clothes which you wear now, and are so careful to keep brushed, since we have become rich and finical, give you half the honest vanity with which you flaunted it about in that overworn suit—your old corbeau—for four or five weeks longer than you should have done, to pacify your conscience, for the mighty sum of fifteen, or sixteen shillings was it?—a great affair we thought it then, which you had lavished on the old folio.

Nor do the perceptions retain that tentative power which enables them to hold, for any length of time, their grasp on the objects of sensual or even of intellectual enjoyments.

Now you can afford to buy any book that pleases you, but I do not see that you ever bring me home any nice old purchases now.

"When you came home with twenty apologies for laying out a less number of shillings upon that print after Lionardo, which we christened the 'Lady Blanche;' when you looked at the purchase and thought of the money,—and thought of the money and looked again at the picture,—was there no pleasure in being a poor man? Now you have nothing to do but to walk into Colnaghi's and buy a wilderness of Lionardoes. Yet do you?

"Then, do you remember our pleasant walks to Enfield and Potter's bar, and Waltham, when we had a holiday,—holidays and all other fun are gone, now we are rich; and the little hand-basket, in which I used to deposit our day's fare of savory cold lamb and salad; and how you would pry about at noontide for some decent house where we might go in and produce our store, only paying for the ale that you must call for; and speculate upon the looks of the landlady, and whether she was likely to allow us a table-cloth; and wish for such another honest hostess as Izaak Walton has described many a one on the pleasant banks of the Lea, when he went a fishing; and sometimes they would prove obliging enough, and sometimes they would look grudgingly upon us, but we had cheerful looks still for one another, and would eat our plain food savorily, scarcely grudging Piscator his Trout Hall? Now, when we go out a day's pleasuring, which is seldom, moreover we *ride* part of the way, and go into a fine inn and order the best of dinners, never debating the expense, which, after all, never has half the relish of those chance country snaps, when we were at the mercy of uncertain usage and precarious welcome.

"There was pleasure in eating strawberries before they became quite common; in the first dish of peas, while they were yet dear, to have them for a nice supper, a treat. What treat can we have

The tendons relax and the sensibilities recoil; and at length the appetite turns in indifference, if not disgust, from that on which it has been satisfied. And the more the taste is pampered, the more fastidious it becomes, the more difficulty it has in finding an object on which it can rest. If the

---

now? If we were to treat ourselves now, that is, to have dainties a little above our means, it would be selfish and wicked. It is the very little more that we allow ourselves, beyond what the actual poor can get at, that makes what I call a treat. When two people, living together as we have done, now and then indulge themselves in a cheap luxury which both like, while each apologizes, and is willing to take both halves of the blame to his single share, I see no harm in people making much of themselves, in that sense of the word. It may give them a hint how to make much of others. But now, what I mean by the word,—we never do make much of ourselves. None but the poor can do it. I do not mean the veriest poor of all, but persons as we were, just above poverty.

"I know what you were going to say, that it is mighty pleasant at the end of the year to make all meet; and much ado we used to have every thirty-first night of December to account for our exceedings; many a long face did you make over your puzzled accounts, and, in contriving to make it out, how we had spent so much—or that we had not spent so much—or that it was impossible we should spend so much next year—and still we found our slender capital decreasing; but then, betwixt ways and projects, and compromises of one sort or another, and talk of curtailing this charge, and doing without that for the future, and the hope that youth brings, buoyant and laughing spirits, (in which you were never poor till now,) we pocketed up our loss; and, in conclusion, with 'lusty brimmers,' (as you used to quote it out of *hearty, cheerful Mr. Cotton*, as you called him,) we used to welcome in 'the coming guest.' Now we have no reckoning at all at the end of the old year; no flattering promises about the new year doing better for us."

other alternative be taken, and a capacity for more continued sensual enjoyment be secured, then comes premature old age and decay, if not remorse.

It may be partly from this fact, and partly from the heroic virtues which a life of austere early culture produces, that it is to these sterile countries that we are to look as the nurseries whence spring the races by which great empires are founded.

These remarks may be taken as introductory to the following observations on the effect of the alternation of seasons.

c^1. *As necessitating labor.*

§ 55. The few countries in which we find a fertile soil and an equal and genial climate, are those in which men are the most abject. Mr. Ellis gives us an example taken from the Otaheitans. They have a soil eminent for its richness, a climate for its equal and generous benignity. They live, however, almost as brutes on the spontaneous produce of the soil, and when urged to work, though only to the slight extent which is necessary to bring them to the comforts of civilization, they reply: "We should like these things very well, but we cannot have them without working; *that* we do not like, and therefore would rather do without them. The bananas and plantains ripen on the trees; the pigs fatten on the fruits that fall beneath them. These are all we want. Why then should we work?"

This inquiry, however, is one which the seasons, in by far the greater part of the habitable globe, do not permit to be put. The keen air of autumn braces the nerves, and the necessities of winter call hunger into that council of war in which the physical energies make their appearance, all whetted and armed for the great battle with nature, for which the early spring is clearing the way. Other allies soon appear. The sun does his part in lifting off the barricades of snow and ice, and softening the frosted gates of the rigid earth so as to let the invader readily in. Necessity, energy, the cheering calls of the opening season, the pleasure and triumph of that fruition which the gradual development of the year makes coincident with toil, combine to spur the husbandman to his post. And not the least beneficent part of this arrangement is the provision which brings on the several harvests in a measured procession. Those who, even under our own evenly distributed harvest system have chanced to visit a village when the wheat is being gathered in—who have seen how all the available male force, from the old man who is all the rest of the summer a fixture in the porch, down to the stable-boy whom the traveler depends upon to put up his horse, are at work harvesting, will understand the object of the arrangement by which the several crops, beginning with the hardy early vegetable, and ending with the no less hardy winter fruit, mature at distinct intervals. For the wheel of the seasons is regularly cogged, and as each cog comes on in its turn, it moves a distinct process of vegetation. Were it not so, the neat but small farm of the growing but still not rich farmer would cease to exist. When the harvest came there would be a sweep made for hands. As the capitalist saw his ripening corn, which a day or two longer would kill, he would force from his weaker neighbor whatever aid his wealth or his power enable him to secure. To bring in the full harvest, also, would require a large increase of the present agricultural population, and would in this way greatly derange the balance so necessary between the several industrial classes. Besides, let us observe the momentous consequences which would follow from a concentration of the several harvests. Now, when one crop fails, another remains. When improvidence or adverse weather kills the wheat that may be planted in the fall, April still remains open for oats, May for Indian-corn and for potatoes. So the storm of August may still follow the benignant sky of July, or precede that of September; and the harvest-home, which may be desolate one month, may abound in beauty and richness the next.

d^1. As generating energy, patience, and a sense of the beautiful.

§ 56. Let us observe, in addition, the moral and social effects produced by this development of the seasons, distinguished as it is by a combination of general laws with special adaptations. Napoleon said during the hundred days, that society can only really move onward under two forces—governmental pressure and popular impulse; and that it was in this respect like the ship which required the application of both wind and helm. So it is with the general laws of the seasons, producing both certainty enough to invoke steady work, and irregularities and special adaptations enough to generate enterprise, and at the same time an intelligent caution. By this same combination, while, on the one hand, the comprehensive wisdom of the Creator is displayed, on the other, by those immediate applications of a special divine will to human agency, man is made to know more deeply his entire dependence upon God.

Nor should it be forgotten that to this alternation of seasons we owe, in part at least, the sanctities of home. Winter comes with ligatures in his hands, to bind not only the stream and the earth, but the family. He drives the fisherman from his nets, the plowman from the field, the child from the play-ground, and collects them around the hearth. There a new senate is convened—the senate of the family. The village may meet to preserve its ways and commons, the farmers may consult as to the best way to put down vermin and keep off horse-thieves; but the family has its special objects, the preservation of home peace, and the culture of the heart. In a little community, so closely bound together for several months each year, it is soon learned how necessary for the good of each as well as of the whole it is, to pass laws requiring self-denial, personal purity, refinement, and thoughtfulness as to others. The veneering of politeness, which is enough for the superficial use of the world, does not do here. There must be an interior refinement by the establishment (and unless in early childhood, how hard is this to be done!) of a good heart. Now is there any school like the family for this, or any school-house but the home? And yet are we not indebted, if not to the school, at least for the school-house, to the pressure of winter?

§ 57. Let us, however, rise, in considering the question, to a higher stand-point. Changing the method of stating the argument for a moment, let us suppose that there is an all-wise Creator, to whom, for purposes of His own, it seems good to excite certain tastes and establish certain principles in His creatures, not by compulsion, but in such a way as to preserve their moral agency. Let us suppose that among these tastes and principles are:—

*a*². Appreciation of and love for beauty, particularly in connection with personal well-doing, and with a due objective exhibition of order and law, so that such beauty may itself be the subject of orderly development.

*b*². The faculty of patient hope and faith in the future, connected with present labor. "It is this," says Dr. Paley, "which creates farmers, which divides the profit of the soil between the owner and occupier; which, by requiring expedients, by increasing employment, and by rewarding expenditure, promotes agricultural arts and agricultural life, of all modes of life the best, being the most conducive to health, to virtue, to enjoyment."

*c*². Fixed habits of industry as a necessary element in probation.

*d*². Belief in the transient and ephemeral character of such present state of probation, and in a more splendid and enduring existence hereafter.

§ 58. Now, what spectacle could be devised grander or more impressive than that of the seasons? We have here a most exquisite, as well as a most sublime mechanism constructed. "The vegetable clock-work," says Mr. Whewell, "is so set as to go for a year." It is a clock-work whose dial-plate is the surface of the earth; whose figures are marked by flowers and fruits, and whose hours are struck in turn by the voices of the air, the field, and the forest. But Mr. Whewell abridges the argument from contrivance when he states that the clock of the seasons goes but for a year; for it is part of a great chronometer which the Artificer of the universe established before the beginning of time. Jean Paul, in one of his apothegms, brings before us an impressive picture of art as developed in the clock of St. Mary's, Lubeck, which will exhibit the movements of the heavenly bodies until 1875, when it must be reset. Dr. Paley, in illustration of the argument from contrivance, takes us to one of the ordinary time-pieces, against which he supposes his philosoper to stumble in crossing a field. Is not the argument strengthened, when the time the watch runs and the number of its combinations are multiplied ten thousandfold? And are we to recognize this progression of proof in the clock of art, which runs for years, and refuse it to the clock of Nature, which runs for ages?

To the beauty of the sights that the seasons unfold we may well turn, as reflecting not only the almighty power and skill of the Creator, but the tenderness with which He provides for His creatures sights of loveliness. The language of poetry, sometimes real, sometimes conventional, has been so intimately associated with the beauty of nature, that practical minds, when they hear anything like an accurate description of any of the exquisite scenes which the ocean, the meadow, or the sky afford, turn from it as if it were sentiment, not fact. But the delicate coloring of the spring flowers; the emerald verdure of the early grain as it springs from the dark mould,—that dark mould itself at once the grave of past vegetation and the cradle of future; the voices of the birds, those cheap orchestras of the poor; the rich and dark foliage of summer, and the gorgeous fruits of autumn,—all these things are FACTS, and are to be treated as such. Let us take, for instance, Bryant's exquisite description of Indian Summer:—

And now when comes the calm, mild day, as oft such days will come,
To tempt the squirrel and the bee from out their wintry home;
When the sound of dropping nuts is heard, though all the trees are still,
And twinkle in the smoky light the waters of the rill;
The south wind searches for the flowers whose fragrance late he bore,
And sighs to find them in the wood and by the stream no more.

§ 59. Now, this is all reality, and each distinct feature, as it stands before us in its individual beauty, will be found to tell its specific message. And this message is not single; for it combines several great truths. It tells us of that tenderness which provides sights of beauty and repose for eyes weary with the sorrows and trials of probation. It accompanies these spectacles with utterances of grandeur which make that tenderness, even if we view it by itself, still more wonderful and still more winning. It tells us of the patient endurance and love of order of the Almighty himself; and it asks us, if the *Creator* is thus forbearing and law-loving, what ought the *creature* to be. And, as the seed bursts both from its burial-place of last year to its resurrection of the next, it proclaims the crowning truth of all:—

"SO ALSO IS THE RESURRECTION OF THE DEAD: IT IS SOWN IN CORRUPTION, IT IS RAISED IN INCORRUPTION; IT IS SOWN IN DISHONOR, IT IS RAISED IN GLORY; IT IS SOWN IN WEAKNESS, IT IS RAISED IN POWER; IT IS SOWN A NATURAL BODY, IT IS RAISED A SPIRITUAL BODY."

c. WATERING THE EARTH.

§ 60. As we stand by the water-works in a large city, as, for instance, in Philadelphia, we find our recognition of the amount of contrivance used to become the more vivid as the simplicity and efficiency of the mechanism become the more clear. We observe the dam by which the river is raised to a height which enables it to supply the water power. By the bank we observe the dark and dripping ribs of the giant wheels as they heavily perform their rounds. Underneath us we can almost see the quivering recoils of the water, as by blow after blow it is beaten up the supply-pipes which lead to the top of the hill. Then comes the reservoir, whence the water is conducted through the great city below. The marble bath-tubs and the sparkling fountain in one mansion do not prove the usefulness of the contrivance more than the rough hydrant which supplies the stream by which the washerwoman plies her trade in another. It is a process which exhibits, in one of its highest grades, not only the skill but the beneficence of civilization.

Let us look, however, from this to the watering-works of the skies. The sun, acting on the rivers and the sea, produces a vapor which, while it raises, cleanses the water, which is then received into the reservoir of the clouds. Here it is held until the process is applied for its dispersion. A watering-pot is said to be an imitation of clouds, but at best the imitation is poor; for the rain drops so softly, so equally, and in showers so patient, as to temper the system as well as to supply the thirst of the vegetation it affects. While the clouds are the reservoir, the sun is the forcing-pump, the vapor the supply-pipes, and the rain the distributing-pipes. And yet, we find contrivance in the water-works of the city, but refuse to see it in the infinitely grander, and, at the same time, more delicate water-works of the skies.

But how is this process of condensation carried on? Let us look, before answering this question, at the peculiar configuration of the North American continent, taking this, for our purpose, as an illustration of the whole globe. We have, so far as the eastern half of the continent is concerned, two great surfaces of water from which rain may be condensed, the Atlantic Ocean and the Gulf of Mexico; and we have two great ranges of mountains acting as condensers. These ranges have no unimportant office to exercise in connection with the watering of the continent to which they belong. For, to adapt to them the eloquent language applied by Guyot to mountain ranges generally, they are "placed by Nature to rob the winds of their treasures, to serve as reservoirs for the rain-waters, and to distribute them afterwards, as they are needed, over the surrounding plains. Their wet and cloudy summits seem to be untiringly occupied with this important work. From their sides flow numberless torrents and rivers, carrying in all directions wealth and life."

§ 61. Let us look, for a moment, at the stream of warm air which arises from the Gulf of Mexico and from the Mississippi Valley. There an excess of rain is peculiarly necessary to feed those great rivers by which that valley is watered. The ordinary processes of condensation would be inadequate for this purpose. It is here, however, that the Alleghanies and the Rocky Mountains come into play. The wind strikes first the lowlands, meeting, perhaps, with currents as warm as itself, and, therefore, incapable of producing that condensation which results, when two volumes of atmosphere of different temperatures and of unlike degrees of moisture come in contact. But soon the trade-winds from the Atlantic, and the moist and warm currents from the Gulf or the plains, ascend, till they touch the higher and cooler layers that hang around the mountain sides. This produces a rapid and copious condensation, and from this, on the eastern slope of the Rocky Mountains, flow the Northern Mississippi, the Missouri, the Yellowstone, the Platte, the Arkansas, the Red River, and the Rio Grande. Here, however, the process stops. Before these winds reach the summit this moisture is exhausted; no more rain falls, because no more moisture is condensed. It is not until the western descent of these plains presents itself to the breezes that arise from the Pacific that rain begins to fall. It falls there, it is true, but lightly, for the southwestern winds are much less fully freighted with moisture than the southeastern, yet in sufficient quantity to supply the comparatively moderate acquirements of the narrow Pacific coast, and to fill the sources of the only two rivers by which the coast is traversed, the Columbia and the Colorado. It leaves, however, between the western and eastern slopes, that area of rainless table-lands which we call the great plains.*

§ 62. It may not be out of place to pause here for a moment to observe that these great plains are not, after all, mere blanks in the expanse of creation. There, the *gramma*,

---

* These views will be found elaborated by an article, by the present writer, in the North Am. Review for July, 1858, p. 66.

or buffalo-grass, raises its spiral and hairlike, but nutritious and perennial moss; there, are water-works adapted to the peculiar wants of this thin and dry vegetation. The snow on the mountain-peaks behind melts at the approach of spring, falling in multitudinous threads over the great plains, and where it does not actually irrigate, softens the dense earth by its temporary vapor. There, the buffalo-grass pierces the hard soil with its delicate fibres, holding its seed in its root. There, as summer comes, the haymakers are at work, though they toil not with human hands, as the sun and the equal drought cure the hay on the ground. Hence it is that these great plains are the barns in which Divine wisdom and benevolence stores away the feed for innumerable wild creatures who there find their meat in due season; there the buffalo, (preserved in these parks from the rapacity of man,) the wild horse, the elk, the deer, and the wild sheep, congregate in numbers which, in the aggregate, are estimated at an hundred million; there the great fur-nursery of the Western future is seated. When the prairies are fenced into farms; when the woods are leveled to pastures, here the wild beasts of the forests will find a refuge, itself as large as all Europe, where their lairs will be undisturbed by the proximity of human habitation. And should a pastoral population, by the aid of the Artesian wells the Government is now projecting, find a home in these plains, it will not be without its appropriate nourishment and mission. "In these elevated countries," says a sagacious observer, "fresh meats become the preferable food for man, to the exclusion of bread, vegetables, and salted articles. The atmosphere of the great plains is perpetually brilliant with sunshine, tonic, healthy, and inspiring to the temper. It corresponds with and surpasses the historic climate of Syria and Arabia, whence we inherit all that is ethereal and refined in our system of civilization, our religion, our sciences, our alphabet, our numerals, our written languages, our articles of food, our learning, and our systems of social manners."

§ 63. But, supposing that these plains remain deserts, interspersed, it is true, as the ocean, by rich and fertile islands, but still, like the ocean, incapable of sustaining man except as a traveler, does it follow that they are of no use? To their west will then lie California and Oregon, great producing, and yet not capable of becoming great manufacturing countries; the former containing the finer, but not the coarser metals, together with breadstuffs abundant for her own support; the latter eminent for her wheat-growths, her fisheries, and her lumber. But in neither California nor Oregon is to be found the coal capable of working, nor the iron for framing those great machines by which the wool of a country can be turned into clothing, by which the hides of the millions of cattle that range the prairies can be used for the shoes and the furniture of the nations on either side, by which the buttons can be turned and the nails cut. On the other hand, on the eastern coast of this great desert-sea, will lie Kansas and Nebraska, of all countries the best suited for the sites of vast manufactories. There, run rivers whose descents and whose copiousness adapt them as well to turn the wheel as to irrigate the land; there, underneath a soil which can support a million of workmen, are spread layers of coal, which will form the fuel for tens of thousands of square miles; there, is the iron which is to form both the engine and the staple, the arm that strikes as well as the material that is struck; there, in fact, are the great furnishing warerooms, where the people of California will exchange their gold and quicksilver, and those of Oregon their fish and lumber, for the hardware, the clothes, and the furniture, which the manufactories of the Missouri Valley will produce. If this view be correct, the scene alone of these prairie sea-ports of the West will not be unlike that at one of our ocean-ports in the East. At the docks of the great cities which will then spring upon this shore of civilization, will arrive fleet after fleet of the future ships of the desert, each dashing over its iron track to the destined port. There, on the levee at which these waves of sand will terminate, will be strewn the boxes containing not only the gold of the Sacramento and of the San Joaquin, and the quicksilver of New Almaden, but the wines which are even now beginning to be drawn from the vineyards of Los Angelos, and the cotton and sugar from the south of Sierra Nevada. There, will be found, in an abundance which New England herself can but rival, the dried and salted fish of the Columbia and the Willamette, and the furs which the Oregon hunting-grounds produce in such rare abundance. There, will be seen warehouses and shops like those which, in New York and Philadelphia, collect for Western inspection the products of Europe and of New England. It will be cheaper for the Pacific merchant to come here and purchase than it would be to visit the cities of the Atlantic. Manufacturers on the Kansas River, on the Blue River, on the Osage, can sell heavy goods at least twenty per cent. cheaper than manufacturers in Connecticut or Pennsylvania. Freight, amounting to five dollars on the hundred-weight, will be a sufficient protection to force the manufactories of the Missouri Valley at once into energetic action. The time will come when the Western merchant, who leaves California by the cars to buy his stock at the East, will find in Topeka, in Nebraska City, in Lawrence, warehouses which will unite the products of the Atlantic States and of Europe with the goods which the abundance of breadstuffs, the proximity of the raw material, and the relief from the burden of freight which bears so heavily on transportation across the Alleghanies, will enable the factories of Kansas and of Nebraska to present on the spot to the exclusion of Eastern competitors.

§ 64. In the people of the great plains the markets of Kansas and Nebraska will not find purchasers only. Those plains, desertlike as they may be, are dotted with islands of great beauty and richness. Even in the sterile wastes, intervening between the south fork of the Platte and the Arkansas, there frequently occur "little valleys," as they are called by Colonel Fremont, "with pure crystal water, here leaping swiftly along, and there losing itself in the sands; green spots of luxurious grass, flowers of all colors, and timber of different kinds." Sometimes these valleys spread themselves into extensive territories, of one of which, on the westernmost slope of the Rocky Mountains, the same explorer tells us that it is twenty miles in diameter, "covered with a rich soil, abundantly watered, and surrounded by high and well-timbered mountains,—a place where a farmer might well delight to establish himself, if he were content to live in the seclusion which it imposes." Sometimes the arable land is distributed in a circle, like that which surrounds the Salt Lake. Not unlike the ocean, this vast sweep of desert is broken by islands that are themselves continents in extent and variety of produce, as well as by islands that are mere specks of rock and sand. It will be to the first eastern coast that checks the waves of sand by which these islands are girt, in other words, it will be to the prairie-banks of Nebraska and Kansas, that this insular commerce of the desert will tend.

§ 65. There is one other view, however, which is calculated still more to enhance the value of our East American land. When the time comes for the inland transportation of the goods of China and India from the Pacific to the Atlantic, it will be found that there is one route whose cheapness will enable it to outbid all competitors. The Pacific shores, unlike those of the more sociable and restless Atlantic, rise up in uniform and dignified seclusion from the approaches of the sea. The coast of the Atlantic is perforated by bays and seamed by rivers. There is scarcely an area of ten miles square, east of the Rocky Mountains, which does not send its tributary to the Atlantic. Far different is the case with the western slope of North America. South of the Columbia River, two ranges of mountains follow the shore, the westernmost of which approaches so closely to the sea as to leave no room for a river of any length to strike inland. The rivers which run into the Bay of San Francisco traverse merely the coast. But the Columbia River, as if for the very purpose of affording an avenue for inland trade, while it forms one vast and navigable stream from the ocean to the centre of the Oregon plain, flares out at the latter point into three forks, each of which offers a pass, and the only passes here accessible, through the Rocky Mountains. It is the Columbia alone that breaks through the mountains of the Cascade and Sierra Nevada; it is the Columbia alone that holds the keys to the passes of the mountains, from which, on the easternmost side, run the tributaries of the Platte. The forks of the Columbia will, therefore, have on one side of them the only navigable waters leading to the Pacific, and, on the other, the only highways through whose mountain gates the locomotive can pass on its way to the Missouri Valley. That the Platte and the Kansas are incapable of navigation, we think is now abundantly proved; but it is equally clear that the valleys through which they run are the natural courses through which the canal must be opened and the railway laid. Thus there will pour into the great depots which these frontier States will present, not only the products of Eastern and Western America, but those of China and India.

§ 66. To these considerations is to be added the fact, that the corn and wheat prairies of Nebraska, Iowa, and Kansas, stand on the banks of that great river, which, with a volume, a force, and through an extent of country which no other stream can equal, shoots down the freight committed to it upon the vast corn-consuming plains of the Southern Mississippi. It is as if the staple and the produce were placed at the top of a great natural inclined plane, and the consumer at the bottom. Never was there such an avenue for such a freight. For five hundred miles these magnificent prairies slope upward from the river banks; for one thousand miles the river dashes down with a velocity which enables even the slower class of steamboats to descend at the rate of from fifteen to twenty miles an hour. It is here that the Missouri has great advantage over the Mississippi. The prairie country is scarcely reached by the latter river, so far as continuous navigation is concerned. The Rapids, at Keokuk, interpose a serious barrier to the continuous shipment of freight from any but the southeast corner of Iowa and the southern lobe of Illinois. Were it not for this, the shallows, above Dubuque, interpose still greater difficulties in the way of the produce of Wisconsin and Minnesota. The navigation of the Missouri, on the other hand, continues nearly one thousand miles beyond where that of the Mississippi stops. Where the languid waters of the latter have scarcely force enough to propel, or depth enough to float a raft, the powerful current of the former enables the heaviest boats to double their speed. Necessary, indeed, is this superior energy in order to reach and drain the remotest regions of Central North America. But by what a stupendous mechanism is this produced!

§ 67. These remarks may be of incidental value in showing how provisions have been made, from the commencement of time, for the sustenance and comfort of the countless multitudes who are hereafter to occupy what may be the final seat of our race. But there is something more than this in the setting apart, not merely of these immense preserves for the sustenance of those creatures upon whom man depends for so large a portion of his clothing, if not his food, but of a land-sea as a commercial highway between the almost equally fertile, though diversely producing regions of the American East and West. If we look upon it as one of the peculiar blessings of our own race that our forefathers, on the shores of Old and New England, were drawn by commerce and the proximity of the coast to assume the hardships, to acquire the discipline, and to amass the wealth of the carrying trade of the ocean, may we not see the same advantages accruing in future to those who are to have the great carrying trade of the land?

But suppose a different arrangement of surface, by which the two ranges of the North American continent were consolidated, as in South America, into one spinal ridge, whose base would be the Gulf of Mexico, and whose water-shed would have sloped equally to the Atlantic and the Pacific coasts. Removed as such a chain would be from either of the oceans by at least a thousand miles, the moist sea-winds would have dropped their rainy contents long before they reached that great condensing apparatus which the mountains would afford. No rains would fall, therefore, on Central North America; and the Valley of the Mississippi, except those portions of it bordering on the Gulf and the great lakes, would be an arid waste. Of all territories those which are the most capable of raising a rich and numerous agricultural population are the States of Ohio, Illinois, and Iowa, of Missouri and Kansas, of Tennessee and Kentucky. But take these domains out of the Valley of the Mississippi, and let them be heaved upward by a central ridge, to which the Atlantic and Pacific winds could never penetrate, and you have instead, either the rainless plains or the desolate and malign ravines,—the *Mauvaises*

Terres, which now make the slopes of the Rocky Mountains uninhabitable. The Mississippi and its tributaries would have ceased to exist, and the habitable portions of North America reduced two-thirds.

d. SOIL.

§ 68. "Man," say McCosh and Dickie, in their work on "Creation,"* "is but the unwitting copyist, on a small scale, of actions which have been conducted on a far greater scale, and apparently with his benefit in view. Those very qualities which a good soil ought to possess, have been induced, in course of time, by various chemical and physical agencies, which have been in continual operation. The debris of rocks yielding calcareous, silicious, aluminous, and other mineral ingredients, have been brought together, and mixed in a way which the husbandman imitates when necessity demands. The furrows drawn by our plowshares are but scratches on the surface of the soil compared with the changes to which that same soil has been subjected in former ages, and to which it owes its varied capabilities of supporting plants and yielding subsistence to the animal kingdom."

Now let us view, in this connection, the soil of our own Mississippi Valley. There, besides the agencies just mentioned, are these great rivers by which this plain is watered, and whose specific mission can be traced in the superb mould which they have been for ages engaged in forming.

---

* Page 346.

For, long before the white man, or that strange, parenthetical people which preceded him,—even before that

> Disciplined and populous race,

which built the great mounds of the West,

> While yet the Greek
> Was hewing the Pentelicus to forms
> Of symmetry, and rearing on its rock
> The glittering Parthenon;

then were these rivers engaged in collecting, in depositing, in manuring the soil. Could a scoffer among the fallen angels, such as those who in these days argue the absence or indolence of God from the apparent wastes of creation, have watched these rivers as amid the pine forests and the lagoons of pre-Adamite life they wore their sluggish way through their marshy bed, until, as time passed on, and the fertilizing action of the water developed itself, rich and dark mosses began to cluster, and mammoth ferns to raise their thick and juicy spires, and the canebrake to thicken, so as to present an impenetrable barrier on the river bank; could he have seen how the waters of these rivers, and of the seas from which they subsided, were only broken by the clumsy dip of bird-mammoths when in pursuit of fish, or by the plunge of the water-horse, he might well have asked, as he compared his own high and refined order of intelligence with the low and inartificial type of creatures before him, what was the purpose of this apparent waste. If so, a view of the distant future would be the answer. Reefs, the workmanship of that coral population which, for hundreds of years, had been rearing in the waters their fretted mansions, would gradually receive a light though fertile soil. Then comes a rich and fat vegetation, producing and precipitating by its oils and salts the most effective of manures. Then, as the rivers narrow, and the bluffs arise, and as the agency of fire begins to be felt, the prairie-grass commences its work of covering this rich soil with a canvas to preserve it for the use of the nations to come. Oak-trees, from three to four hundred years old, have been found with this prairie sod so placed underneath their roots as to show that it was there when the acorn was dropped. For centuries, therefore, the long and strong threads of the grass-root have been knitted to and fro, until at last they have become a fabric, the tenacity of which no loom can rival. For centuries birds have rendered their aid to complete the work by dropping down seeds of an infinite variety of stunted but thick-set little plants that clinch and rasp the sod above and beneath. For centuries fires have periodically blazed over the whole surface, forcing vegetation, in very self-defence, to betake itself to underground work, where its enemy cannot reach it, packing itself away in cellars two or three stories deep.

§ 69. Now, let us observe the soil that by this process has been produced. On the bottom lands we have a soil of sand and clay, richly impregnated and saturated with carbon and with the vast quantities of decayed vegetable matter which the rivers are constantly precipitating. Corn, not unusually to the amount of an hundred and fifty bushels to the acre, is here produced, with scarcely any more preparation than the turning of the soil, which is already so soft and pliable as to require only the ordinary plow-work. From this, which forms, more strictly speaking, the river-basin, there rises not unfrequently a second, or subsidiary bottom, at an average height of fifty feet from the river level, and sloping back to the bluff heights which form the base of the inland prairies. Of the fertility of this formation, as well as of that of the vast inland expanses that are covered by the prairie sod, it is not necessary here to speak. It is sufficient to say, that nations, exceeding in population all Europe and Asia, will find food in the great valley which Divine wisdom and beneficence has thus prepared.

e. FUEL.

§ 70. The traveler who passes up the Upper Missouri into regions where the crack of the woodman's ax is as yet but rarely heard, will recollect how the progress of civilization is marked by the frequency of the little wood-piles which are placed along the shore to meet the wants of the steamboat as she pushes her away against the strong and muddy current. "There," is the cry, as the pile of fuel exhibits itself on the river-bank, "there is the mark of man; there exists, not far off, a human home, and here is the sign of thought and contrivance." No one would listen contentedly to the suggestion that these little heaps were drift-wood, broken by some violent storm into these peculiar shapes, and then swept by chance to these particular spots in the heaps in which they are now found.

It is hard, however, to see how we can admit contrivance in the wood-piles by the river-side, and deny it to the wonderful deposits of fuel which we find adapted to the growing wants of human society. As the forests are hewn down, and more particularly as the great and treeless prairies are peopled, we may well pause to admire that wise mercy which provided an inexhaustible field of fuel at the very spot where it is the most required. And yet it is no slight proof of the patience and majesty of the procession of the Divine will, that it is only lately that man has been able to understand the object of this great contrivance. Those huge cone-bearing trees, those rich and varied mosses, that flowerless and fruitless vegetation, so luxuriant and so immense, for what were they meant? And then, those layers of black stone, cropping out by the hill-side, what object have they? But now the answer comes in the hum of "15,000 steam-engines, with a power equal to that of 2,000,000 of men, and thus is put into operation machinery equaling the unaided power of 300,000,000 or 400,000,000 of men."* The answer rises with the smoke of the cottage where labor plies its task, and from the whistle of both the magnificent steam-hotel that navigates the Mississippi, and the energetic and bustling little propeller that darts up into the narrowest of the inlets that feed the inhospitable shores of Lake Superior.

So it is, interpreting the meaning of the past by the development of the present. If, as we are entitled to do, we take the converse, and judge of the development of the future by the meaning of the present, how still more majestic becomes that Providence by which both present and future are determined! Thick beds of coal, we are told,

* Hitchcock's Rel. Truth Illustrated by Science, p. 111, etc.

underlie 200,000 square miles in the United States, which have been actually probed, irrespective of the vast area to be hereafter examined. Taking, as does Dr. Hitchcock, 1100 cubic miles of coal as the measurement of that already discovered, and assuming with him that one cubic mile would supply the country for a thousand years, we are able to look forward over a period of a million of years during which this fuel would remain unexhausted.*

§ 71. Nor is the care shown in stowing away this fuel less worthy of our admiration. The masses of these soft, but gradually hardening vegetable-coal, were overlaid with strata of rock, forming a roof to the vast vaults in which they were deposited for future use. These vaults, or coal-cellars, are placed in the vicinity of the points where their contents are to be needed. The tropics know them not, and the semi-tropics but slightly. But in those Northern climes, whose vicissitudes most encourage labor, there, where the great factories of the world are to be placed, where its commercial depots are to spring up, and population, in its most concentrated shape, is to be collected, this fuel has been stored. And then, with a careful providence which anticipates, though on so much more splendid a scale, the forethought of the manufacturer, who, before putting his machinery to work, collects together his staples as well as his fuel, we find that iron and limestone are almost invariably placed in proximity to the coal.†

---

* See Hitchcock's Rel. Truth Illustrated by Science, p. 112.

† The bearing of the above on the political future of the United States is strikingly exhibited in Professor Le Conte's

We may well, then, unite in applying to these great and beneficent arrangements for the comfort of man that remarkable passage in which the Saviour of men—He who, during His human life, was so comfortless among those

late lectures on coal, before the Smithsonian Institute.* "There are, within the limits of the United States, no less than four coal-fields of enormous dimensions. One of these, the Apalachian coal-field, commences on the north, in Pennsylvania and Ohio, sweeping south through Western Virginia and Eastern Kentucky, Tennessee, extends even into Alabama. Its area is estimated at about 60,000 square miles. A second occupies the greater portion of Illinois and Indiana; in extent almost equal to the Apalachian. A third covers the greater portion of Missouri; while a fourth occupies the greater portion of Michigan. Just out of the limits of the United States, in New Brunswick and Nova Scotia, there is still a fifth, occupying, according to Mr. Lyell, an area of 36,000 square miles. Besides these, there are several others of less extent. If we now compare the relative coal areas of the principal coal-producing countries, the superiority of our own will be still conspicuous. The annual production of coal in Great Britain is more than seven times that of the United States, although her coal area is so much less. It is estimated that even at this enormous rate of production the coal-fields of Great Britain will yet last for five hundred years. There is little danger, then, that ours will fail us shortly. Now, industry, as the basis of the organization of society, forms the distinguishing feature of modern civilization. Coal is the very aliment of industry. The material prosperity of any country may, therefore, be tolerably accurately estimated by the amount of coal consumed. According to this method of estimation, Great Britain is superior to all other countries in actual material civilization. But if the consumption of coal is a measure of the *actual* civilization of a country, *the amount of coal area* represents its *potential* civilization. How far are we

* Smith. Inst. Rep. 1857, p. 129.

whose comforts He suffered so much and worked so grandly to promote—thus speaks :—

"The Lord possessed me in the beginning of His way, before his works of old. I was set up from everlasting, from the beginning, or ever the earth was. When there were no depths, I was brought forth; when there were no fountains abounding with water. Before the mountains were settled; before the hills was I brought forth; while as yet He had not made the earth, nor the fields, nor the highest part of the dust of the world. When He prepared the heavens I was there: when He set a compass upon the face of the depth: when He established the clouds above: when He strengthened the fountains of the deep: when He gave to the sea His decree, that the waters should not pass His commandment: when He appointed the foundations of the earth: THERE I WAS BY HIM, AS ONE BROUGHT UP WITH HIM: AND I WAS DAILY HIS DELIGHT, REJOICING ALWAYS BEFORE HIM; REJOICING IN THE HABITABLE PART OF HIS EARTH; AND MY DELIGHTS WERE WITH THE SONS OF MEN."

---

superior to all other countries in this respect! What a glorious destiny awaits us in the future,—a destiny already predetermined in the earliest geological history of the earth!"

CHAPTER VI.

FROM THE PROGRESS OF SOCIETY.

a. Arts and sciences.

§ 72. There are but two ways of accounting for the comparatively recent development of the arts and sciences: the one is, that man, though as a race, of indefinite age, has only of late years been endowed with faculties for this purpose; the other is, that the race itself is of recent creation.

Take, for instance, the first alternative. Who endowed the race with these new and special powers? Does not a new and substantive addition to the properties of mind prove an originator as much as does its original establishment?

But, in point of fact, there is no such recent accretion to the store of human intellect. It is true that Christianity has given an industrial value and beneficence to modern art, and that this has almost indefinitely increased the number of useful inventions; but is art itself developed in our own times to any greater degree than we would expect from the accumulation of the experience derived from so long a lapse of years? Compare, for instance, the elegance of the art of our own days with that of what is called ancient times, and see wherein we have gained. It is not in architecture, however it may be in house building. It is not in sculpture, however it may be in the industrial use of stone.

It is not in the embossing and moulding of gold, however it may be in the working of iron. In the mere line of ornament it is a question whether the *lost* arts do not almost equal the *retained* arts.

§ 73. Nor can we say that the inventive faculties of the human race have diminished. Nothing has since exceeded the fertility of invention and the vividness of the grouping of the Iliad,—nothing has equaled the sublime and pathetic theodicy of the Book of Job. Of Aristotle, we are told by Archbishop Whately, that his is the only human intellect which, at the same time, originated and perfected an art. Nor can we now explore the remains of Pompeii or of Nineveh, without seeing that the inventive faculty among the artists who dwelt in those ancient cities was as strong as their power of decoration was great.

But if, as is thus shown, the faculty and habit of invention are not of late introduction; if we are to presume them coeval with our race, does not this bring the creation of man down to a comparatively recent period? Could intellects as flexible as those which framed the Iliad, or ambition as remorseless and patient as that which built the Pyramids, have worked for centuries without leaving a mark? Let us see how we apply the same test to other matters of human observation. Robinson Crusoe finds one day the print of a human foot on the spot which a day before was unmarked, and he concludes that, between the first and second visits, man had been there. So in our own land, we measure the duration of the several races which possessed it by the monuments of art they left. When we find that, compared with the geological record, the history of human art is very brief; when we see how every year heralds in important inventions, showing a progression which, in itself, involves a commencement, we must conclude that our race is not indefinite in its duration, but that it had a definite and specific beginning.

b. Reproduction.

§ 74. Taking the ratio of increase of man, as exhibited during the section of history concerning which we have been able to collect statistics, we have no difficulty in determining that, within a specific range of time, man must have commenced to exist. Here geology, as will be noticed more fully under another head, comes in to point out to us exactly the period of animal creation in which the introduction of man took place.

c. Written history.

§ 75. Beyond three, or, at the utmost, four thousand years back, we have no trace of the existence of any authentic history. If man was eternal, with those same capacities for narration which the earliest records display in at least an equal degree with the latest, there is no other way of accounting for this silence except on the hypothesis of some great convulsion which tore apart the lines of communication. But if so, the vivid memory of this great disruption would have been recorded by those who stood on this side of the chasm. They would have left for us, in language the most enduring, their testimony to an event so momentous. But, instead of this, we have tradition, both written and unwritten, all tending the other way.

§ 76. To these remarks may be added the following striking observations of Dr. Chalmers :—"After all, they are the direct testimonies, handed down from one to another in the stream of Jewish and Christian authors, which constitute the main strength and solidity of the historical argument for the historical fact of a creation. There might be fitter occasions for entering into the detail of this evidence, but we hold it not out of place to notice even at present the strong points of it. In tracing the course upwards from the present day, we arrive, by a firm and continuous series of authors, at that period, when not only the truth of the Christian story is guarantied by thousands of dying martyrs, but when the Old Testament Scriptures—these repositories of the Jewish story—obtained a remarkable accession to their evidence, which abundantly compensates for their remoteness from our present age. We allude to the split between two distinct and independent, or stronger still, two bitterly adverse bodies of witnesses at the outset of the Christian economy. The publicity of the New Testament miracles; the manifest sincerity of those who attested them, as evinced by their cruel sufferings in the cause, not of opinions which they held to be true, but of facts which they perceived by their senses; the silence of inveterate and impassioned enemies, most willing, if they could, to have transmitted the decisive refutation of them to modern times; these compose the main strength of the argument for our later Scriptures. And then, besides the reference in which they abound to the former Scriptures, and by which, in fact, they give the whole weight of their authority to the Old Testament, we have the superadded testimony of an entire nation now ranged in zealous hostility against the Christian faith, and bent upon its overthrow. * * * * Now, the truth of the continuous narrative which forms the annals of this wondrous people would demonstrate a great deal more than what we are in quest of: that the world had a beginning, or rather, that many of the world's present organizations had a beginning, and have not been perpetuated everlastingly from one generation to another by those laws of transmission which now prevail over the wide extent of the animal and vegetable kingdoms."*

---

* 1 Nat. Theol., p. 183. Constable's edition.

CHAPTER VII.

FROM GEOLOGY.

a. Anterior uninhabitability of the earth.

§ 77. The conditions of heat and cold prescribe that where the former is brought into contact with the latter, through a conducting medium, the heat will be lost unless there be a process inside for its continued generation. Thus, if we go into a room where the atmosphere is at zero, and find in it a stove-drum with a superficial heat of 80°, we conclude either that the drum is now supplied with heat, bringing it up to this temperature, or that it is gradually cooling from an anterior higher degree of heat. We know that the cold air and the hot drum could not have remained in contact any long period without an approach toward the equalization of their temperatures; and, finding that the drum is not connected with any fire, we, therefore, conclude that it has been gradually cooling. Now, the atmosphere around the earth is of a temperature of at least fifty-eight degrees below zero. That of the earth runs up from twenty to an hundred degrees above zero. One of two alternatives is, therefore, correct: either the earth has had a beginning, or it has not. If it has had a beginning, this involves a maker. If it has not, but is indefinitely old, then, as it is not pretended that it contains the power of the indefinite renewal of heat, the alternative follows that there must have been a period when it was in a state of incandescence. Hence, in either way, we come back to the alternative of supernatural interference at such definite anterior period.

b. SUBSEQUENT CREATION OF SPECIFIC FORMS OF ORGANIZED LIFE.

a[1]. *Man.*

§ 78. "All observation," says Dr. Hitchcock,* "teaches us that he (man) was one of the last of the animals that was placed upon the earth. In vain do we search through the six miles of solid rocks that lie piled upon one another, commencing with the lowest, for any trace of man. And it is not until we come into the uppermost formations,—we mean the alluvial, nay, not until we get almost to the top of that, merely in the loose soil that is spread over the surface, —that we find his bones. And yet these, formed of the same materials as the bones of other animals, would have been as certainly preserved as theirs, in the lower rocks, had he existed there. The conclusion is irresistible, and it is acquiesced in by all experienced geologists, that man did not exist as a cotemporary of the animals found in the rocks. At least five vast periods of time, with their numerous yet distinct groups of organic beings, passed over this globe before the appearance of man. This is not a dreamy, hypothetical conclusion, but a simple matter of fact, which has been scrutinized with great care, and by some unfriendly to revelation, who would gladly have found it

* Rel. Truth Illustrated from Science, p. 120.

otherwise. But no fossil man or works of man have been discovered below alluvium, (in which we include drift;) nor would any really scientific man risk his reputation by maintaining the existence of the human species earlier than the alluvial period. What an astonishing exhibition does this scientific fact bring before us! Suppose we could explain by chemical and organic laws how the inferior animals were gradually developed from one another in the successive periods of our world's history. Yet here we have the phenomenon of a being introduced at once, superior somewhat in organic structure to the other animals, but raised immeasurably above them all by his lofty intellectual, and moral powers,—a being destined to take the supreme control of all inferior natures, and, so far as need be, to subject them all to his will; and, in fact, to convert the elements into servants to do his pleasure. The anatomist can, indeed, describe his organization; the physiologist can point out the functions of his organs; and the zoologist can assign him rank at the head of animate creation; but how is the psychologist baffled when he attempts to unravel the wonders of his spiritual power, and the theologian when he looks into the depths of his moral and immortal nature! * * What greater miracle does even revelation disclose?"

b[1]. *Inferior animals.*

§ 79. I propose, under this head, to restrict myself to the examination of a few of the fossils lately discovered in a single and not very large section of territory,—the Bad Lands of Nebraska, called by the French trappers the *Mauvaises Terres.* The geological formation of these lands is of the tertiary period, and of all sections of

America as yet explored, they present objects of the greatest interest to the student of cosmical as well as geological science.* The traveler who descends from the vast and now dreary level of the surrounding prairie, is appalled by the sight of a basin of fossil cemeteries, sinking nearly two hundred feet below the adjacent surface. On the sandy soil of this basin rise an infinite series of minaret-pointed peaks, some jutting up two hundred feet, and many painted on the side with prismatic hues. The quaint-looking towers; the winding alleys which separate block from block; the occasional buttresses which round off one line of streets; the chimneylike turrets that rise over the level of the larger and more compact masses, give all the evidences of some vast but deserted metropolis. When, however, the observer descends to the supposed city, the delusion vanishes. The perpendicular walls fall backward into slanting, weather-beaten rocks. The pavements crumble into sands, which, in the torrid heats of August, parch the traveler's feet as much as the vertical sun oppresses his brain. The chimneys are but blocks of rock, and the minarets splinters of spar.

These castellated structures, though they are not the evidences of human civilization, are the metres by which are noted the progress of events far more stupendous than those of mere mechanical enterprise. The turrets and columns of the Bad Lands are incrusted with the fossil remains of races submerged by the fresh waters of the early tertiary period.

---

* This subject is more fully considered by the present writer, in the Episcopal Review for Jan., 1858, to which the reader is referred.

Animals which preceded the mammoth and mastodon—and between which and the mammoth and the mastodon there exists a chasm which neither class has overpassed—are here to be found in unequaled completeness. Thus, for instance, in the Archiotherium, a specimen discovered by David Dale Owen, in his exploration, and examined by Dr. Leidy,* are united characters belonging to the pachyderms, the plantigrades, and the digitigrades. With these are grouped a series of other individuals, which demonstrate, to use the language of Mr. Owen himself, by no means an intentional supporter of the Mosaic account, that "at the time these singular animals roamed over the *Mauvaises Terres* of the Upper Missouri, the configuration of our present continents was very different from what it now is. Europe and Asia were then, in fact, no continents at all, being represented only by a few islands, scattered over a wide expanse of ocean. The Atlantic seaboard of the United States, back to the mountain ranges, and up the Valley of the Mississippi as high as Vicksburg, was yet under water.—In Europe, during the period following the extermination of the eocene Fauna of Nebraska, the Alps have been heaved up nearly their whole height; and in Northern India the whole Subhimalayan range had been elevated."

§ 80. So it is that on the Bad Lands we find the water-guage, which marks the rise and fall of a deluge which, if not that of Noah, relieves that great phenomenon from the main cosmical difficulties with which it has been invested by the earlier skeptics. A deluge which, if not universal, was

---

* Owen's Geo. Sur., p. 198.

at least extensive enough to have submerged all the living members of a population as large and widely spread as that of Europe at the present time, not only is possible, but is shown to have actually taken place.

We have corroborating evidence as to the seniority of the American continent in the coal formations which Kansas and Iowa exhibit in common with the Atlantic States. Vegetable life in the Valley of the Euphrates did not begin until race after race of extinct species of plants had been buried in the Valley of the Missouri. This is thus noticed by Agassiz, in his work on Lake Superior. "It is a circumstance," we are told by this acute observer, "quite extraordinary and unexpected that the fossil plants of the tertiary beds of Œnigen resemble more closely the trees and shrubs which grow at present in the eastern parts of North America than those of any other parts in the world, thus allowing us to express correctly the difference between the opposite coasts of Europe and America, by saying that the present Eastern American Flora, and, I may add, the Fauna also, have a more ancient character than those of Europe. The plants, especially the trees and shrubs, growing in our days in the United States are, as it were, old-fashioned; and the characteristic genera, Lagomys, Chelydra, and the large Salamanders with permanent gills, that remind us of the fossils of Œnigen, are at least equally so; they bear the marks of former ages." And, on the same point, Hugh Miller says: "Not only are we accustomed to speak of the Eastern continents as the Old World, in contradistinction to the great continent of the West, but to speak also of the world before the Flood as the Old World, in contradistinction to that postdiluvian world which has succeeded it. And yet, equally, if we receive the term in either of its acceptations, is America an older world still; an older world than that of the Eastern continents; an older world, in the fashion and type of its productions, than the world before the flood. And when the immigrant settler takes ax amid the deep back-woods, to lay open for the first time what he deems a new country, the great trees that fall before him; the brushwood which he lops away with a sweep of his tool; the unfamiliar herbs which he tramples under foot; the lazy fishlike reptile that stirs out of his path as he descends to the neighboring creek to drink; the fierce alligatorlike tortoise, with the large limbs and small carpace, that he sees watching among the reeds for fish and frogs, just as he reaches the water, and the little harelike rodent, without a tail, that he startles by the way, all attest, by the antiqueness of the mould in which they are cast, how old a country the seemingly new one is,—a country vastly older, in type at least, than that of the antediluvians and patriarchs, and only to be compared with that which flourished on the eastern side of the Atlantic long ere the appearance of man, and the remains of whose perished productions we find locked up in the *loess* of the Rhine, or amid the lignites of Nassau. America is emphatically the Old World."

§ 81. There is a peculiar emphasis in the teachings of the Bad Lands as to the fact of the creation and extermination of races now extant. "Every specimen as yet brought from the Bad Lands," says Mr. Owen, "proves to be of species that *became exterminated before the mammoth and mastodon lived, and differ in their specific characters not only from all living animals, but also from all fossils obtained even from contemporaneous geological formations elsewhere.*" In other words, the Bad Lands record a miracle with as sharp precision as do the first chapter of Genesis, the fourth chapter of the Second Book of Kings, and the eleventh chapter of John. It is a creation, not by the ordinary process of generation, but by a divine fiat, of a new family of living creatures. The calling of life into the widow's child was not, by any means, so violent a disruption of what philosophers call the laws of nature, as the awakening of a new period of animal life in the then untrodden bottom of the Missouri. Lazarus, rising from his grave, broke not so much in upon these same laws as the starting up from his miry bed of the gigantic hornless rhinoceros—the Rhinoceros Nebrascencis, described by Dr. Leidy—who was the Adam in that race whose last as well as whose first members now lie in the eocene tertiary of the Bad Lands. The record of such creations and extinctions as these is the record of miracles as distinguished from history, which is the record of the working of natural laws. The latter narrates the march of second causes; the former, of first. In this view we have a most complete refutation of Mr. Hume's famous position, that no human testimony can prove a miracle, because, what is contrary to universal experience cannot itself be shown by substantive proof. The universal experience of man, as he would argue, which establishes the uniformity of animal generation, would exclude the reception of any evidence whatever of a creation by a direct Divine interposition. But this is as if an insect, whose term of life is a moment, and the history of whose race occupies but half a day, should declare that the clock, whose ticking sounds so sonorously in his tiny ears, and which, from the memory of his remotest ancestors, never ceased to strike in the same equal beats, is an institution of perpetual existence, any deviation in whose course no evidence can be received to prove. Tell him that at some remote period that clock was wound up by extrinsic power, and he will tell you that such a winding up is contrary to all insect experience, and that he will hear nothing to prove it.

§ 82. Now, while human history details the ticking and movements of the clock, as moved by its inner machinery, the geological record notes its windings-up. It presents to us, not the details of intermediate life, but the epochs of successive creations and extinctions. It shows us the shadow of that august Presence as, from the secret chamber of His eternal purposes, He passed over the face of the earth to create a new race in place of one that had run its course. We can watch the awful solitude that covered all that then existed of the now busy continent of North America. The Alps were still but low promontories, and the now fiery head of Etna, not yet deserted by the waters which washed into its crater, had not commenced to burn. The main land of North America stopped at the East with the Alleghanies, and the waters penetrated northward into the Valley of the Mississippi, nearly to the mouth of the Arkansas. It was in the Valley of the Missouri that life, in this early tertiary period, first broke. There, in the rank vegetation of the river-bottom, and under the shade of mammoth trees, among swamps, from which rose upward in all their coarse strength, obelisklike reeds, or among terraces of immense cone-bearing trees, and forests of ferns,—there, with canines adapted to seize upon the fish with which the waters were filled, and grinding teeth, like the elk, only vastly larger, so as to cut through the huge vegetation, strode the oreodon, a creature of an order between which and all others a definite chasm exists, which nothing but a new creative power could have passed. There were to be seen mammalia of the lachydermal tribe, twenty feet in length and ten in height, with massive scales on their backs, and jaws five feet long, armed with teeth for grinding and cutting flesh and bone as well as for chewing cud. There, in the semi-aqueous earth, waddled or wallowed huge turtles, (*Testudo Nebrascencis*, Leidy,) gifted with amphibious parts, which even now make the acute mind of Dr. Leidy to hesitate as to the order to which they really belonged.

All of these species, with their contemporaries, preserve their specific features from the beginning to the end of this fossil history. They are identical with nothing else, either before or after. They begin with all their idiosyncrasies entire, and they end with them such. The last individual buried in this tertiary grave has the same features as the first; but neither of them is the same as anything else. There is no intermediate stage, showing how they developed out of some prior and simpler condition of animal life, or afterwards matured into something riper and more complex. On the contrary, they leap, with their individuality complete, into existence, and leap, with their individuality in like manner complete, out of it. It is the sharp and clear fiat: "AND GOD MADE THE BEAST OF THE

EARTH AFTER HIS KIND." It is the history of a miracle engraven by the Divine hand upon the perpetual rocks.

§ 83. It will be seen, therefore, that there is one other error which these fossils confute: the theory of psychological development, so wildly flung out by Dr. Oken, as well as that more artfully propounded by the author of the "Vestiges of Creation." No lineage through prior eras can be traced for the mammalia of Nebraska. None of them, or no approaches to them, have a place in the secondary period of the geologists. When God created them, to use the strong language of Sir Charles Lyell, He threw away the die. The race was formed in a mould by itself. "There is nothing," to adopt the language of Agassiz, when applied to another class, "like parental descent connecting them (the several periods.) The fishes of the paleozoic age are, in no respect, the ancestors of the reptiles of the secondary age, nor does man descend from the mammals which preceded him in the tertiary age. The link by which they are connected is of a higher and immaterial nature; and the connection is to be sought in the will of the Creator himself."

Of the continuity, and, at the same time, the identity of the several families of the Nebraska mammalia, the perceptive sagacity of Dr. Leidy has furnished us with several illustrations which meet the only objection which can be urged to the theory of miraculous creation. In the Bad Lands of Nebraska lie not occasional specimens of animals swept there by some great estuary, but the remains of an entire race. They form the family burying-ground of the early eocene tertiary. There are to be traced, in their full delicacy, all the modulations from childhood to maturity, from maturity to old age. They venture to all the limits of family variation, but they never venture out of it. The cub and the dam, the infant and the adult, the young rhinoceros, scarce able to sprawl on the ground, and the aged parent, hardly strong enough on its crooked legs to support the weight of its armor-clad trunk, all lie, side by side, in this vast mammal cemetery. And now, through the skill of the comparative anatomist, we have not only the picture of the individual, but the picture of the family-group of young and old, infant and parent, as they sank in the soft soil of the bottom of this ancient valley. Thus, of a single animal, the Rhinoceros Nebrascencis, Dr. Leidy gives us the plates of portions of no less than twelve different individuals. We have the "adult" and the "nearly adult," the "very old," the "very young," the "male," and the "female," as they browsed sometimes on the club ferns of the bluffs, or pursued their fishy prey below. We can draw, therefore, from these explorations of the Bad Lands, more than one important truth. We can learn that the graveyard into which we enter contains remains not of stray individuals only, but of all contemporaneous neighboring creation.

§ 84. We learn that the members of this creation are united by no lineage with periods that precede and follow them. We learn that so skillful is the art of the comparative anatomist, that he is now able to distinguish between even the phases of sex and age, and *a fortiori* would be capable of tracing the deviation into a new species. We have, therefore, the material to act upon, and the power to act. And then, with this power, and this subject-matter, when we lift the curtain and gaze upon these wonderful archives of geological scriptures, there opens upon us not merely the written truth that God created each living thing after his kind, but the august reality of creation itself, begun, continued, and closed by the Great First Cause in person.

CHAPTER VIII.

THE RELATIONS OF GOD AND MAN AS DETERMINED BY NATURAL THEOLOGY.

§ 85. *a.* In the preceding chapters the following propositions may be considered as established :—

a[1]. That there is an all-powerful God who seeks the pleasure of His creatures.

b[1]. That this God is a sovereign, directing all things by His will.

c[1]. That He governs by general laws.

d[1]. That besides this, He has established in each breast a moral tribunal, armed with powerful sanctions, for the purpose of directing right and prohibiting wrong.

§ 86. *b.* On the other hand, it is clear that a comprehensive survey of the phenomena already examined brings before us the following apparently contradictory truths :—

a[1]. That what appear gratuitous pain and sorrow are often inflicted on the animal creation.

b[1]. That man is endowed with freedom of will and action, which, however, he frequently perverts to his own ruin.

c[1]. That human conduct is to a great degree affected by what are called "accidents," *i.e.* events not to be accounted for by any general law.

c. RECONCILIATION OF THESE APPARENT CONTRADICTORIES.

a[1]. *The attempt to reconcile them by the hypothesis of an imperfect Creator illogical.*

§ 87. These supposed contradictions have been used to prove the imperfection of the creative power. If a contrivance, it is argued, proves a contriver, so an imperfect contrivance proves an imperfect contriver.

Now, there is a fallacy in the very statement of this proposition, which Dr. Johnson pointed out when touching upon a kindred dogma. The line, "Who rules o'er freemen should himself be free," was quoted in his presence; and he disposed of it by the parody, "Who drives fat oxen should himself be fat." It is not necessary that the ruler should partake of the character of the ruled, or the creator of the created. A glass-blower, for instance, may produce a thick shingle of glass, for a roof, so tough and hard that it may resist all blows, or he may produce a wide sheet which will make an excellent mirror, but will crack if struck by a pebble. Now, if the mirror was intended for the roof, or the roof for the mirror, we would infer an imperfect artificer; but if they are each adapted to their specific purposes, we can infer nothing more than a wise economy of means toward end. Before, therefore, determining whether the imperfectness of the machine proves the imperfectness of the machinist, we must inquire for what the machine is meant.

§ 88. This same proposition may be further illustrated as follows:—A river is let into a canal; at a distance of twenty miles from the feeder the water is lost. Now, this may be attributed either to a deficiency in the original stream or a leak in the canal. And the presumption that it is the latter, increases as, on going nearer and nearer to the feeder, we find the volume of water proportionally enlarge.

§ 89. Now it is remarkable that, in contemplating the great area of the universe, the nearer we get to man the more these irregularities and imperfections multiply: the farther off we get the more they decrease. It would seem as if God governs the inanimate creation through the vice-agency of subalterns, in the shape of second causes, whose letters of instruction are known to all, while He commands mankind in person. The laws that control the former are open to the observation of science; not so with the laws that control the latter. The philosopher may tell where a comet will drop a thousand years hence, but he cannot tell where his own days will end. He can lay down the laws of celestial harmony, but not those of life and death. There seems to be something about the moral atmosphere which surrounds man which excludes the entrance of these general laws.

Rien n'est certain que l'imprévu,

says a French proverb. "There is nothing certain but the unforeseen." An "accidental" surfeit of pork so deranged Napoleon I.'s stomach as to lose him the battle of Leipsic. The "accidental" delay of an aid-de-camp lately saved Napoleon III.'s life. History is but the analysis of "accidents," and biography their narrative. As we come down to domestic life, these interruptions of general law increase. The movements of large bodies of men may be determined beforehand by law, but not the movements of individuals. In ten thousand individuals we can positively say that there will be ten who will die in a given period; but there is no one to whom we can say, "this day one year, or ten years hence, you will cease to exist." No one who looks back on the past will deny that by "chance," as distinguished from "law," the main results of his history have been produced. No one can look forward to the future and deny that it is by the uncertain that it is to be controlled.*

§ 90. If, then, it is at the human end of the system that this uncertainty exists; if, as we approach nearer man, these laws yield more and more to irregularities, we are pointed to an inquiry into the human constitution in order to see whether an explanation of these apparent contradictions may be found. We find the signals in the telegraph weakening as they reach a particular point, and we look to see if there be a leakage at that point before we decide that there is a defect in the electric fluid. And this course seems the more appropriate from the fact that, until other methods of accounting for these defects fail, it seems unreasonable to charge the Creator of all things with imperfection.

b^1. These apparent contradictions may be reconciled by the following assumptions:—

a^2. Man is in a state of exile from God.

§ 91. During the French Indian wars, a party of Indians made an attack on a Moravian cottage in Northeastern Pennsylvania, at the time of family worship, and succeeded in carrying off a little girl of three or four years of age. Season after season the parents of the child endeavored to discover her, but in vain. Ten years, however, had

---

* See *post*, § 213–14–15.

passed, when it was reported that a white girl, very weather-beaten and worn, had been captured from some Indians in the neighborhood of Pittsburg. The mother of the lost girl proceeded there, but was unable to recognize in the captive any traces of her own child. At last she bethought her of the hymn tune that was sung on the fatal evening of the Indian descent. She began to sing it, and at once the mass of superincumbent rubbish on the child's memory was removed. The far past became the immediate present, and the exile was recalled home.

There is something like this in the ordinary human consciousness. There are phenomena which it is hard to account for except on the supposition that man has a Heavenly Father, but that from that Father's home he is now banished. He speaks not, at least in his normal condition, the language of heaven, and yet that language awakens in him strange memories. Even without revelation he worships an unknown God. He has memories, subtle and strange, that call back the language of a lost home. There is an almost universal consciousness that a God exists, and yet there is a feeling that the avenues to that God's throne are blocked. So it is with all, from the polished Greek, who erects a temple even to the deities of the stranger and the outcast, to the rude Indian, who worships God in tree and wind.*

* Bishop Butler thus writes:—"That He is infinite in power, perfect in wisdom and goodness, makes no alteration, but only that He is the object of these affections raised to the highest pitch. He is not, indeed, to be discerned by any of our senses. *I go forward, but He is not there; and backward, but I cannot see Him: on the left hand, where He doth work, but I cannot be-*

§ 92. This banishment from God of man, does not, it is submitted, arise from any inability of his merely intellectual powers. These he possesses amply enough for even indefinite comprehension; for time and space form no barrier to human intellect. It takes, it is said, two millions of years for the rays of the most distant of the recently discovered stars to reach us; the human mind conceives of and pictures to itself such a star in an instant. And, to show the triumph of intellect over the material it uses, matter itself is the agent by which matter is to be subdued. A bit of glass, on the one hand, expands an atom into worlds, and, on the other hand, uncovers worlds to an atom. Steel, in one form, carves on stone, or traces on paper, or restores from the geological record the history of remote ages; on the other, it brings the thoughts of continents together in one common pulse. Through this, century answereth to century; land to land; sea to sea. When we see such an agency as this, indefinite in its power of reaching over time and space, dropping helpless at the mere approach to the throne of the Most

---

hold Him: He hideth Himself on the right hand, that I cannot see Him. O that I knew where I might find Him! that I might come even to His seat! Job, xxii. But is He then afar off? Does He not fill heaven and earth with His presence? The presence of our fellow-creatures affects our senses, and our senses give us the knowledge of their presence; which hath different kinds of influence upon us: love, joy, sorrow, restraint, encouragement, reverence. However, this influence is not immediately from our senses, but from that knowledge. Thus, suppose a person neither to see nor hear another, not to know by any of his senses, but yet certainly to know that another was with him; this knowledge might, and in many cases would, have one or more of the effects before mentioned."—*Sermon on the Love of God.*

High; when we see how that avenue is covered with the broken fragments of the speculations of intellects the boldest and strongest, we may well believe that there has been here some great disruption that has severed man from his God, and driven him an exile from a heavenly home. It is as if, by a deserted telegraph line, we see the posts fallen, and the wires lying tangled and broken on the ground. We can well believe that once the magnetic fluid passed through that now broken wire. We can feel that the very point where we now stand was once brought into immediate communication with the great centres of human society. Now, however, all that remains is a broken instrument, incapable itself of bearing a message, but significant of two great truths: first, former capacity for communication; and, second, a shock by which this capacity has been destroyed.

Now, are not these same phenomena observable in man? Do we not see, first, the remains of former grandeur, the traces of former communication and sympathy with God, of a heart that throbbed in a reciprocal pulsation with that of the Most High himself; and do we not see, also, evidence of some great catastrophe by which this exquisite instrument was shattered? In other words, do we not find here the base of two great propositions which will go a great way toward solving these difficulties,—an original creation in holiness and in unison with God, and a subsequent fall and perversion, followed by a judicial exile?*

* "Consider once more the religious aspirations and capacities of religious attraction that are garnered up, and still live in the ruins of humanity. How plain it is, in all the most forward demonstrations of the race, that man is a creature of religion; a

§ 93. Let us take, for illustration, one of the several topics which have been already discussed as exhibiting the goodness and wisdom of God. Take the ocean, and view it on one of its charts, and see how its face is marked with dangerous shoals, with sunken rocks, with stormy coasts. View, also, the iceberg; undoubtedly, as it sallies forth into Southern seas, a great mitigator of tropical heat, and yet,

---

creature secretly allied to God himself, as the needle to the pole, attracted toward God, aspiring consciously or unconsciously to the friendship and love of God. Neither is it true that, in his fallen state, he has no capacity left of affection or religious attraction, till it is first new created in him. All his capacities of love and truth are in him still, only buried and stifled by the smoldering ruin in which he lies. There is a capacity in him still to be moved and drawn, to be charmed and melted by the Divine love and beauty. The old affinity lives, though smothered in selfishness and lust, and even proves itself in sorrowful evidence when he bows himself down to a reptile or an idol. He will do his most expensive works for religion. There is a deep panting still in his bosom, however suppressed, that cries inaudibly and sobs with secret longing after God. Hence the sublime unhappiness of the race. There is a vast, immortal want stirring on the world and forbidding it to rest. In the cursing and bitterness, in the deceit of tongues, in the poison of asps, in the swiftness to blood, in all the destruction and misery of the world's ruin, there is yet a vast insatiate hunger for the good, the true, the holy, the divine, and a great part of the misery of the ruin is that it is so great a ruin; a desolation of that which cannot utterly perish, and still lives, asserting its defrauded rights and reclaiming its lost glories. And therefore it is that life becomes an experience to the race so tragic in its character, so dark and wild, so bitter, so incapable of peace. The way of peace we cannot know till we find our peace where our immortal aspirations place it, in the fullness and the friendly eternity of God."—*Bushnell's Sermons on the New Life*, p. 63.

at the same time, as with its comrades it issues in grim procession from its fastnesses in the North, a remorseless devastator of whatever life or wealth it may happen to strike. In the silence and calm of a windless and currentless sea these gaunt and awful marauders of the ocean march onward, impelled, as it would seem, by some interior energy that propels them by its elemental force. The motive power, in fact, is one of those under-currents so essential to the due purification of the sea, which strikes the submerged base of the iceberg, generally so much greater than its glittering heights, and drives it onward with such tremendous power. It would seem as if these giant corsairs from the North are drawn by the force of currents to a special rendezvous at the "great bend," near latitude 43°. Here, touching the edge of the Gulf Stream, some of the most beneficent forces in Nature combine to invest them with peculiar peril. When under full head, a steamship would be overtaken by them, and woe to that vessel which comes into collision with their brilliant but pitiless bulwarks. Among the numberless vessels that have thus fallen may be placed two of the finest that modern skill has constructed—the President and the Pacific.

§ 94. Let us take another illustration from the same quarter. The vessel bound from England to the Capes of the Delaware or Chesapeake is "met by snow-storms and gales which mock the seaman's strength and set at naught his skill. In a little while his bark becomes a mass of ice; with her crew frosted and helpless, she remains obedient only to her helm, and is kept away for the Gulf Stream. After a few hours' run, she reaches its edge, and, almost at the next bound, passes from the midst of winter into a sea at summer-heat. Now the ice disappears from her apparel; the sailor bathes his stiffened limbs in tepid waters; feeling himself invigorated and refreshed with the genial warmth about him, he realizes, out there at sea, the fable of Antæus and his mother earth. He rises up and attempts to make his port again, and is again as rudely met and beaten back from the northward; but each time that he is driven off from the contest, he comes forth from this stream, like the ancient son of Neptune, stronger and stronger, until, *after many days, his freshened strength prevails, and he at last triumphs and enters his haven in safety; though in this contest he sometimes falls to rise no more, for it is often terrible. Many ships annually founder in these gales.*"*

It is the same wherever man and the inanimate creation come in contact. Nature bears, it is true, the horn of plenty in the one hand, but she carries in the other the rod of discipline. The coal mine yields up its inexhaustible stores, but below issues a gas ready to poison or explode, and above beetles the earth, ready to fall in and bury. Mr. Huskisson is torn to pieces on a railway, which his clear head and resolute purpose led him to be foremost to appreciate and carry through; the great gun of the Princeton, exhibited as one of the first products of mechanical art, bursts and destroys the chief of the very department under whose auspices the exhibition was made. Iron, proclaimed by the late Francis Horner to be the chief engine of modern civilization, is the great agency which pro-

* Maury's Geog. of the Seas.

duces by far the greater proportion of violent deaths. Even climate, while it marches forward, sowing the seeds of life, carries also a scythe by which, in the moist winds of spring, the sultry heats of summer, the bitter storms of winter, multitudes are swept into their graves.

§ 95. The inquiry then comes, is there anything in the character of man, the only agent existing on the face of the earth as the subject of moral discipline, which can explain phenomena such as have been noticed? Let it be remembered that the analogies of science lead us to this very kind of inquiry. If the comparative anatomist, for instance, discovers an anomalous bone, he does not declare that here is an evidence of imperfection or caprice on the part of the Creator, but he looks to the properties of the specimen, and judges of the remainder of the animal by the peculiarities he thus observes. "This," he decides, "is the part of an animal that is granivorous; that of one that is carnivorous." So it is with respect to the physical properties which certain atmospheres engender. We look at Jupiter, and, as we observe the tremendous pressure of the gravitation which bears upon his bottomless seas and his light soil, we conclude that, if he be populated at all, it must be by animals light of weight and strong of muscle. We turn to Saturn, and when we observe that his density is scarcely above that of cork, and that the amount of light and heat that reaches him is only a nineteenth of that of the earth, we conclude that his inhabitants, if possessed of the same type of organization as our own, must have the senses manifold more acute, and the sensibilities to the same degree more obtuse. We turn to Mars, and, as we find that the gravity at his surface is only half of that with us, we make allowance for a double bulk on the part of those who dwell amid the sparkling snows which astronomers have been able to detect at his poles, or under the sultry clouds that float around his equator. In other words, instead of judging of the *Creator* from a section of the thing *created*, as some of those who have drawn these very conclusions would ask us to do, we judge of the thing created from such properties placed about it by the Creator as we are able to accept as a basis of examination.

§ 96. Let us suppose that an inhabitant of one of these planets, after witnessing the scarred and corrugated moral atmosphere of our own globe; after seeing only fissures of sunlight through lowering banks of clouds; after seeing how crushingly grief or oppression gravitates the heart downward in one place, and how genially home and social influences unite in another to cheer and elevate it, and yet how certainly these influences are, sooner or later, destroyed; what would an intelligent observer be likely to conclude with regard to the moral character of those to whom this atmosphere was adjusted? Would not such an observer, after witnessing these phenomena, and noticing the marks of Divine wisdom and love rising superior to the whole, conclude that man is in a state of exile from God, continued on his part voluntarily, and accompanied by severe penalties—that home is meant to teach, and not to worship—and that all the mechanism of Nature is so adapted as to instruct and discipline, but, at the same time, to prepare for another life?

§ 97. b^2. *The human heart, so far from maintaining a*

communion with God, is inclined more and more to place its affections on things earthly.

Why else is it that life is made so short? Why is it that while there may be special "runs of luck," as they are called, the longest and most fortunate of lives meets, sooner or later, with its heavy cross, or, if that cross come not, goes at last naked out of that world where its attire was so splendid,—goes from the home of luxury to the cold and loathsome grave? How can we account for the *inadhesiveness*, as it were, of all earthly good,—for that quality which apparently intervenes to loosen and break off the attachments of man to whatever those attachments cling? Does not this discipline of affliction,—of disappointment, of casualty, of wind and storm, of earthquake and blight, of disease and pestilence,—does not this discipline, viewed from the stand-point thus taken, demonstrate a settled tendency toward the idolatry of human wealth and comfort on the part of those to whose moral standard this system is adapted? We visit a lunatic asylum, or a prison, and judge of the character of the inmates from the character of the restraints placed on them. "This man," we say, if we start with proof *aliunde* of the benevolence and wisdom of the government of the institution, "has a temper violent and ungovernable; this is gentle but melancholy. Restraints we find in one place; encouragements in another." May we not say the same, when we view the system of mingled encouragements and restraints with which the world abounds?

§ 98. c^2. *There is a future retribution which demands that the free agency of those subject to it should remain unimpaired, while there are such general influences about it as will promote patience, submission, and earnest endeavor.*

It would have been practicable to have created a groove out of which human purpose could not run. We can suppose such an observer as we have described, could he see a compulsory mechanism which would exact a specific course and no other, declare, "Here are no moral agents; these are automata who are as much the creatures of positive control as are the stars in their orbits." But when he observes the moral atmosphere around man, his opinion would greatly change. "Here," he would say, "is an agency, not to compel, but to invite patience and energy. Here comes the spring, with its slow vegetation, interrupted by occasional frosts and storms, but at the same time showing how industry and endurance will bring forth the tardy crop. Here comes the storm at sea, admonishing man how incompetent are science and skill to secure an always favorable voyage. Here are varied elements, such as climate and soil, combining to preserve individuality, to excite energy, to counsel submission." Under so artificially constructed a system of *influences* such as these,—not *powers*,—there must dwell a moral agent, and one whose destiny corresponds in its grandeur to the splendid apparatus of which this system consists.

§ 99. d^2. *These disciplinary influences, however, are insufficient without the special Divine aid.*

Let such an observer, for instance, view such a storm as that which destroyed the San Francisco. Let him notice the sublime and awful spectacle produced by the crash of thunder, the fierce swell of the billows, the violence of the wind. Or let him pass to those cities that have been desolated by the plague, or to those scenes of Eastern torture, such as the Black Hole of Calcutta, where death in its most appalling shapes is slowly pressed into a mass of human beings. If he reverse the process of inquiry, he will find that while such scenes produce with some awe and submission, with others they generate a fierce and brutal despair. The scenes of lust and outrage on board the sinking San Francisco; of levity in Florence during the plague, as depicted by Boccaccio in his Decameron; of pillage in London and Philadelphia under similar circumstances, as described by De Foe and Charles Brockden Brown,—go to show that without some special spiritual influence, even the most awful of material phenomena would fail of their effect. While, therefore, the visible creation is made to bear its part in the aid of human probation, the work is not one of mechanical constraint, but room remains for the distinct and special introduction, under conditions consistent with probation, of Divine aid.

§ 100. e^2. *A written revelation, as a final educationary process, is a priori probable under such a dispensation.*

God, we may assume from the phenomena of the material universe, is equally unlimited in His command of resources, and in His capacity for comprehensive as well as for particular government. The elaboration of the minutest atom, and the comfort of the humblest form of animal life, are no more below His providence than the pre-arrangement of the spheres above it. His administration, as has been further shown, is one of general laws written on the skies and earth. He has not thought it beneath Him to engrave on the rocks, in letters which myriads of years have not effaced, the history of the successive miracles by which He filled the earth with organic life. It is not *a priori* improbable, therefore, that He should lay down laws for the *moral* government of a race for whose *physical* interests He has shown such a tender concern, nor that He should place these laws on record. He is like a father, whose children, emigrating we may suppose to a distant colony, where they must necessarily be dependent on their own energies for support, stand peculiarly in need of that advice which their father's superior wisdom can best give. What so likely as that such a father, knowing how fluctuating is memory, and how liable it is to be modified by passion or interest, should place in writing that information as to their history and ultimate destiny, and those precepts for their government, which their necessities require? And is not this presumption strengthened when we discover throughout the narrative of this father's relations to his children, the traces of a mind not only eminently systematic and law-loving, but prone to register for his children's study, even though a most complicated mechanism be required for the purpose, those laws and systems by which his own conduct is governed?

This view is strengthened when we turn toward the condition and constitution of man. He is, as has just been seen, incapable of self-renovation. The world in which he lives has been said to be a temple desecrated by sin; and if so, how sad must be his fate, who, as the sole moral agency in this world, stands as it were by the altar to which the aisles of this vast but sin-desolated pile converge. Inadequate to the work of restoring either himself or the splendid ruin in which he dwells; not only corrupt himself but corrupting even the traditions of truth that he retains, what so natural as that the loving and Almighty Father who placed him here,—that law-loving and law-recording Father,—should not merely give him spiritual solace and instruction, but should so perpetuate that solace and instruction that they may be preserved uncorrupted and intact. That such a revelation, incorporating the laws necessary for the government of the human race, should be written, the analogies of man's nature seem to indicate. Men, in all their variations of race and family, resort to writing as the best means of giving permanency to their own laws, and recording their own thoughts. The dangers, which the experience of society proves, of the perversion or the loss of mere oral tradition, would enter into the governmental calculations of an intelligent observer, to say nothing of an omniscient God. What, then, would be more likely than for such a God, in speaking to such a race, to use such a medium as would be most consistent with His wisdom and tenderness, and their infirmities?

"But," it may be objected, "if this be true, a written revelation would have been coeval with the human race." But can we apply the tests of time to a being who is unconditioned by time? And is it not plain, if we are to judge from cosmical history, that the plan of the Divine Architect of the universe is to introduce successively improving periods by terraces or grades, adopting neither on the one hand a simultaneous and complete production, nor on the other a gradual development? The earth was first created without form and void. Then a rough and drossy scum writhed and quivered over the molten ocean beneath. Then, as this scum toughened into a crust, it was fractured by fissures through which burst volcanic fires showering upward torrents of fused rock and metal afterwards to harden into mountains. Thousands of years passed before the fat alluvial soil began to cover this skeleton of bone and iron; thousands of years more before life appeared in the flood or on the fast land; thousands of years more before we find the vestiges of man. It is not for us to seek a reason for this, to us, slow dignity in the march of the Divine purpose. It may be, it is true, that of the Almighty, to whom time and space are nothing, the patient majesty and the rising cycles of laws, may be an essential attribute in the progress of His own administration as well as in the education of His rational creatures. But be this as it may, the analogy of God's dealings with the material creation leads us to suppose *a priori* that the dispensations by which He would communicate His solaces and directions to man would be in a progressive series, and not in a revelation complete at its first utterance. The educational processes of revelation would be likely to correspond with those of natural religion in the terracelike ascents by which they would rise in completeness. Man as a race, as it is with man as an individual, would have several distinct class-books of instruction. At first he would receive, though with powers as yet incapable of precise perception, the communications of his God and Father speaking inarticulately at a period when the forms of language were unknown. Then we can suppose an era of tradition, until the moment when through the infirmities and corruptions of our nature these traditions would lose their virtue. Then we can suppose an education by example and precept, not directly, for this would hamper moral agency, and be at variance with the analogy of civil society, but through a specific order or nation, who, favored with greater religious light, (as in all times there have been nations favored with greater intellectual light and geographical advantages,) could become a medium for the religious tuition and enlightenment of others. Then next we may suppose a written revelation. Such a series of dispensations would be at least not at variance with the divine polity as developed in cosmical history. And yet this series is no more than what we find in the Patriarchal, the Jewish, and the Christian economies.*

But, it may be further objected, that this position proves too much, for it goes to show that written revelation, like the dispensations of the material world, is subject to a gradual development, and hence that the Romish view of traditional and progressive interpretation is correct. But the answer to this is complete. If the analogy is worth anything, it goes to show that these dispensations rise, to carry out an illustration already given, not as a *slope*, but as a series of *terraces.* "It is a truth which I consider now as proved," says Agassiz,† "that the *ensemble* of organized beings was renewed not only in the interval of each of the great geological divisions which we have agreed to term formations, but also at the time of the deposition of each

---

* See on this point, *post*, § 173.

† Twelfth Report of British Association, p. 85. See also *ante*, § 30–40.

particular member of all the formations. I cannot admit the idea of the transformation of species from one formation to another." And so a very recent and capable observer, already quoted,* tells us that "*species did not pass into one another by transmutation, but that each species was introduced in full perfection, remained unchanged during the term of their existence, and died in full perfection.*" "As far as the evidence of geology extends, *each species was introduced by the direct miraculous interference of a personal intelligence. There has indeed been a constantly increasing series, but the connection between the terms of the series has not been physical or genetic, but intellectual; not founded in the laws of reproduction, but in the eternal counsels of the Almighty.*" What we would be led by geological analogy to believe would be that each specific dispensation (*e.g.* the written) would remain intact and unprogressive, until the same miraculous power that called it into existence should, by the same supernatural interposition and attestation, replace it by another. The clouded gloss of language may be removed, and the creature may see the Creator face to face. But this will not be by any gradual self-clarifying power of the text, nor by the action of the human reader, but by the direct and miracle-attested agency of the Almighty Himself, as preliminary to a new and final stage of existence.†

I have now brought this inquiry as far as the limits of natural religion permit me to go. But the practical ques-

---

* Professor Le Conte, Smithsonian Instit. Rep. 1857, p. 168.

† See *post*, § 227.

tion remains, if there be a written revelation, can this be anything else than the Christian Scriptures?

If the propositions which have been stated in this chapter may be fairly inferred from the phenomena of creation,—if, in other words, it be considered as thus established that man is in a state of exile from his God,—that the human heart, so far from maintaining a communion with God, is inclined more and more to place its affections on things earthly,—that the soul is reserved for a high future destiny, which demands that its free agency should remain unimpaired, but that there should be such influences about it as to educate it to patience, to submission, and to earnest endeavor,—that these disciplinary influences, however, are insufficient without special divine aid,—we are able to find not merely an explanation of but a reason for that very union of general laws with special providences,—of blessings with warnings, of beneficence with discipline, of sunshine with storm,—by which the operations of the material world are marked. Such a view, in fact, only completes the proof of that adaptation of cause to effect, and of that beneficent and general contrivance, which even when viewed in their merely material relations, go so far to establish the existence, the wisdom, the mercy, and the justice of God.

BOOK SECOND.

SKEPTICAL THEORIES.

CHAPTER I.

"AN IMPERFECT CREATOR."

§ 101. An imperfect creation, it is said, argues an imperfect Creator. The logical force of this position has been already noticed.* It will further be examined under the following heads :—

a. Inability of the finite to measure.

§ 102. We stand, for instance, at the centre of one of our great Western prairies. We look at the distant horizon, and discover on it lines which appear to us, as in sharp precision they stand up against the vivid sky, like the castellated roof of a Gothic mansion. As we approach, the object gradually loses its architectural precision, and subsides, perhaps, into a low range of hills, perhaps into a

---

* *Ante*, § 87.

series of cabins. On the other hand, under a less luminous atmosphere, the building of real splendor and beauty may, in the distant view, appear but as a hovel.

This is still more striking in the opinions we form of questions of possibility which are not within the range of visual observation. Many men of science scouted at the idea of crossing the Atlantic by steam: some men of science believed in the pretended moon discoveries of Locke. One of the most agreeable of our French North American explorers tells us a story of an Indian council which illustrates this. A young brave had been sent to Washington to confer with the Great Father. He returned, with a remarkable account of witches and wizards whom he had seen in endless processions in the East. All this was listened to with profound respect and confidence. He went on, however, to add that, among other things, he had observed a canoe sailing in the air with a ball of wind on top of it. At once the demeanor of his audience changed, and it being pronounced that so great a liar ought not to live, the narrator was forthwith shot. A Japanese king, we are told, was almost equally demonstrative of his disapproval of those who told him that in England water became solid in cold weather. Herodotus narrates—with all the gossiping vivacity of the most satisfied credulity—stories of monsters, dwarfs, giants, cannibals, of beasts that were three-quarters men, and men wholly beasts; of rivers that were scarcely less than oceans, and of palaces that were greater than pyramids. But, at the same time, after relating the observation of the Phœnician mariners, that in doubling what is now the Cape of Good Hope they had the meridian sun on the north, the same historian, himself not the least philosophical of his order, says, "anybody else may believe this, but to me it is perfectly incredible." To those who look upon such confusions of belief with unbelief, as the accompaniments of a primitive or barbaric state, it is only necessary to point out the period when the most cultivated people of the seventeenth century persecuted those who would *not* believe in witches, and those who *would* believe that the earth revolved round the sun.

§ 103. This imperfection of vision is a necessary incident of that limitation which, as will presently be seen, belongs to created things. This is admirably illustrated in the following remarks by Dr. Ferguson:—"If the human fœtus were qualified to reason of his prospects in the womb of his parent, as he may afterwards do in his range on this terrestrial globe, he might no doubt apprehend in the breach of his umbilical cord, and in his separation from the womb, a total extinction of life, for how could he conceive it to continue after his only supply of nourishment from the vital stock of his parent had ceased? He might indeed observe many parts of his organization and frame which would seem to have no relation to his state in the womb. For what purpose, he might say, this duct which leads from the mouth to the intestines? Why these bones that each apart become hard and stiff, while they are separated from one another by so many flexures or joints? Why these joints in particular made to move upon hinges, and these germs of teeth, which are pushing to be felt above the surface of the gums? Why the stomach through which nothing is made to pass? And these spongy lungs, so well fitted to drink up the fluids, but into which the blood that passes everywhere else is scarcely permitted to enter? To these queries, which the fœtus was neither qualified to make nor to answer, we are now well apprised the proper answer would be: The life which you now enjoy is but temporary; and those particulars which now seem to you so preposterous, are a provision which Nature has made for a future course of life which you have to run, and in which their use and propriety will appear sufficiently evident."*

§ 104. This analogy might be pushed so as to give materials from which, by a very simple induction, we may draw the proposition, that in our present limited and probationary state the imperfection of our vision is such as to prevent us from comprehending at any period the conditions of any subsequent stage through which we are to pass. The boy sees not the trials he will have to encounter as a man, and when he is told of struggles and defeats ahead, he turns from the scene as belonging to a distinct existence. The man of mature years sees not before him the picture of his own frame slowly descending the path that leads to the grave. He listens, perhaps, to the story of affliction, but he comprehends it not until the crushing grief at last comes. Then there is an almost infinite depth of experience opened to him of which before he knew only by the memorials erected by others on its outer surface. It is this that gives to old age what is so often a stony and unsympathizing wisdom—a wisdom not so remarkable for its practical value as for its apparently supernatural detachment from the concerns of active life. And yet, even this wisdom, when merely human,

* See Conybeare's Theol. Lect., pp. 81, 82.

has its range of observation closed by the tomb. Every life is thus divided into stages separated by periods through which the vision does not pass. We cannot comprehend, when in childhood, the conditions which in manhood will take us from love of pleasure to the pursuit of wealth and honor; we cannot comprehend in manhood the conditions which in old age will make us seek rest; we cannot, on this side of the grave, comprehend the conditions which will surround us in a future world. We only know that we are proceeding onward by progressive periods of development, and, like the traveler ascending a mountainous range by a series of terraces, we at the moment see only the particular sweep before us, thinking that to be the last ascent, and observing not the next, until we find that what appeared the summit is only the base of another rise.

The imperfection of our finite faculties should thus ever be kept in view when we undertake to determine on the appropriateness of the plans of the Eternal and Infinite; and this view is strengthened by the additional important fact that our nature is so constituted as to confine its powers of actual comprehension to the conditions belonging to it at the particular moment.* It will be presently shown that this limitedness of vision is a necessary incident of probation.†

b. Incapacity of the infinite for measurement.

§ 105. Let us take one of the extremest cases that can be afforded us of physical evil. Let us observe a lifetime of patient suffering, harrowed, it may be, by poverty, by lingering disease, by loss of friends. Let us imagine this life to

---

* See *post*, 245. † *Post*, § 109.

be protracted far beyond the ordinary limits, and the exquisiteness of its appreciation of distress refined far beyond the usual bound. But what then? Next comes the grave, and then eternity. It is as if we should be summoned before a gigantic counter, on which stand the scales of the universe. On one side we find this life of misery, which may be represented by a weight of any degree of definite immensity that may be chosen. But then comes the other scale. There come mountains upon mountains of weight, each in turn waiting to be calculated, and each forming part of an infinite range behind. The question is not whether this particular life's grief is to be outweighed by the infinite counter-balances of eternity. For this is done before the process of outweighing is even begun. The scale never even begins to quiver. If we adapt such a process of measurement to our own standards, it is as if we dropped into one pan a grain so imperceptible as not even to overcome the friction of the pivot, while an indefinite number of other weights stood ready on the other to be interposed.

Incomprehensibility is an essential attribute in the infinite. When it is comprehended, it becomes finite. There is always, as has been noticed, an indefinite extension of time beyond the period at which we stand, and this indefinite extension of time forms material amply compensatory for any irregularity. Nor does *time* come in alone for this purpose. There is also an indefinite compensatory medium in *space*. A globule, for instance, to the unarmed vision of the ancient sages appeared a mystery; and the best they could do was to declare that here the animated creation ceased. The milky-way, to the astronomers of old, was a desert of the skies, whose dreary wastes were only traversed by those nomadic comets whose fierce retinues were regarded as carrying destruction wherever they swept. But the globule, under the microscope, is now a new world of life,—through the telescope the milky-way is a city of planets, and the tails of comets are nothing more than impalpable mists.

Let us look, again, at the fact of disturbance, which, when it was first observed, was supposed to interfere with the application of Newton's great law of gravitation to the heavenly system. But it was soon found that this disturbance of the motion of the planets, which arose from their mutual attraction, and which was looked upon as threatening some great convulsion, was compensated for by a provision made specially to counteract it. It required, however, all the present perfection of the telescope to show that this aberration is part of the celestial harmony, not a deviation from it. What right have we, then, to say that when a keener vision enables us to see the ultimate bearing of these difficulties, they will not, in like manner, vanish?

§ 106. Religion, in fact, comes to teach us *practice*, not *speculation*—*duty*, not *philosophy*. For reasons not given to us, but perhaps from the fact that if it taught the latter instead of the former, the great work of a hardy, earnest, faith-depending probation, would sink into a dreamy idealization, or an inexorable fatalism,—religion, both natural and revealed, confines itself to practical teaching. Man, when set down in this life to his work of probation, is like an emigrant who goes forth to settle in one of the territories of our Western frontier. It is desired, we may assume, to furnish him with such facilities as will be most likely to make him an effective farmer. We will suppose him, with a party of other colonists, to be placed on one of the islands of verdure which intersperse the arid plains that are divided by the River Platte. A government survey has lately been made of that remarkable region, and so much of this is handed to him as will enable him to discharge his particular work. Information as to the character of the soil and climate is placed in his hands. The soundings and courses of the sluggish river by whose side he is seated—those of the impetuous Missouri into which it runs—are laid before him as important in showing where and how his produce is to find a market. But beyond this immediate locality and those with which it is brought in business contact it is not necessary to supply him with details. There are many reasons why it would not be desirable for him to take with him a topographical survey of the entire universe. One is, that it would be so cumbrous that he could not carry it; another is, that if he undertook to study it, it would leave him no time for farming; another is, that the speculative habit which, if so employed, he might acquire, would unfit him for the humbler work of tilling the ground. It is true, there is a great deal that is incomprehensible in the phenomena about him, but nothing that is so is of a character whose explanation would facilitate his farming. He may or may not know what is the true source of the Mississippi. It is enough for him to know where he can most conveniently strike that river, and to what markets it will carry his produce. Photographs of the stars, such as science is now producing, might form interesting objects of curiosity, or of philosophical speculation, but may be postponed to an almanac, giving him the rising and setting of the sun, and the most concise and appropriate information as to the crops to be planted in his immediate locality. What he would be furnished by those who wished him well in his new enterprise, would be information as to the field he has to work, and the duties expected of him in connection with it.

§ 107. Now what we would expect man to do, supposing him to act kindly and beneficiently to his fellow-man, we may well expect from the Divine Ruler of the universe, under similar circumstances. As the chart of universal knowledge is in His hands, and as that chart is infinite, there must be some portions of it which, in submitting it to a finite creature, must be withdrawn. Man, with his three-score years and ten, could not go through a course of study which would take him an eternity. A certain portion must be therefore selected for his aid, and what so fit as that which relates to the practical duties incumbent on him in the special period of time in which he is placed? He will be told his duty toward his God and his duty toward his neighbor,—he will be taught, through the phenomena of the seasons, of the earth and the seas, the importance of faith, of patience, of industry, of doing to his fellow-man as he would be done by, and of reverence to his God. But there will be a horizon somewhere, and we would expect that the horizon would be placed just where the practical passes to the speculative. Of course, as in the map of the county or state placed in the emigrant's hands, the sources of the larger rivers are left out; so in the guide-book of the emigrant in this world of probation, there is a great deal in the causes of things existing, and in the reasons for prescribed duties, which will pass beyond the limits of observation.

A priori, therefore, this incapacity of the infinite for comprehension, is what we would expect from the nature of the work in which man is in this life concerned.

c. SUPPOSING, HOWEVER, SUCH IMPERFECTIONS TO EXIST.

§ 108. a^1. *They cannot overcome the positive evidence of Almighty wisdom and goodness.*

Cotton Mather tells us that he preserved his equanimity by keeping two heaps in his mind, one for the incomprehensible, and the other for the incurable. If a friend treated him unjustly, and he had no opportunity of explanation, he took the offence off the surface of his sensibilities, where it might perhaps be acting with corrosive mischief, and placed it at once in the heap of the incomprehensibles. If the whole thing was a mistake, of course he took it off this heap altogether and dismissed it from his possession. If, on the other hand, he found it was an intended and unjustifiable insult, he took it from the heap of incomprehensibles and placed it among the incurables. Either way it was not permitted to vex his feelings or disturb those general principles of conduct which he had previously deliberately adopted with regard to the temper in which he was to regard his fellow-men.

Now the temper in which we are to regard God may be governed by the same rules. Let us take at the outset a comprehensive view of creation, and see whether we can draw from it any settled conclusions as to God's nature and attributes. When we have done this, let us recollect that what is *incomprehensible*, cannot be received to disturb what is *positive*. And this position is one which in science we do not hesitate to accept. Thus the existence of an unexplained interruption of the sidereal system is not permitted to shake our belief in the Copernican system. It makes no difference that the interruption is inexplicable. Thus aërolites, or masses of iron or iron-stone, falling from the sky, of all sizes, from several hundred weight to a few ounces, have been cast on the earth in various places with such velocity as sometimes to bury them deep into the soil. Whence or how they come, is inexplicable. No rational solution of it has as yet been approached. And yet no astronomer, on account of this unexplained phenomenon, will allow his belief in the harmony of the celestial phenomenon to be disturbed.

§ 109. b^1. *They are reconcilable with the Divine perfections.*

This may be the proper place to notice the theories of the reconciliation of evil with the Divine perfections which come to us with the greatest philosophical weight. Let it be observed, at the outset, that the inquiry is in a great measure irrelevant, since the *incomprehensibility* of the topic, leaving it to stand unexplained, forms no ground, as has just been seen, to dispute the positive evidence of Divine wisdom of Goodness. "But," says Dr. Chalmers, "an hypothesis might subserve a great logical purpose in theology. And accordingly the one framed by Leibnitz respecting the origin of evil, even though admitted to no higher rank than a mere unsupported imagination, may yet be of force to nullify all the objections wherewith this topic is conceived to be pregnant, and so as to leave in their undiminished strength all these affirmative props on which the system of theology is based." This hypothesis, with those of a kindred purpose which have been most prominently before the philosophical mind, will now be noticed.

§ 110. *a².* *Evils and imperfections are necessary to moral agency.*

b². *They are ordained of God, as forming part of a scheme, of all others the best and most perfect.*

These two points may be considered together. It is assumed that out of all possible schemes, God chose that which on the whole was best,—that to this scheme moral agency is a necessary incident,—that to moral agency a liability to temptation,* if not a certainty of sin, is essential. God has the POSSIBLE, in all its modifications, open before Him, and He chooses that phase which of all the others is best. This scheme, as enforced by the scientific genius of Leibnitz, the rhetorical opulence of Chalmers, the logical energies of Jonathan Edwards, has been the base on which theologians of far divergent schools have founded their speculations. We may well pause for a moment, therefore, to consider on what it rests, and how far it goes.†

---

* Between "liability to temptation," and "certainty of sin," a distinction has been taken which, as will presently be seen, divides two theological schools.

† The most philosophical exposition of this position comes from Leibnitz, who, even by the skeptics, is ranked as the first philosopher of his age, while among Christians his orthodoxy is unimpeached. Both sides, therefore, defer to him, the one testifying to his capacity in the search for truth, the other to his integrity in its delivery. He had indeed a splendid as well as a well-poised

§ 111. The proposition may be illustrated, taking in the aid of the only class of analogies open to us,—those drawn

---

intellect; and though his almost universal genius laid him under tribute to all the great controversies of his times, and though he therefore was unable to leave behind him any complete treatise on any single branch, yet the sparks incidentally generated by him in the heat of controversy, or in the ardor of special investigation, often throw out an illumination more complete than that which the concentrated energies of the lives of less extraordinary men were able to produce.

According to Leibnitz, the divine contemplation must necessarily, from all eternity, have included all possible forms of cosmical existence. To that infinite eye, which embraces the conjectural as well as the real, all combinations of worlds were presented, in each of which the elements of good and evil were mingled in proportions always distinct but always such as to reach the common result. From these forms that of the present universe was selected, as that on which the character of good was most impressed. "God then is not the author of the essences so long as they are but possibilities—but there is nothing actual which He has not decreed and given existence to; and He has permitted evil, because it is enveloped in the best plan which is found in the region of possibles, and that divine wisdom could not fail to have chosen." (*Essay*, art. 338.)

Evil in this way is a contingency of the infinite rather than a concomitant of the finite. Thus, Leibnitz tells us, "Chrysippus has reason to allege that vice comes from the original constitution of some spirits. It is objected to them that God has formed them; and he can only reply, that the imperfection of matter does not permit him to do better. This reply is good for nothing; for matter itself is indifferent to all forms, and besides, God has made it. Evil comes rather from forms themselves, but abstract; that is to say, from ideas that God has not produced by an act of His will, no more than He has produced number and figure; and no more, in one word, than all those possible essences which we regard as eternal and necessary, for they find themselves in the ideal region of possibles; that is to say, in the divine understanding. God is then not the author of these essences, in so far as from human society,—somewhat in the following fashion. The executive of a home government, we may suppose, is engaged in drawing up a constitution for a distant colony. He arrays before his mind the several possible schemes on which such a constitution can be constructed. He possesses, we may assume, liberal, humane, and enlightened views, controlled by a severe sense of right and of justice. Would it be best for him to institute, in this distant province, a pure democracy; an absolutism, of which he is to be the head; or a mixed system which would unite the elements of individualism and centralism? Each of the three has its objections: to the first there is a danger of tumult, of disorganization, of waste of power from decentralization of energies. The second, the nearer it would approach to perfection, the nearer would it approach to a dead mechanism. The third, no matter how skillfully constructed, would be open, not merely to the incidental vices of all governments, but to a constant collision of forces,—men arraying themselves, as their interests or temperaments prompted them, on the side of progress or of conservatism, and making the very union of liberty with authority the cause of revolt and disorder. Notwithstanding these evils, this form of government may, of all others, be the best, and as such may be

---

they are only possibilities; but there is nothing actual but what He discerned and called into existence, and He has permitted evil, because it is enveloped in the best plan which is found in the region of possibles; that plan the Supreme Wisdom could not fail to choose. It is this notion which at once satisfies the wisdom, the power, and the goodness of God, and yet leaves room for the entrance of evil.

selected with its known evils. All the possible schemes have their evils: this is taken because it has the least evil and the most good.*

Now, for reasons which it is not necessary for us to penetrate, God has chosen moral agencies as the best of all systems for the government of an intelligent creation. It may be sufficient for us, as an hypothesis, to assume that He may not choose to be a prince over stocks and stones. It may not be consistent with the exercise of His perfect powers and infinite love to gaze down upon a bleak and desolate universe, the mausoleum of possible existences, to Him *actual* because *possible*, whom death arrested and froze before yet they sprang to life, their unheaved bosoms crossed by their unnerved arms, emitting no response to Him,—reasonless, fearless, loveless, hopeless, wantless. To Him, to whom what MIGHT BE is always equivalent to what IS, it may be no pleasure to see stretched before Him the corpses of even the possible, they, the sole representatives of organic life, rocked forever on the waves of a shoreless eternity, gazing upward to Him, the universal Father, with eyes none the less glassy, and frames none the less rigid and dread, from the fact that by the arctic severity of a merely mechanical universe, the decree of non-existence was one which forbade rather than destroyed life. All the splendor of the architraves above, all the grandeur of the cosmical architecture, all the garniture of its jewels, might not, to the divine vision of infinite love, compensate for the childless-

* See this view elaborately expanded by Leibnitz, in his Theodicea, and stated by Dr. Chalmers in his Natural Theology, book v. chap. ii.

ness and desolateness of this stricken world. To Him the cold, metallic ringing of the spheres, as in their tenantless grandeur they roll over the frozen track of their eternal courses, may be no substitute for even the weak and discordant cries of men. Is it inconsistent with the idea of His divine wisdom that He should give life and moral agency in preference to the death of a mere mechanical obedience?

§ 112. Thus far, *i.e.* in the assumption that God selected that form of polity which, of all others, was the best for the government of intelligent creatures, and that the form thus chosen was that of moral agency, the leading minds who have entered on the question agree. Here, however, they divide; one class holds that to moral agency only a liability to sin is essential; that it would not only have been possible to have created moral agents without the certainty of sin, but that moral agency as such was so created, and that the ordinary government of God continues so to control the moral agents thus created as to make all their actions the result of His permissive if not His directive power. The other class holds that moral agency is endowed with the absolute power of choice as an essential element in its existence; that not only is temptation necessary to such agency, but that actual sin is so, and that, therefore, sin is the act of the creature alone, over which the Creator has no control. The first view has been maintained by Augustin, by Calvin, by Leibnitz, by Pascal, by Jonathan Edwards, and, to a modified extent, by Chalmers and McCosh; the second by Samuel Clarke, by John Young,*

* The Mystery of Evil and Good, by John Young, LL.D.; Phil. 1856.

and in our own country, of late days, by Mr. Bledsoe,* by Dr. Bushnell,† and incidentally by Dr. Hickok.‡

§ 113. a^3. *Necessitarian view.*

Of the writers who maintained the first of these theories, there is one who has obtained an eminence which justifies us in treating him, if not as the type, at least as the representative of the large, and, in some respects, not very harmonious school who have arrived at the same result. "The honor of being the most effective defender of Christianity," says Dr. Chalmers, who was in the main one of his disciples, "we should ascribe to Jonathan Edwards;" and such, limiting the remark to what it was intended to apply—the doctrine of grace as expounded by the Calvinistic and Augustinian schools—has been the uniform judgment of those who have followed Edwards in the support of the same opinions. Nor is the tribute paid to the great American metaphysician by his adversaries less emphatic. "His power of subtle argument," says Sir James Mackintosh, "perhaps unmatched, certainly unsurpassed among men, was joined, as in some of the ancient mystics, with a character which raised his piety to fervor." He was a "very candid and acute reasoner," says Dugald Stewart, who regarded Edwards's dogmas, both evangelical and metaphysical, with peculiar animosity. It cannot be out of place, therefore, to pause a moment to consider the solution of this great difficulty proposed by so eminent an intellect.

* A Theodicy, etc., by A. T. Bledsoe; New York, 1854.

† Nature and the Supernatural, as together constituting the one system of God, by Horace Bushnell; 1858.

‡ Rational Cosmology, etc., by L. P. Hickok; 1858.

The fundamental principle of Edwards's argument is that there can be no event without an adequate cause, and that hence there can be no independent spontaneous volition on the part of man. Hence it is, that instead of each moral agent being capable of spontaneous action, his will is under the control of a moral necessity which on the one hand, is alleged to be subordinate to the sovereignty of God, and yet, on the other, to be consistent with the freedom of man. How this view accords with the Divine perfections is thus explained :—

§ 114. "It properly belongs to the Supreme and Absolute Governor of the universe to order all important events within His dominion by His wisdom ; but the events in the moral world are of the most important kind, such as the moral actions of intelligent creatures, and their consequences.

"These events will be ordered by something. They will either be disposed by wisdom, or they will be disposed by chance ; that is, they will be disposed by blind and undesigning causes, if that were possible, and could be called a disposal. Is it not better that the good and evil which happen in God's world, should be ordered, regulated, bounded, and determined by the good pleasure of an infinitely wise Being, who perfectly comprehends, within His understanding and constant view, the universality of things in all their extent and duration, and sees all the influence of every event, with respect to every individual thing and circumstance, throughout the grand system, and the whole of the eternal series of consequences, than to leave these things to fall out by chance, and to be determined by those causes which have no understanding or aim ? Doubtless, in these important events, there is a better and a worse, as to the time, place, subject, manner, and circumstances, of their coming to pass, with regard to their influence on the state and course of things. And if there be, it is certainly best that they should be determined to that time, place, etc., which is best; and, therefore, it is in its own nature fit that wisdom, and not chance, should order these things. So that it belongs to the Being who is the possessor of infinite wisdom, and is the creator and owner of the whole system of created existences, and has the care of all; I say it belongs to Him to take care of this matter; and He would not do what is proper for Him if He should neglect it. And it is so far from being unholy in Him to undertake this affair, that it would have rather been unholy in Him to neglect it, as it would have been a neglecting what fitly appertains to Him; and so it would have been a very unfit and unsuitable neglect.

"Therefore, the sovereignty of God doubtless extends to this matter; especially considering that if it should be supposed to be otherwise, and God should leave men's volitions and all moral events to the determination and disposing of blind, unmeaning causes, or they should be left to happen perfectly without a cause; this would be no more consistent with liberty, in any notion of it, and particularly not in the Armenian notion of it, than if these events were subject to the disposal of Divine Providence, and the will of man were determined by Divine Wisdom, as appears by what has already been observed. But it is evident that such a providential disposing and determining men's moral actions, though it infers a moral necessity of those actions, yet it does not in the least infringe the real liberty of mankind,—the only liberty that common sense teaches to be necessary to moral agency, which, as has been demonstrated, is not inconsistent with such necessity.

"On the whole, it is manifest that God may be, in the manner which has been described, the orderer and disposer of that event, which, in the inherent subject and agent, is moral evil; and yet, His so doing may be no moral evil. He may will the disposal of such an event, and its coming to pass for good ends, and His will not be an immoral or sinful will, but a perfectly holy will. And He may actually, in His providence, so dispose and permit things, that the event may be certainly and infallibly connected with such disposal and permission, and His act therein not be an immoral or unholy, but a perfectly holy act. Sin may be an evil thing, and yet, that there should be such a disposal and permission, as that it should come to pass, may be a good thing. This is no contradiction or inconsistence. Joseph's brethren selling him into Egypt, consider it only as it was acted by them, and with respect to their views and aims, which were evil, was a very bad thing; but it was a good thing, as it was an event of God's ordering, and considered with respect to his views and aims, which were good. Gen. i. 20: 'As for you, ye thought evil against me; but God meant it unto good.' So the crucifixion of Christ, if we consider only those things which belong to the event as it proceeded from His murderers, and are comprehended within the compass of the affair considered as their act, their principles, dispositions, views, and aims; so it was one of the most heinous things that ever was done, in many respects the most horrid of all acts; but consider it, as it was willed and ordered by God, in the extent of His designs and views, it was the most glorious and admirable of all events, and God's willing the event, was the most holy volition of God that ever was made known to men; and God's act in ordering it was a divine act, which above all others, manifests the moral excellency of the Divine Being."*

§ 115. This scheme, as it will at once be seen, lies open to at least two imposing objections: (a^4,) that it renders useless all means for avoiding sin, reducing men to mere machines; and (b^4) that by bringing the Divine Being himself under the operation of necessity it destroys the Divine individuality altogether. These objections are stated by President Edwards, with his characteristic candor, and are met by him with an exquisite delicacy and yet strength which, so far at least as the mere mechanism of logic is concerned, are probably unsurpassed. The several links of this subtle chain it will not be practicable at present to examine. It will be sufficient, briefly here to notice the main points made by this great reasoner in reply to the objections which have been just stated.

As to the position that the scheme of necessity renders useless all means for avoiding sin, reducing men to mere machines, the question is first put whether, instead of breaking, as is insisted, the connection between the means and the end, the doctrine of necessity does not knit them all the tighter. "My effects," says the objector, "can do no good, if I am under necessity." But it is *because* we are

* Edwards, on Freedom of the Will, p. 160, § 9, iv.

under moral necessity, *i.e. because* there is a necessary connection between effects and results, that these effects *are* successful. "Means are foregoing things, and effects are following things; and if there were no connection between foregoing things and following ones, there could be no connection between means and end; and so all means would be wholly vain and fruitless. For it is by virtue of some connection only, that they become successful; it is some connection observed or revealed, or otherwise known, between antecedent things and following ones, that is, what directs the choice of means. And if there were no such thing as an established connection, there could be no choice as to means; one thing would have no more tendency to an effect than another; there would be no such thing as tendency in the case, all those things which are successful means of other things, do therein prove connected antecedents of them; and therefore to assert that a fixed connection between antecedents and consequents makes means vain and useless, or stands in the way to hinder the connection between means and end, is just as ridiculous as to say, that a connection between antecedents and consequents stand in the way to hinder a connection between antecedents and consequents." And the refusal to do an act, on account of its uselessness, is an admission, it is argued with great subtlety, that the party so refusing negatives his hypothesis by his own act. "If prior necessity, that determines all things, makes vain all actions or conclusions of ours, in order to anything future; then it makes vain all conclusions of ours, in order to our future ease. The measure of our ease, with the time, manner, and every circumstance of it, is already fixed, by all-determining necessity, as much as anything else. If he says within himself, 'what future happiness or misery I shall have, is already in effect, determined by the necessary cause and connection of things; therefore I will save myself the trouble of labor and diligence, which cannot add to my determined degree of happiness or diminish my misery, but will take my ease, and will enjoy the comfort of sloth and negligence.' Such a man contradicts himself; he says the measure of his future happiness and misery is already fixed, and he will not try to diminish the one or add to the other; but yet, in his very conclusions, he contradicts this; for he takes up this conclusion, to add to his future happiness, by the ease and comfort of his negligence; and to diminish his future trouble and misery by saving himself the trouble of using means and taking pains. In short, the principles are such as cannot be acted on, in any respect, consistently."

In meeting the remaining difficulty, that of the alleged annihilation of the Divine will, by subjecting it also to necessity, President Edwards has the assistance of Dr. Samuel Clarke, a conjunction which, in such questions, was a rare one, between the two greatest theological metaphysicians in the English tongue. "It might have been objected," says Clarke, "with more plausibleness, that the Supreme Cause cannot be free, because He must needs do always what is best in the whole. But this would not at all serve Spinoza's purpose; for this is a necessity, not of nature and of fate, but of fitness and wisdom; a necessity consistent with the greatest reason and most perfect choice. For the only foundation of this necessity, is such an unalterable rectitude of Will and perfection of Wisdom, as makes it impossible for a wise Being to act foolishly." And with this may be taken the following observations of Edwards himself.

§ 116. "If God's will is steadily and surely determined in everything by supreme wisdom, then it is in everything necessarily determined to that which is most wise. And certainly, it would be a disadvantage and indignity to be otherwise. For if the Divine Will was not necessarily determined to that which in every case is wisest and best, it must be subject to some degree of undesigning contingence; and so in the same degree liable to evil. To suppose the Divine Will liable to be carried hither and thither at random, by the uncertain wind of blind contingence, which is guided by no wisdom, no motive, no intelligent dictate whatsoever, (if any such thing were possible,) would certainly argue a great degree of imperfection and meanness, infinitely unworthy of the Deity. If it be a disadvantage for the Divine Will to be attended with this moral necessity, then the more free from it, and the more left at random, the greater dignity and advantage. And, consequently, to be perfectly free from the direction of understanding, and universally and entirely left to senseless, unmeaning contingence, to act absolutely at random, would be the supreme glory. It no more argues any dependence of God's will, that His supremely wise volition is necessary, than it argues a dependence of His being that His existence is necessary. If it be something too low, for the Supreme Being to have His will determined by moral Necessity, so as necessarily, in every case to will in the highest degree holily and happily; then why is it not also something too low for Him to have His existence, and the infinite perfection of His nature, and His infinite happiness determined by necessity? It is no more to God's dishonor to be necessarily wise, than to be necessarily holy. And if neither of them be to His dishonor, then it is not to His dishonor necessarily to act holily and wisely. And if it be not dishonorable to be necessarily holy and wise, in the highest possible degree, no more is it mean and dishonorable, necessarily to act holily and wisely in the highest possible degree; or, which is the same thing, to do that, in every case, which, above all other things, is wisest and best.

"The reason why it is not dishonorable to be necessarily most holy, is, because holiness in itself is an excellent and honorable thing. For the same reason, it is no dishonor to be necessarily most wise, and, in every case, to act most wisely, or do the thing which is the wisest of all, for wisdom is also in itself excellent and honorable."

§ 117. The doctrine of Necessity, as laid down by Edwards, has been not a little modified, first by Dr. Chalmers, and afterwards by Dr. McCosh, who may be taken as giving the views of the present school of Scotch orthodoxy on this point. According to the last writer, the older Necessitarians, including Edwards himself, erred in a too close approach to the position that man has all his thoughts and feelings determined by an external cause. The true doctrine, it is maintained, is that the cause of any given mental phenomenon, its *unconditional antecedent which will always produce it, and without which it cannot recur*, is composed of two things,—the immediately preceding state, and a mental power or faculty. Should the latter be held as truly the cause, then the other falls to be regarded as the circumstances, in the common aphorism, that the same cause produces the same effect in the same circumstances. In many cases the cause is still more complex, and embraces other elements, as, for instance, the previous habits of the soul; nay, the very casual associations of the mind in all its previous history, and the forgotten incidents of childhood, may be swaying more or less powerfully the actual state produced at any given moment.* It will be seen from this that the doctrine of necessity, as taught by Edwards, is here opened, and the self-determining power of the human will let in as a causal element.

§ 118. The practical conclusion deduced from this distinction is the pushing of the doctrine of philosophical necessity one step farther back. The action has its cause, without which it cannot exist, but that cause, in whole or in part, is the will. This will itself is acted upon by causes, not sufficiently powerful, however, to destroy its freedom, but, at the same time, strong enough to establish between it and them the relation between cause and effect. On the one hand, man has "a power of will and self-agency; and his conscience announces that he is responsible." On the other hand, the law of cause and effect reigns in mind as it reigns in matter. "We can produce the separate proofs of the two separate truths advocated by us; and, when looked apart, these proofs are acknowledged to be irrefragable. Should it be demanded of us that we reconcile them, we answer that we are not bound to offer a positive reconcilia-

---

* McCosh, on the Divine Gov., fourth Am. ed., p. 541.

tion."* In this view, man, while in everything acting under the direction of the Divine Sovereignty, is at the same time, chargeable with his own sins.

b^3. *Libertarian view.*

§ 119. The libertarian view, as taught by Christian theists of the present day, approximates so closely to those just stated as to leave the difference rather nominal than real. Taking it in reference to the origin of evil, Mr. R. A. Thompson, whose late treatise on Theism may be regarded as based on this special hypothesis, tells us that it consists in "laying it (sin) to the charge of finite wills," and by this means "reconciling the prevalence of mischief with the perfections of the Creator."† To an American writer, however, Mr. A. T. Bledsoe, we owe the broadest enunciation and the most systematic defence of this doctrine, so far as it may be received as an element in Christian theism.‡

The main difficulty, as is stated by Mr. Bledsoe, and as is noticed at the commencement of this discussion, is the position of the atheist, that if God possessed perfect holiness He would prevent all moral evil, unless His power were limited. Now, says Mr. Bledsoe, "this influence is a false premise, namely, that if God is omnipotent He could easily prevent moral evil, and cause virtue to exist without any mixture of vice. This assumption has been incautiously conceded to the atheist by his opponent, and hence his argu-

---

* McCosh, on the Divine Gov., fourth Am. ed., p. 279. See *post*, § 243, 244, etc.

† Thompson's Theism, book iii., chap. vi., § 9.

‡ A Theodicy, etc., by A. T. Bledsoe, Professor in the University of Mississippi. New York: Carlton Philips, 1854.

ment has not been clearly and fully refuted." The proper refutation of the argument, it is said, involves two assumptions: "first, that it is no limitation of the Divine Omnipotence to say that it cannot work contradictions; and, secondly, that if God should cause virtue to exist in the heart of a moral agent, He would work a contradiction."

§ 120. The first position, that God cannot work impossibilities, may be for the present passed. The second, viz., that "if God should cause virtue to exist in the breast of a moral agent, He would work a contradiction," is thus defended: "In other words, the production of virtue by any extraneous agency, is one of those impossible conceits, those inherent absurdities, which lie quite beyond the sphere of light in which the Divine Omnipotence moves, and has no existence except in the outer darkness of a lawless imagination, or in the dim regions of error in which the true nature of moral goodness has never been seen. It is absurd, we say, to suppose that moral agents can be governed and controlled in any other way than by moral means. All physical power is here out of the question. By physical power, in connection with wisdom and goodness, a moral agent may be created and endowed with the noblest attributes. By physical power a moral agent may be caused to glow with a *feeling* of love, and armed with an uncommon energy of will; but such effects, though produced by the power of God, are not the virtue of the moral agent in whom they are produced. This consists not in the possession of moral powers, but in the proper and obedient exercise of those powers. If infinite wisdom, and goodness, and power, should muster all the means and appliances in the universe, and cause them to bear, with united energy, on a single mind, the effect produced, however grand and beautiful, would not be the virtue of the agent in whom it is produced. Nothing can be his virtue which is produced by an extraneous agency. This is a dictate of the universal reason and consciousness of mankind. It needs no metaphysical refinement for its support, and no scholastic jargon for its illustration. On this broad principle, then, which is so clearly deduced, not from the confined darkness of the schools, but the open light of nature, we intend to take our stand in opposition to the embattled ranks of atheism."

This course of reasoning, as will be observed, still lies open to the inquiry, why, if the capacity to sin is inseparable from moral agency, did God create moral agents at all? This objection Mr. Bledsoe, like his antagonists in this issue, very satisfactorily disposes of by recourse to the theory of optionism. "God did not choose," says Mr. Bledsoe, "to prevent sin in this way, but to create the world exactly as He did, though He foresaw the fall and all its consequences, *because the highest good of the universe* required the creation of such a world."

The objections which may be urged to this scheme may be classified as follows:—

§ 121. a^4. *It still traces back sin to God.* Undoubtedly a capacity to sin "is essential to moral agents." But does it follow that there must hence be actual sinning, especially to the extent to which it is carried among men? While the capacity to sin would remain, it will surely not be denied that God, by an infusion of gracious affections, could have averted the overt act. If He could have done so, but did not, He becomes as much open to the charge of permitting sin as He is under the necessity hypothesis.

§ 122. b^4. *It contemplates an abeyance in the Divine Power inconsistent with the idea of an infinite and perfect Deity.* It requires us to presume that the all-observant and managing Governor, who, it is assumed, controls the destinies of the myriads of animals, great and small, who are ranged around the great amphitheatre of nature, not only withdraws from man all moral influence, but delivers to him an independent power of volition which must enable the creature to control the movements of the Creator's realm. This, it is insisted, involves difficulties far greater than those of the necessity hypothesis.

§ 123. c^4 *It aggravates man's impotence.*

It requires no extensive induction to prove that men, as they now stand, are incompetent for the work of their own moral renovation. It is not merely the declaration of Scripture, but the testimony of experience, that for this purpose there is needed the interposition of Divine grace. But, by surrounding man by a non-conducting atmosphere of moral agency, through which this grace does not penetrate, do we not expose ourselves to Coleridge's sarcasm, that while the doctrine of necessity is the lamb in wolf's clothing, that of liberty is the wolf in lamb's clothing?

Of these objections, the *first* is equally chargeable to all hypotheses of the origin of evil, and may, therefore, be canceled altogether. The *second* is common to every scheme which recognizes moral agency. The *third* is, however, more serious, and can only be avoided by invoking the aid of the apparently contradictory truth of a special and constantly succoring Divine Sovereignty, in the same way that those who acknowledge such sovereignty reciprocally invoke the aid of free agency to meet the common consciousness of individual being.

d^4. It is in the omission to appeal to this established though apparently conflicting truth, (*i.e.* that of Divine Sovereignty,) that Mr. Bledsoe, while preserving the symmetry of his hypothesis, has failed to adapt it to all the exigencies of consciousness. The difficulty here is twofold.

§ 124. *a^5*. Such omission is in conflict with our own experience as to the power of man for self-renovation. Who is there who cannot testify to his moral inability for this purpose,—to his attempting, for instance, to conquer some specific evil habit—to his using whatever powers he could summon for this end,—and yet to his ultimately failing?

§ 125. *b^5*. The theory in like manner conflicts with our consciousness as to the existence, in part at least, of the relation of cause and effect to the actions of the human mind. Mr. Bledsoe, and those who agree with him in the advocacy of a systematic and absolute libertarianism, assume the entire absence of causation in the human mind. Now this is in opposition both to consciousness and to experience. We are conscious of causation—*e.g.* the influence of others, early prejudices or associations—producing certain results. We calculate on the action of such causes on others, when we predict that under certain circumstances others will commit certain acts. In some cases, such as the absence of counteracting causes, we all must admit, there is a probability approaching to a moral necessity of these agencies producing their specific effects. How then, in harmony with our own conscience, can we assert the will to act absolutely free from any superior causality?

To Mr. Young's exposition of the same view, marked as it is with singular dialectic skill and great felicity of expression, the same objections apply though with greater force. To him the human judgment, throughout its whole probation, is free from any supernatural divine causation. God works on man even in the office of renovation, not by moving the *will*, but by illuminating the *understanding.* Original sin is represented as "ignorance, or false views of the Most High."* Resurrection to life is effected by "just views of the Almighty." "Spiritual truth is the medium and even the very material of the soul's life." The ministry of Christ consists in "pouring a flood of light upon the world in which its darkness might be quenched." The office of the Holy Spirit consists in "pouring down the light of truth and the force of love, commanding all the appliances of infinite wisdom, infinite patience, and infinite power, *and ceaselessly distributing, combining and modifying moral influences of all kinds, in order that at length man might be won back to his Creator, to duty, to reason, to life.*"

§ 126. It is not within the province of the present work to consider how far this is consistent with Christian theology. It is enough to say that it is in conflict both with psychological experience and with analogy. There are few who have spoken of their own religious history, who do not say that their will was at times actěd on, not by

* Mystery of Evil, Phil. edition of 1856, p. 316.

"light,"—not by evidence, not by argument,—but by a power distinct from either, a power which was above themselves, and which could not be accounted for by merely human and natural conditions. And the analogy with other decisive phenomena which operate in the formation of character, tends to strengthen this view. Two minds, trained under the same process, illuminated by the same degree of light, differ widely in their reception of it. With regard to the degree to which this light is cast, a still greater variety exhibits itself. The inhabitants of Central Africa in our own day,—those of Germany before the Christian era,—had no concern in selecting the points of time or of territory in which they were placed. Among civilized countries even now, we unite in predicting certain phases of character as likely to arise from birth and involuntary education. We know all of us how much our own character and opinions have in this way been moulded. The question now is not whether an all-observant and humane God may not vary the inner light communicated by Him, and proportion His ultimate judgments, so as to compensate for the inequalities in which His creatures were placed. But the question is whether those inequalities do exist so as to affect character. And it is submitted that consciousness and observation show they do.

§ 127. Two still more recent American writers, however, by recognizing this element, have, with more or less qualification, pushed the libertarian hypothesis almost to the point where the necessitarian is left by McCosh. Dr. Hickok, whose profound work on "Rational Cosmology," places him in the front rank of modern theistical metaphysicians, declares "the reason-idea of spiritual agency" to be "spontaneous activity self-directed," and announces that in this we have an "utterly new kind of *cause*, viz., a *cause* originating or causing to be from itself, and not a cause conditioned or caused to cause from something back of itself. It is activity in liberty, which can make a beginning from conditions within its own being. We have in this conception no impossibilities, nor absurdities of the *last-first*, in affirming that we may intelligently apprehend how an utterly new thing can absolutely begin existence. With all rational spirits there is such capacity of initial causality, and thus of all free and responsible beings, we affirm that their personal acts are their own origination, and can no more be transferred to any other person than their separate identity. Man and angel can, in this sense, truly create. Their good and bad deeds are of their own origination. Whatever another agent may do in throwing his own conditions on them, he does not originate their acts within them But man cannot originate new forces, and thus man cannot create matter."*

Here we have free agency limited by the conditions which belong to it as a *spiritual* as distinguished from a *corporeal* organization. In a late very striking exposition of the same topic,—an exposition also from the libertarian point of view,†—we have an additional qualification attached which makes moral freedom, as here defined, almost tantamount to philosophical necessity, as defined by McCosh. In the treatise now under notice, after declaring free agents to be

* Hickok's Rational Cosmology, by L. P. Hickok; 1858, p. 99.

† Bushnell's Nature and the Supernatural; N. Y., 1858, p. 234.

"powers," who "act as being uncaused in their action, which excludes any control of them by God's omnipotent force," the author states that in the lapsed condition in which the soul now finds itself, God alone can restore it to life and liberty. "By the freedom of the will we understand simply its freedom as a volitional function; but mere volitions, taken by themselves involve no capacity to regenerate or constitute a character. Say what we may of the will as a strictly self-determining power, raise what distinctions we may as regards the kinds of ability, such as natural and moral, antecedent and subsequent, we have no ability at all, of any kind, to regenerate our own state, or restore our own disorders."

§ 128. c^3. *Present approximation of the two schools.* Philosophical necessity, as now stated, consists of the Divine Sovereignty, incorporating within itself and recognizing as an independent power, Free Agency; Libertarianism, of Free Agency, capable, within its own range of action, of voluntary choice, but dependent, for self-renovation, on Divine grace. In other words, each system consists of the same two great truths, apparently hostile, yet even consistent in human consciousness—God is Sovereign, the Will is free. If, in respect to the question of the primacy of these truths, there should be great diversity of opinion,—if by one class of thinkers the one is placed first and gazed at with peculiar reverence, if by another the other,—this is no more than we find in civil society, where the two parallel truths of individual liberty and governmental subjection are subject to the same treatment. The question is one of temperament. In sociology, we find on the one side, those who look up with peculiar reverence to the conservative power of government, who distrust the capacity of bodies of men for self-government, who turn fondly to the past and sadly to the future; on the other side, those who holding that true conservatism requires constant change in order to withstand the dilapidations of time, have an *a priori* tendency to reforms, and look upon the past mainly as a platform on which to raise the achievements of the future. To the struggles of these two classes of opinion—the conservative and the reforming—we owe a great part of the healthy action of society. No man would now affirm that either class possesses the truth solely, or that the apparently hostile truths of human independence and of human subordination are not practically recognized in political economy. Among those engaged in marshaling the two cardinal propositions of metaphysical theology, we may look for the same diversity.

In the present discussion, the metaphysical errors of the two schools have been produced very much in the same way as the economical errors of the two political schools which have been noticed. At one time the over-pressure of centralism requires a vigorous and unqualified assertion of individual liberty; at another, the over-pressure of individualism requires a similar assertion of the supremacy of the law. It has been so in the history of the necessitarian controversy. At a time when the Divine Supremacy was almost overlooked, Edwards, by his matchless logic, vindicated the causal connection of the Divine Purpose and the human will. Afterwards, when the danger was from the contrary direction, and when, under the lead of Condillac and Hume, there was a practical denial of the power of self-determination, the truth was again approached by the vindication of that particular branch of it which was then in peril. To this last reaction, almost simultaneous in England, Scotland, and Germany, we owe the extraordinary logical acuteness and profound analysis with which Kant established the "autonomy" of the will, and its own supreme law-giving functions;* with which Reid, with grave and luminous precision, vindicated moral agency,† and with which Coleridge, with more comprehensiveness than either, (for he recognized the countervailing proposition of Divine sovereignty,) brought his own lustrous rhetoric to the rescue of the truth then in peculiar peril.

But from the very force of their mission, the advance-guard of each school erred: that of the necessitarians in rejecting *intuition*, as an original idea produced in the human mind; that of the libertarians in rejecting *sensation* as having a like office and power. A more liberal philosophy has told us that the two methods of reaching truth co-exist; riper theology tells us that the two great truths of God's sovereignty and man's free agency are, in like manner, coexistent.

§ 129. So far as concerns the supposed conflict of predestination with free will, the difficulties have been greatly lessened by modern scientific research. Geology, as the annihilator of time, and astronomy, as the annihilator of space, tend to relieve this position from its doctrinal difficulties by showing that, to a Divine eye, there can be no blanks over

---

* See particularly his Grundlegung zur Metaphysick der Sitten; Riga, 1785.

† See his Essay on Liberty of Moral Agents, Essays, etc., No. 4, part iii.

which either predestination or retrospection can act. There can be no prophecy where there is no future; there can be no history where there is no past. All is an immediate present, ranging in a concave surface before the observation of the Almighty, the points in it separated from each other, but all at the same distance from Himself.

We have an illustration of this as to space, from the magnetic telegraph. The operator at the wires no longer finds mountains and forests lifting themselves between himself and the terminus of the line, but his fingers talk through their dumb formula across a continent with as substantial rapidity as if that continent did not exist.

But it is from astronomy that we learn most impressively the great truth that infinitude is natural and normal, and time and space artificial. Light, which, could it be reined and guided, would curve round the earth in a moment,—which, even when on its by-roads, makes its cross journey from the sun to the remotest known planets and from thence to the earth, in less than a day,—is yet many thousands of years in reaching us from those as yet unresolved nebulæ whose elements the most space-penetrating of telescopes cannot do much more than suspect. These telescopes, then, spread before us worlds that existed before the creation of man. This faint suffusion on the distant skies is, as we now see it, coeval with those periods when only animal life issued over the earth's surface, or perhaps with that still more remote period when that surface was a mass of fire. It is a singular illustration of the inadequacy of our formulas of time to note even the ordinary phenomena of the heavens; that not only is the star that we now see a cotemporary with events a thousand years back, but may be at this moment extinct. Other stars, under past astronomical observation, have, within a few hundred years, been annihilated; this we now look upon may be but the spectre, created by the finiteness of our senses, of that which once was.

§ 130. Nor does this thought strike us the less if we suppose the position reversed, and the observer to stand on one of these distant stars watching our own globe. Supposing he has a telescope of almost infinitely augmented power, what does he see? Let him take one of the more remote of these stand-points, and the earth hurries across the range of his instrument with her then thin crust, at one place palpitating and heaving over the seething of the boiling rock beneath; at another, gashed and seamed by fissures, through which torrents of molten basalt, porphyry, and granite, break upward and then fall down in blazing but ponderous spray; at another, suddenly overwhelmed by some ocean-lake which the upheaval of new mountain ranges has driven from its seat. Let him pass from this desolate and awful scene, and station himself at a stand-point, perhaps a thousand years nearer, as measured by the passage of light. No longer the earth is covered with dark clouds, broken only by volcanic fires. A new and tranquil scene follows,—the scene of a giant though languid and otiose infancy. The fierce energies of all that awful subterranean laboratory, with its powers of earthquake and volcano, and its then uncombined agents of fire, water, and rock, have done their work. The chemical as well as the mechanical transformation is complete, and the earth now calmly sleeps prior to the great morning of organic creation. Vast rivers drop lazily through continents of alluvium and drift. These club-masses, (Sigillariæ,) in height one hundred feet, and five or six feet in diameter,* supply, in the concentric layers of their cylindrical trunks, the base of the coal strata of the future. Their gigantic boughs flap, over the rich soil, their awninglike leaves. And then, from another stand-point, a new stage of creation appears. The primeval faunæ, corresponding, in their comprehensive but simple structure, with the preliminary and typical forms of human society, first display themselves to the telescopic eye. The present observer, if we can suppose such, may now, from one of these ranges, see prowling in the quiet waters the Placoids and Ganoids, who, in those paleozoic days, were the sole representatives of the vertebrate type. The cumbrous rhinoceros wallowing in the rich mud by the side of the lagoon; the tortoise sprawling in the sunshine; family after family of mammals, ending with man himself, as by successive creations they appear; each stand at present before these planetary observers. And, if light paints in those distant spheres with the same infinite accuracy and delicacy as it does in ours, we see, as we look on these remote nebulæ, not merely the witnesses, but the representations of our cosmical history. There is no TIME in that great daguerreotype gallery of the heavens; but there, as at the present, are spread the responsive paintings, changing as the original changed, of each period of the earth's creation and development.

§ 131. To the human mind, therefore, using the aid of

* See Professor Le Conte's Lecture on Coal, Smithsonian Institute Proceedings, 1857, p. 159.

geology and astronomy, time and space dwindle and disappear in the very proportion in which the instruments by which they are measured become the more perfect. To the Divine mind, they must cease to exist altogether. Astronomy, by showing us how the gravitation which binds together the atoms of earth, keeps in harmony the remotest stars, tells us that the reins that guide us unite in that same great hand that orders the entire universe. Geology takes us still farther; for it shows not merely the unity of mechanism through space, but the unity of design through time. *Time*, indeed, cannot apply its notations to the contemplation of this immutable and supreme Governor of the universe. Thousands upon thousands of years back the geologist carries us and shows us the prior stages of a continuous life of which we are ourselves members. In this continuousness there is neither break or disharmony. It is but the flash of a conception and the stroke of a decree that intervenes between the earliest and the latest geological eras.

Let us remove, then, space and time from our calculations; let us cease to apply the measuring-rods of our own finite senses to the Unchangeable and the Almighty, and then prophecy and history, foreknowledge and retrospection, must coalesce in immediate observation. The event will then be cotemporaneous with the foreordination; it will be foreordained because it exists, as well as exist because it is foreordained.

§ 132. *d^3. The mere fact of the opposition of Divine Sovereignty and of human reponsibility, does not justify the rejection of either the one or the other of these truths.*

It may here be observed that philosophy as well as theology leads to the belief that the highest truth, to finite minds, is based on two subordinate propositions, each true, and yet apparently irreconcilable. It may be, to adopt an illustration already given, that the arch which unites the pillars is beyond the reach of the human eye, and that though all that we can see is the pillars themselves, distinct and almost defiant, yet that at a height beyond our observation they join and harmonize. The following may be taken as illustrations of the existence of such hostile and yet at the same time necessarily reconcilable truths.

The philologist infers, (and, on the supposition of there being no supernatural interference, without the possibility of reply,) from the diversity of languages now existing on the globe, the existence of the human race for hundreds of thousands of years. He looks at the fact that nations, from religious and patriotic associations, if not from literary use, cling to their languages with a pertinacity so great that during the periods of which authentic history speaks, the changes have been but slight; he notices the fact that since the time of Alfred, through a series of extraordinary vicissitudes, nine-tenths of the words used in the English language have remained essentially the same; he traces the similarity between the Homeric dialect and the Romaic, between the most ancient Latin and the most modern Italian; between the laws of Menu and the three thousand years' posterior essays of Rammohum Roy; he reminds us that the farther back we go in time, as the chances of mutual combinations and outside influence become less, so the process of internal change becomes more protracted; and from these facts he calls upon us to conclude that the human race, unless some miraculous multiplication of tongues be supposed, must have lived during a period of which its present recorded history is an inconsiderable fraction. On the other hand, geology shows, beyond the possibility of doubt, that the race is of but recent origin, and this view is strengthened by the testimony of history and tradition. And yet these truths not only coexist, but find their common origin in a divine fiat—that of the multiplication of tongues at Babel—which in this special case revelation has discovered to us.

We find another instance of opposite truths, which nevertheless must in fact harmonize, in the phenomena of the centrifugal and centripetal forces. Are we in these, and similar cases, to hold that because we cannot *reconcile*, we must *reject*? Does not the presumption hold good that when the veil is uncovered the solution of the apparent contradictions will be discovered?

"The proposition that men are responsible for their moral character, taken by itself," says Dr. Hodge, "is so capable of demonstration, that all men do in fact believe it. Every man feels it to be true with regard to himself, and knows it to be true with regard to others. All self-condemnation and self-approbation rest on the consciousness of this truth. All our judgments regarding the moral conduct of others are founded on the same assumption. It is, therefore, one of those truths which is included in the universal consciousness of men, and has in all ages and nations been assumed as certain. Men cannot really doubt it, if they would. On the other hand, it is no less certain that our character does depend in a measure upon circumstances beyond our control; upon our original constitution, upon education, upon prevalent habits and opinions, upon Divine influence, etc. All this is proved by experience and observation. Here then are two facts resting on independent evidence, each certain, and each by itself securing general assent. Yet we see men constantly disposed to bring up the one against the other; and argue against their responsibility, because they are dependent, or against their dependence, because they are responsible. In like manner the proposition that man is a free agent, commands immediate and universal assent, because it is an ultimate fact of consciousness. It can no more be doubted than we can doubt our own existence. Side by side, however, with this intimate persuasion of our moral liberty, lies the conviction, no less intimate, of our inability to change, by merely willing to do so, either our belief or our affections, for which, as before stated, every man knows himself to be responsible. Perhaps few men,—perhaps no man,—can see the harmony of these truths; yet they are truths, and as such are practically acknowledged by all men. Again, all experience teaches us that we live in a world of means; that knowledge, religion, happiness, are all to be sought in a certain way, and that to neglect the means is to lose the end.

"It is, however, no less true that there is no necessary or certain connection between the means and the end; that God holds the result in His own hands and decides the issues according to His sovereign pleasure. In all the ordinary affairs of life, men submit to this arrangement and do not hesitate to use means, though the end is uncertain and beyond their control. But in religion, they think this uncertainty of the result a sufficient excuse for neglect."*

With this comes the following profound thought, expressed by Sir W. Hamilton with the felicity and sustained by the power of which he is so great a master: "It will argue nothing against the trustworthiness of consciousness, that all or any of its deliverances are inexplicable—are incomprehensible; that is, that we are unable to conceive through a higher notion how that is possible which the deliverance avouches actually to be. To make the comprehensibility of a datum of consciousness the criterion of its truth, would be indeed the climax of absurdity; for the primary data of consciousness, as themselves the conditions under which all else is comprehended, are necessarily themselves incomprehensible. We know, and can know only that they are, not how they can be."†

§ 133. e^3. *Incidental moral consequences of evil.*

"De vitiis nostris scalam nobis facimus, si vitia ipsa calcamus," says St. Augustine; or, to take Mr. Longfellow's paraphrase,—

Saint Augustine! well hast thou said
  That of our vices we can frame
A ladder, if we will but tread
  Beneath our feet each deed of shame.

We may here find the ground-work of a peculiar com-

---

* Hodge's Way of Life, p. 99.

† Hamilton's Reid, p. 745. See *post*, § 241, etc.

munion with God; a communion so intimate, and so humble, as to exceed in its tender and pathetic love and its grand meekness even the sublimest adoration of the untempted and sinless of the angelic creation. "There is no temptation," says John of Wesel, one of the greatest of the pre-Lutheran reformers, "so great as not being tempted at all." In other words, there is nothing so dangerous to the love which is life, as that security which needs nothing to cling to, and which has no recollection of personal unworthiness and misery forgiven and relieved by a pity at once so tender and sublime. This experience of sin is a great teacher. One, who if he may not be cited as a Christian poet, may at least come before us as a sagacious and experienced judge of our common nature, thus writes:—

I asked the Lord that I might grow
  In faith and love and every grace;
Might more of His salvation know
  And seek more earnestly His face.

I hoped that in some favored hour
  At once He'd answer my request,
And by His love's constraining power,
  Subdue my sins and give me rest.

Instead of this, He made me feel
  The hidden evils of my heart;
And let the angry powers of hell
  Assault my soul in every part.

"Lord, why is this?" I trembling cried,
  "Wilt Thou pursue Thy worm to death?"
"'Tis in this way," the Lord replied,
  "I answer prayer for grace and faith.

"These inward trials I employ
From self and pride to set thee free,
And break thy schemes of earthly joy
That thou may'st seek thy all in me."

§ 134. And ONE other, who, if He did not, according even to modern positivism, speak divine truth, at least uttered words of deep wisdom, said:—

"SIMON, I HAVE SOMEWHAT TO SAY UNTO THEE. AND HE SAITH, MASTER, SAY ON.

THERE WAS A CERTAIN CREDITOR WHICH HAD TWO DEBTORS: THE ONE OWED FIVE HUNDRED PENCE, AND THE OTHER FIFTY. AND WHEN THEY HAD NOTHING TO PAY, HE FRANKLY FORGAVE THEM BOTH. TELL ME THEREFORE, WHICH OF THEM WILL LOVE HIM MOST?

SIMON ANSWERED AND SAID, I SUPPOSE THAT HE TO WHOM HE FORGAVE MOST. AND HE SAID UNTO HIM, THOU HAST RIGHTLY JUDGED."

c^2. *As the necessary incidents of limited creatures.*

§ 135. The argument in this connection may be thus stated: The scheme of an ascending scale of beings, each of a distant order and degree of power, is of all others the one most consistent with the general good. To such a graduated order of beings, metaphysical evil, at least, is essential. Therefore metaphysical evil is essential to the highest standard we can propose for the general good.

We will examine the two premises in succession. The scheme of an ascending scale of beings, each of a distinct order and degree of power, is of all others the most consistent with the general good.

How far this scale *ascends* may be considered under another head. It is enough to say, that as it *descends* almost infinitely, and as from the lowest mollusc upward to man there is a gradual rise, the presumption is that this ascent continues. This, however, is not necessary to the strength of the present argument. We may suppose that the scale of creation terminates with man, and, even on this supposition, draw the following inferences:—

§ 136. a^3. *By a graduated scale there is room for the exercise of charity and an interchange of favors.*

Wordsworth touches very delicately on this in that fine passage in which he speaks of the hardness of temper of those who herd and browse only

In the grove of their own kindred.

The association merely with those who stand with us in a high scale of comfort hardens the heart, and, in hardening it, closes up many avenues of pleasure. Cicero* carries this to the irrational as well as the rational creation:—"Accedit ad non nullorum animantium, et earum rerum quas terras gignit, conservationem et salutem, hominum etiam solertia et diligentia. Nam multæ et pecudes, et stirpes sunt, quæ sine procuratione hominum salvæ esse non possunt." And even in the inanimate creation a similar teaching may be found. It is in the inequalities of the heavenly bodies that consists their harmony. The earth and its sister planets, inferior as they are in size and lustre, derive a comfort from the sun such as perhaps its splendor may not enable it to impart to itself. The moon waits on the earth,

---

* De Nat. Deorum, lib. ii. c. 52.

ministering, as it were, to its wants, lifting up and down its tides so as to rinse the reedy banks of the remote river, as well as to agitate, and thereby refine the ocean. And, on the other hand, it is by these inequalities that the grander bodies are kept in their orbits.

§ 137. Now, these analogies are not without value in determining the important relations of the different grades of rational as well as irrational creatures. "Reduce the creation to a *perfect equality*," says Dr. Chauncey, (on the *Benevolence* of the Deity, p. 201,) "and all participation of that part of the Creator's happiness, the *communication of good*, is at once necessarily destroyed. For, where the same perfection and happiness, both in *kind* and *degree*, is at all times equally possessed by all beings, it is evident that *good* cannot possibly be communicated from one to another. And can it be imagined that the Deity would pitch upon a plan for the communication of good, which would render it impracticable for any of his creatures, either to resemble Him in that which is His greatest glory, or to partake, in any measure, of that which is His greatest pleasure? There is no truly benevolent mind but will readily be reconciled to a diversity in beings, rather than the pleasure of communicating good should be excluded from creation. And excluded it must be, if there is not some diversity. Upon any other supposition, not one being in the creation could be the object of another's beneficence; and, consequently, the noblest and most truly Divine pleasure, that which arises from doing good, could not have place in the whole circle of existing creatures. So that it is evident a diversity of beings is so far from being an objection against infinite benevolence that it really flows from it as its proper cause. There could not have been the manifestation of so much goodness, if there had not been *some difference* between the creatures brought into existence. And the least attention will obviously lead any one to determine that, if goodness may be the cause of any diversity at all, no stop can be made without continuing it down through all variety of orders, so long as the balance shall turn in favor of happiness, or, in other words, so long as existence can be called a good, and pronounced better than not to be."

§ 138. b^3. *By a graduated scale the earth will be most thoroughly populated, and human comfort best promoted.*

"Its different elements and different climates," says Mr. Fleming, in his excellent Plea for the ways of God, "are obviously fitted for affording the means of life and enjoyment to different orders of beings, and, accordingly, every element and every climate have their appropriate inheritants. Multitudes of swift and brilliant creatures tread the sands of the southern zone: striped zebras and spotted leopards; while the frost-bitten regions of the north are traversed by the dull ox and the dark wolf. Even the cold ice is tenanted by the shaggy bear. The horse gallops across the plains, while the eagle builds his nest on the crags of the rock; the insect sports in the sunbeam, while the leviathan takes his pastime in the mighty waters."

§ 139. Now, this view might be extended so as to introduce the human race. The restless and adventurous temper of the pioneer leads him to those Western forests where, himself passing beyond the blazed oak, he surveys, by the instruments only of a hunter's instinct, the road which a coming nation is to travel. He dies poor, and his solitary grave lies unmarked in the woods, but he has enjoyed a life of wild pleasure which he would not have exchanged for one on a monarch's throne, and he leaves his grave as the base on which civilization couches as it is about to make a new spring. And on each member of the procession that follows him, individuality sets its special stamp and gives to him its peculiar impulse. The brawny arm and strong nerve of one stations him in the blacksmith's shop, where, day after day, he strains and bakes himself over the anvil in an occupation most useful to the community, but, at the same time, very ungenial to those who may not be led to it by a special taste. An instinct for bartering and peddling drives forth another in the advance-guard of the same procession, and the clothing-store opens its windows and displays its goods in the new-built village. So it is throughout. Were there an equal uniformity of taste, of means, of capacity, either the northern seas would not be fretted with the harpoon, or, if we suppose the passion to be universal, the pursuit of the gigantic ocean-game would engross the great mass of the young energies of the land. So with that remarkable mechanical dexterity which, when whetted by poverty, moves, to take a single illustration, into the cotton field, and there, with a series of revolving spikes, disentangles the knotted fibres of the cotton-plant; then passes to the landing, and packs the bales on the deck of the low-pressure boat that disturbs the sluggish Southern stream; then drops to the factor's warehouse, and calls into its aid a new class of energies, those of ocean commerce; then puts in motion the factory, with its myriads of workmen, and, at last, the sewing machine, which supports the solitary seamstress. Without diversity of gifts, and without the inequalities of fortune, on the one side to supply the capital, on the other the labor, this great element of national prosperity and personal comfort could not have existed. And the same reason applies to every other industrial enterprise by which the general good has been advanced. Inequality is the soul of enterprise and the spring of prosperity; horizontal wealth and uniform capacity would be nothing else than unbroken penury.

c^3. *By a graduated scale a stimulus is afforded for enterprise and room for improvement.*

§ 140. This proposition, in its first branch, has already been touched upon. In its second, it is self-demonstrative. Perfection must necessarily be stationary. To leave room for progress requires imperfection. Mr. Addison, with his usual elegance, likens the soul, in its relation to its Creator, "to one of those mathematical lines that may draw nearer to another, for all eternity, without a possibility of touching: and can there be a thought so transporting," he inquires, "as to consider ourselves in these perpetual approaches to Him who is not only the standard of perfection, but of happiness?"

Having now shown that an ascending scale of beings, each of a distinct order and degree of power, is, of all schemes, the most consistent with the general good, we proceed to the minor premise, viz., that to such a scale, metaphysical evil, at least, is essential.

§ 141. Take, as the lowest phase, the mere evil of *incapacity*. That this is an evil,—that the struggling in even a single direction against an impassable barrier,—the imprisonment even of one class of energies within a cell against whose grated windows they are ever chafing and torturing themselves in order to escape to the infinite beyond,—that these things are evils, no one can doubt. But some limitation is essential to all created beings. For, even supposing the creature to have no actual corporeal or even psychical limit, it is inseparable from the very fact of createdness that there should be the moral limit of a consciousness of having been created, accompanied, it may be, with that oppressive sense of dependence which Milton points out to us as the cause of the revolt of the Archangel Satan.

But besides this, *bounds* are necessary to the existence of all created things. To people the world with a series of vagrant and penetrable spirits, each capable of occupying or passing through the other, with no coherence or shape, even if it were wise, would not be possible. For individuality there must be shape; for shape, deprivation; to deprivation, metaphysical evil is an essential requisite.

§ 142. But, it may be said, this difficulty might be obviated by creating only the highest of all orders of creation, and imparting to it the greatest degree of happiness. Now it has already been shown that this would not produce the desired end of the maximum of aggregate happiness. But the creation of an order such as is here spoken of is itself an absurdity. The pleasures of self-denial, of benevolence, of self-reliance, could not enter into the character of these desolate and unpitying inhabitants of such austere and baseless heights. And nothing is more limited than the very compact and unvarying mass of maximum beatitude which the hypothesis assumes. "A triangle," says Mr. Hayes, in his very ingenious essay on Divine Benevolence, "may be made as large as you please, yet the largest possible cannot be; for such a one could not be a triangle, which is a surface bounded with three straight lines. In like manner, we may, I apprehend, speak in relation to the happiness and perfection of the universe. God may make it as happy and as perfect as He pleases, and may continually increase this in any proportion He thinks fit; but still, I apprehend, it is capable of this increase, without limits, and without end; and that to suppose the greatest possible quantity of happiness or perfection diffused through it, is to suppose that there is a certain fixed and determinate quantity of happiness and perfection, beyond which it is impossible even for the power of God to proceed, which, I must own, seems to me absurd. So that to argue against the goodness of God because there is not the greatest quantity of happiness and perfection in the universe, is to use an argument that can have no force, since, if put into form, one of the premises is unintelligible."

d[3]. *What may to the human eye be a lower and inferior scale of happiness, may to a higher vision occupy a reversed position.*

§ 143. "We can see," says Hugh Miller, in the last and most graphic of his works,* "how in the pre-Adamic ages higher should have succeeded lower dynasties. To be low was not to be immoral; to be low was not to be guilt-stained and miserable. The sea-anemone on its half-tide rock, and the fern on its mossy hill-side, are low in their respective

* The Testimony of the Rocks, p. 262.

kingdoms; but they are, notwithstanding, worthy, in their quiet, unobtrusive beauty, of the God who formed them." And even after the human period this truth holds good. The aged pauper in the work-house, who, when taunted with his uselessness, and asked what he was doing, replied, "only waiting," may in the divine scale be a happier as well as sublimer object than even the archangel, who, with the most splendid powers and the most exquisite sensibilities for delight, is engaged in the active service of the Most High. Milton touches on this in these fine lines,—

> When I consider how my light is spent,
> Ere half my days, in this dark world and wide,
> And that one talent which is death to hide,
> Lodged with me useless, though my soul more bent
> To serve therewith my Maker, and present
> My true account, lest He, returning, chide;
> "Doth God exact day-labor, light denied?"
> I fondly ask: but patience, to prevent
> That murmur, soon replies, "*God doth not need*
> *Either man's work, or His own gifts; who best*
> *Bear His mild yoke, they serve Him best: His state*
> *Is kingly; thousands at his bidding speed,*
> *And post o'er land and ocean without rest;*
> *They also serve, who only stand and wait.*"

§ 144. Now even assuming that the nominally inferior classes, whether in the moral or physical creation, are endowed with a degree of happiness which, though lower in grade, is still definite and positive, are we to limit the divine power, and say, that after the creation of the higher and more perfect order, the divine energies are exhausted and are incapable of further creative action?

To these remarks it may be added—and on this point I must acknowledge my indebtedness to an eminent living psychologist, Mr. Isaac Taylor—that in a human state limitation is an ingredient in a full perception of beauty. "The beautiful in nature seldom presents itself otherwise than under some conditions of imperfection and limitation. The flower-garden has its cankers and its blights, and its fading and decaying splendors. The bright landscape of June suggests a contrast with the rigors and discomforts of February. The beauty of the material world is just bright and fair enough to stimulate that imaginative faculty the creations of which could never be acclimated to earth. So it is that this sense, which opens to us so much of pure and intense enjoyment which can never be realized unless it be in some brighter and distant sphere. From the cottage flower-garden such as shows itself on a summer morning, there is a pathway which the imaginative man does not fail often to tread, leading to the unknown and infinite, even to a world of absolute beauty, and of beauty never to decay.

On a path that is still more direct, the human mind finds its way toward the unknown and the infinite, when we stand in presence of those objects in nature which give rise to the emotions of sublimity. In front of Alpine altitudes, with their vast upheaved masses, commingled cloud, rock, glacier, cataract, there is excited not simply admiration and awe, but there is a feeling that these terrestrial marvels are samples only, shown off upon this planet in order to suggest to man the idea of scenes in some other world still more stupendous. If earth has its Alps, and its Andes, and its Himalayas, what shall be the spectacle of awe which a world unknown might open to our gaze?

Telluric catastrophes, volcanic eruptions, earthquakes, deluges, and whatever else combines ideas of destructive force with the conception of sublimity, has a further influence in carrying the mind, if it be sensitive in this manner, into those abysses of imaginative terror where the unknown and the infinite may be conceived of as unveiling their powers to the utmost.

There is yet a path which may be trod with less trepidation and with more fruit and advantage. The nocturnal heavens may, at first glance, seem more magnificent than sublime; but undoubtedly it is sublime when, by aid of reason, we penetrate this magnificence and become cognizant of the reality beyond. Now, there is here to be noted a change in our modes of thought which has been long in progress, and which is now advancing toward its consummation. This consummation will bring with it a consciousness of relationship, to the unknown and infinite of a far more substantial and impressive kind than hitherto has been admitted."*

d^1. The defects and evils complained of are, in many cases, productive of positive good.

a^2. Sorrow.

§ 145. Longfellow gives but a sad view even of sorrow in the following lines:—

The air is full of farewells to the dying,
  And mournings for the dead;
The heart of Rachel, for her children crying,
  Will not be comforted.

---

* World of Mind, p. 316.

> Let us be patient! these severe afflictions
> Not from the ground arise,
> But oftentimes celestial benedictions
> Assume this dark disguise.
>
> We see but dimly through the mists and vapors
> Amid these earthly damps;
> *What seem to us but sad, funereal tapers*
> *May be heaven's distant lamps.*

Far different is the confidence of the Christian:—

> I KNOW, is all the mourner saith,
> Knowledge by sorrow entereth,
> And life is perfected in death.

§ 146. Sorrow may also be not only the guide to, but the test by which true religion may be discovered. It may be opaque enough when merely worldly comforts attempt to illuminate it; but when a light from above falls on it, it not only receives that light itself, but, like the camera, collects and exhibits the truth all the more vividly from the darkness in which it is itself enveloped. Sorrow thus has come to us possessed with a wonderful gift of discrimination. The soul goes to the world for aid, and turns sadly away with her face all the darker, for there she finds no response. It is otherwise in religion. It is not that the religious man does not grieve. He does so, and all the more deeply from the fact that the narcotics taken by men of the world have no effect on him. But the very profoundness of his grief gives him a depth and fullness in his hope. He may be crushed by the death-bed of one whom he loves, but there is a grand

18*

anthem, ringing in his ears, sung by the spirits of the departed as well as of those present in the body: I KNOW THAT MY REDEEMER LIVETH. It may be that in this we find a primary purpose of sorrow. And let it not be said that this purpose is unimportant. For, assuming that there be a future state, how immensely important it is that there should be a monitor to point out the real sanctions by which that state is governed.

Sorrow, however, besides this, exercises a direct subjective influence on the human heart, which, in itself, is evidence of a Father's care. A painter, to adopt an illustration from another, was working at fresco on the ceiling of a lofty church. He was standing on a scaffolding, toward the unguarded edge of which he was slowly backing, absorbed in perfecting the figure on which he was engaged, and unconscious of the danger he was approaching. In a moment he would have been dashed on the pavement below, when one of his companions, seeing but one way to save him, suddenly threw a wet brush against the picture. The painter sprang forward to prevent the mischief, and, in so doing, saved his life. And it may be one of the chief evidences of the gentleness of the probationary government of God, that in this way, by apparently defacing an earthly image, the heart is turned from the idolatry of the human to the love of the spiritual and infinite. Nor is this all. Human affections, *e.g.*, those of the child to the parent, and of the parent to the child, are thus the instruments by which the impulses of true and disinterested love are called out and placed in training for a future more exalted sphere. They are, in this

sense, the trellises around which the affections are at first supported, until, by the Divine discipline, and by the cutting away of the merely earthly stay, these affections turn upward to heaven.

§ 147. The effect on others of the discipline may also be taken into account. To this the grand emotion of compassion is mainly due. Thus, Dr. Paley says, "One man's sufferings may be another man's trial. The family of a sick parent is a school of filial piety. The charities of domestic life, and not only these, but all the social virtues, are called out by distress. But then misery, to be the proper object of mitigation, or of that benevolence which endeavors to relieve, must be really or apparently casual. It is upon such sufferings alone that benevolence can operate. For, were there no evils in the world but what were punishments, properly and intelligibly such, benevolence would only stand in the way of justice."

And besides the refinement of human nature that is thus produced, it should not be forgotten that of all champions of the truth there is none more effective than the propagandism of meek and wise suffering. Conscious attempts to manage others, even if these attempts are successful, are but ephemeral in their effects, for there is always a feeling that some part at least of the object of the actor is display, if not advancement. Hence it is that even real reforms, when pressed by artificial agitation, move forward with so much uncertainty. But it is otherwise with those which are *lived* as well as *preached;* which are vindicated, not on the battle-field or in the senate-chamber, but in the lives and death of that noble company of obscure confessors, whose office it is, on the sick-bed, in the hard home of poverty, under the stress of many afflictions, to show that beyond all the institutions of the statesman, is a meek and hopeful submission under adversity, and a calm trust in Heaven.

b^2. Pain.

a^3. It preserves identity.

§ 148. The sense of pain is vested, with one or two exceptions to be hereafter noticed, entirely in the skin. Even in some of apparently the most painful operations, when the surgeon cuts the deepest, the pain disappears after the skin is cut through, only to reappear when the instrument, on extending its incision, touches the orifice from beneath. Even the *heart*, whose connection with the sensibilities is so remarkable that its expansion or contraction at sudden good or bad news often produces death, is not susceptible of actual pain. A nobleman of the Montgomery family, we are told, whose chest had been so opened by a fistulous affection that the heart was exposed to the touch, was brought to Dr. Harvey for examination. The organ was found to be entirely insensible. "I then brought him," said this accurate observer as well as great discoverer, "to the king that he might behold and touch so extraordinary a thing, and that he might perceive, as I did, that unless we touched the outer skin, or when he saw our fingers in the cavity, this young nobleman knew not that we touched the heart." So it is that the brain, when in like manner exposed, may be even pared away without sense of pain.

§ 149. Now, in this view let us contemplate the wisdom of the process by which the features which compose the human face are thus sealed and sheltered. In itself, this individualism of the countenance is an impressive proof of a Divine contriver and of a future destiny. When we recollect that of the millions who inhabit the face of the earth, no two have ever been found so exactly alike as to baffle, when full opportunities were given, the power of discrimination; when we recollect how numerous are the purposes which this individualism of countenance subserves, how without it the sanctities of home, the security of commerce, the peace of society would be destroyed,—we may admire the wisdom and the benevolence by which this most exquisite of mechanisms is constructed. The design of one original distinctive human face, as it rises forth under the sculptor's chisel from the marble block, draws from us a recognition of the artist's genius almost in proportion as the marks of individuality of expression are blended with the signs of ideal power. How much greater should be our admiration of the handiwork of the Great Artificer by whom this sculptury, not on the solid block, but on the much more subtle and yielding material of the face, is indefinitely multiplied and perfected! And there is a point in this individuality of expression which takes us a step beyond this. It is as if we should enter into a large chamber where are collected an immense number of keys, each with a ward of a distinct pattern. We would at once draw two inferences—first, that of a designing and contriving cause; and, second, that of a purpose, *i.e.* a room which each key is meant to open. And thus in the distinct individuality of the myriads of faces with whom we meet, we may recognize not only the divine workmanship, but the future distinct destiny of each.

"In my Father's house are many mansions." The severance of the mansions which these distinct individualities will open,—the continuance, in other words, in the next world of that individualism which exists here, may be drawn from an examination of this complex mechanism with almost as great certainty as may the existence of a contriving first cause.

§ 150. It is in the preservation of this individuality that we can find a reason for the sense of pain. An injunction is thus laid on all attempts to alter the distinctive marks of the countenance. Were the face as insensible to pain, and as susceptible of change, as the hair and nails, the whole of human confidence would be destroyed. The murderer would go into the surgeon-artist's hands and come out a philanthropist; men would be personated by others in the families, in the bank, in the exchange, in the senate. Sheridan, when recovering from a debauch, after a late session of the House of Commons, when asked his name by the watchman by whom he was picked up, answered "Wilberforce." The joke, for such it was, became for a moment a reality, and the excellent and pure statesman whose name was assumed, found himself for a day or two the subject of quite an unusual notoriety. But what would it be if false personation could be so sustained by a little plastic skill as to baffle the perceptions of the most acute?

§ 151. Now how, *a priori*, could a means be adopted to preserve this individuality? Human wisdom might suggest to seal it with an impenetrable cement. But Divine wisdom has doubled the guard. Not only is the surface so composed as to be in the highest degree unplastic, but the sense of pain is so stationed as to prevent any attempt at change of identity. And it is a remarkable fact, that among the numberless devices to which criminals have resorted to prevent detection, we do not find a case recorded where this was attempted by an alteration of the features.

b[3]. *Pain defends life.*

§ 152. Let it be suspended, and we then will be ready enough to admit the value of its active aid. The delicious lull of the sensibilities which is experienced by those who yield to the drowsiness produced by extreme cold, indicates the approach of death, because it arises from the silencing of those sleepless monitors by whom the gates of life are guarded. Several parallel cases are recorded of persons who have laid down to rest in cold weather on lime-kilns, and who, stupefied by the carbonic acid, have either been killed by the heat, or have had their limbs partially consumed, of which fact, however, they were not aware until they attempted to use them. By patients who have had limbs removed when under the influence of chloroform, the same subsequent unconsciousness is exhibited. "A man who had his finger torn off," we are told by Sir Charles Bell, "so as to hang by the tendon only, came to a pupil of Dr. Hunter. I shall now see, said the surgeon, whether this man has any sensibility in his tendon. He laid a cord along the finger, and blindfolding the patient, cut across the tendon. Tell me, he asked, what have I cut across? Why, you have cut across the cord, to be sure, was the reply." Not only therefore is the *action*, but the *location* of pain, adjusted to warn against real danger, and then, when its office is completed, the watchman withdraws, inflicting no

further distress than is actually necessary to discharge his mission.

§ 153. We have another illustration of the importance of pain, in the mischief following its suspension, in the cases of those paralytics in whom sensibility is lost in the numbness of disease, and whom, therefore, in order to prevent mortification of the flesh from the constant pressure produced by lying in one position, it is necessary constantly to move. In persons in health, nature performs the same office, at the promptings of pain, by those constant though unconscious movings by which even the deepest sleep is accompanied.

c^3. *Pain economizes strength.*

§ 154. Fatigue, for instance, is the grand protector of the muscular system against premature decay. An instance has lately been mentioned of a chemist who, in order to perfect an experiment, kept himself awake and in the active exercise of his faculties for day and night during an entire week, but who dropped down dead at the close of this period, broken as it were to pieces in the same way that a spring breaks on which is placed a constant and unrelieved pressure. Such, to speak of the higher faculties of the mind, was the case with Hugh Miller, who plied a frame which in its earlier years was used only to physical labor, until at last, at the close of his final and most brilliant intellectual effort, the nervous system suddenly crashed.* "I have got rid of my headaches," said a man of eminent talents in our own country not long since to a very capable observer, "and I can now work uninterruptedly." "You have got rid of

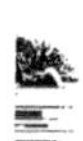

* See *post*, § 157.

your safety-valves," was the reply, "and now prepare for an explosion." Pain thus guards the intellect from the invasion of excess; and if the sentinel is drugged into silence, the fortress is in danger.

§ 155. The same rule holds good with regard to the muscular powers. How vast, in the vivacity of youth, would be the springs, how violent the blows struck by the hands and feet, how protracted the exertion, were it not for this sense of pain that comes and says, "Stop here; this is too much for your strength; your hand or your foot will be crushed by that shock; your body will be dashed to pieces by that fall; your muscles will be worn out by those continued strains!" The sense of pain acts in this way as a sort of subsidiary agency to keep up the integrity of the animal system; and without it we would have men strewn along the stream of life in wrecks,—limbs crushed in, sinews sprung, shape deformed. And, by a singularly subtle contrivance, these functions of preliminary injunction against waste are vested just in the authorities who can most efficiently exercise them, and are vested nowhere else. Acting, as this power does, through a severe and summary discipline, it is no slight proof of the Divine wisdom, that it is so economized as to be vested only in those organs and in those quarters where its action is essential. Thus the muscles and ligatures, so necessary to the easy working of the limbs, and the cushions of cartilages in which the ends of the bones play, communicate no pain when cut, for against an incised wound, so far at least as is requisite to prescribe prudence on the part of the patient, they are protected. But it is otherwise with regard to strains and concussions, against

which the elastic skin, so sensitive to cuts, utters but slight protest, while they are greeted by the muscles and ligatures with a most clamorous outcry. The sprained foot, by which prudence in jumping and leaping is taught, is equally emphatic with the sore cut which tells us it is necessary to be cautious in the use of edged tools. And both serve a still higher purpose in preserving the identity and individuality of the human frame, and in checking empirical experiments. Euripides tells us that the daughters of Pelias, on prescription of Medea, who undertook to cure old age, cut their aged father up, and put the pieces in a caldron, expecting him thus to come out young. Had the instincts of pain given to Pelias himself been consulted, or had the head surgeon and her assistants been made the first subjects of the operation themselves, the experiment never would have proceeded.

§ 156. The same remarkable distribution of this precautionary police, each department of it in the location to which it is peculiarly adapted and nowhere else, is to be found in the throat and windpipe. The texture of the windpipe is insensible to cuts, against which exterior guards are appointed, but is keenly sensitive to the slightest speck or crumb that threatens to pass the orifice. Now, how are such invaders to be repelled? The practical answer is to be found in a most ingenious system of defences by which this main entrance is guarded. The epiglottis acts as a trapdoor, which lifts up during breathing, but flies immediately to during swallowing. Then there is an exquisite irritability in the slit at the mouth of the windpipe, so that at the approach of the most insignificant assailant, it at once bristles up and slams to its door. As, however, this slip must open at the next breath into the lungs, it is necessary that a new set of guards should be set in motion, and this is effected by a sympathy between the upper vein of the windpipe and a reserve body of muscles below, who, in case of the invader passing the first defence, throw themselves into a state of vehement and clamorous resistance, of which the well-known convulsive windpipe cough is the outer manifestation.

§ 157. d^3. *The experience of pain, to limited agents, is necessary to the appreciation of pleasure.*

It has been already observed how the *common* blessings of life pass by unnoticed. It is, in fact, an inseparable attribute of a limited being, that his attention, and power of relish and appreciation, with his other faculties, grow weaker in proportion to the period in which they are kept on the stretch, until at last they cease to exist altogether. This we know is the case with the eye, in which, if turned to a specific object for any length of time, the power of vision relaxes and is gradually dissipated. We have still more remarkable illustrations of this in the intellectual and nervous powers. Unintermitted attention to any specific object,—suppose it be a chemical experiment, as in a case already mentioned, if it does not result in a torpor of the particular faculties exercised, is apt to produce general insanity. From this we may infer the principle that to enable the perception to continue acute and vigorous, its forces must be periodically recalled to receive their tone either in a period of tor-

por and inaction or through a positive corrective discipline.* Now, both these methods are adopted. Sleep comes with its torpor; dreams with their relaxation, when the traces are unhitched, and the faculties are permitted to wander purposeless over the great commons of speculation; and reverie, where the same faculties are let loose with equal freedom from immediate restraint, but still in a specially assigned field. Then, as a disciplinary adjunct, comes pain, a part of whose purposes in this respect have already been noticed. *Rest,* in fact, seems to answer the purpose of recuperating the powers; *pain,* that of refining and invigorating them. The one may be compared to the sunlight and the dew when acting on the plant; the other to the skill of the gardener, which deepens the crimson of the rose, mottles its damask, and almost indefinitely multiplies its petals; which grafts on the hardy stock of the coarser stem the delicate stock of the weaker, and thus unites the strength of the one with the perfectness in quality of the other, until, from the hard and sour wild fruit, come the apple in its fullest and most golden luxuriance, and the peach in its richest and most luscious blush. If we look, in fact, at the finest developments of human genius, we shall find that they have been accompanied, in most instances, by some physical deformity or more than usual proportion of pain: Milton and Homer (if Pausanias be correct) by blindness; Scott and Byron by lameness; Chatham by gout.

§ 158. Even still more remarkable are the physiological alleviations of pain, some of which are thus strikingly ex-

---

* See *ante,* § 154.

hibited by Paley, in a chapter which is not diminished in interest by the fact that it was written during an acute disease which afterwards proved fatal:—"It is seldom both violent and long-continued: and its pauses and intermissions become positive pleasures. It has the power of shedding a satisfaction over intervals of ease, which, I believe, few enjoyments exceed. A man resting from a fit of the stone or gout, is, for the time, in possession of feelings which undisturbed health cannot impart. They may be dearly bought, but still they are to be set against the price. And, indeed, it depends upon the duration and urgency of the pain whether they be dearly bought or not. I am far from being sure that a man is not a gainer by suffering a moderate interruption of bodily ease for a couple of hours out of the four-and-twenty. Two very common observations favor this opinion: one is, that remissions of pain call forth, from those who experience them, stronger expressions of satisfaction and of gratitude toward both the Author and the instruments of their relief, than are excited by advantages of any other kind: the second is, that the spirits of sick men do not sink in proportion to the acuteness of their sufferings, but rather appear to be roused and supported, not by pain, but by the high degree of comfort which they derive from its cessation, or even its subsidency, whenever that occurs: and which they taste with a relish that diffuses some portion of mental complacency over the whole of that mixed state of sensations in which disease has placed them."*

* Nat. Theol., chap. xxvi.

c[2]. *Death.*

a[3]. *In its existence.**

§ 159. Death is necessary to probation. Let us look, for a moment, at the difficulties which would arise from a perpetuity of life. Let us notice, in the first place, the repugnancy of such perpetuity to anything like a beneficent distribution of property. As it is, history tells us how injuriously society has been affected by the attempt to establish an accumulating fund for even a limited period of time. The Thelluson case is an illustration of this. The testator left a will providing that his large personal estate should be vested in trustees with directions to accumulate the fund for a hundred years. It was soon found that this would absorb all the floating capital of England. No step remained but to break the will, and this was effected by a decision of the House of Lords, which, though necessary, was clearly unconstitutional. A statute was subsequently passed to declare all such trusts void, *ab initio.*

Suppose that such a capitalist as Girard should live forever. If the division of talents and tastes continue as at present, in which such a man as himself, amid all the varieties of parsimony and avarice on the one side, and of profuseness and thriftlessness on the other, would stand preeminent for his acquisitive and retentive powers, what a scene would the world present, when such a genius, so intense, so capable, and so persistent, would be forever eating into the very vitals of others and gorging with them its

* A portion of the remarks under this head was published by me in the Episcopal Review for July, 1858.

already mammoth frame! Only one of two alternatives would exist: one would be a series of violent proscriptive confiscations, which would drive the capitalist in howling rage before the face of a flock of prodigal pursuers, the very necessities of whose character would soon again place them at the feet of a foe made still more rapacious and remorseless by the maltreatment he had received.

§ 160. Suppose, however, that the other alternative be good, and that the man of wealth be permitted to go on and accumulate indefinitely, as would be the case in a well-ordered government in our own time. Soon all small properties would be absorbed in his immense estate. His rents, we will suppose, would amount to a million of dollars in one year. He cannot spend this amount, and he turns it, therefore, to the purchase of new land, with a freshly augmented rental. Now, this can only end in the destruction of all small tenures, and, with them, would fall one of the most efficient engines we have for the welfare and comfort of society. No one can pass along the country road or the city street without seeing that to the tenant of the small farm, or of the small house, a much more than average amount of happiness is allotted. He has just the amount of comfort about him that best promotes health, without possessing that luxury which generates disease and languor. Labor—voluntary, and because voluntary, sweet—sufficient to employ, but not enough to exhaust, is his. Hope is his. And yet this condition of life, so peculiarly conducive to the well-being of society, would be destroyed by a perpetuity of life, unless under circumstances very different from our own.

Let us view, however, the effect of perpetual life on the

controversies and wars of men. Death, we cannot but feel, is a great pacificator. The sturdy Massachusetts volunteer, the resolute British guardsman, the reluctant Hessian, all lie peaceably together under the corn-fields of Monmouth. Napoleon, with the hatred of his intense and almost demoniac ambition, Charles X., with that of his stolid and narrow bigotry, now lie quietly almost side by side. The two duelists, who glared and fired at each other across the table, now rest tranquilly, with their arms folded across their breasts, in the same grave. Death quenches many a fire which otherwise would have desolated the globe. Ambition, when confined by the conditions of mortality, may, like the steam-engine, traverse its appointed track usefully, if not innocently. But, let the trains meet, let the snorting and shrieking monsters dash to and fro over lines intersecting each other indefinitely, and dismay and ruin ensue.

§ 161. See also what would be the condition of the church. At the same moment, and that moment a perpetuity, she would be meeting each of the several shocks which, in God's providence, have been heretofore distributed among ages. There would be the coarse abuse of Paine; the sly inuendo of Gibbon; the subtle sophism of Hume, armed by the imperial malignity of Julian. In meeting and repelling assaults so varied and so incessant, the danger would be that the entire spiritual character of the church would be lost. Fenelon, Leighton, Pascal, Martyn, would give place to men such as Hildebrand, as Atterbury, as Swift, as Bossuet, as Peter the Hermit. The saint would be merged in the confessor, the confessor in the crusader.

The constant presence, in fact, either in things civil or

things ecclesiastical, of a hateful and hating adversary, is of all influences the most calculated to destroy the peace and embitter the temper. To be conscious, even for a few days, of the immediate and lowering attendance of a hostile eye, of an eye sleepless, malign, and fierce, produces a restless anxiety, under which there are few who will not writhe. But let that eye be glaring on us ceaselessly and forever; let its torn and bloody lids, Reguluslike, never close; let such eyes be indefinitely multiplied, and let the object of their hate be placed within their concentrated focal gaze, and we ask whether there is any misery which would be greater than the mere patient endurance of such an acute and eternal watch? Yet such would be the sentinels that a perpetuity of life would place around each of us, were the rivalries and animosities of our nature, unchecked by death, to be permitted to grow and develop forever.

§ 162. We may thus be permitted to regard death as the wisest and most essential of checks introduced by the Divine Government to preserve the harmony and equal relations of society. Men are in this way bound over to keep the peace; and the penalty of their recognizance is their existence now and their happiness hereafter. The necessity for the introduction of such a change is thus displayed by a late brilliant writer:—"The whole earth was filled with violence; and, but for a change in the method of government, this violence might have become, beyond measure, intolerable. In the new dispensation, the bow in the cloud was the sign that the earth should not henceforth be visited by such a catastrophe; but contemporaneously with it, and in order to render such an interposition no longer needful, there was to be a shorten-

ing of man's life; and apparently, too, a greater uncertainty as to the time of the approach of death. Man's gigantic plans of wickedness were not henceforth to be arrested by so terrible an event as the flood; but means, too, were taken to prevent their schemes from attaining so tremendous a magnitude. May we not discover, too, in the confusion of tongues at Babel, and the consequent dispersion, a special arrangement of Heaven for keeping the inhabitants of this world from combining to produce such an amount of disorder and violence as would have prevented this world from fulfilling the ends contemplated by its Divine Governor?"

§ 163. Let us view the effect of such a system on the oppressed. There is no wretchedness so great as that of satiety. The canker-worm, when it reaches the tree-top, drops and dies. The canker-worm of ambition does the same. It weeps when there are no more worlds to conquer, and expires in a debauch. There is no more impressive sight than that of desolate power looking to the grave for rest. For the higher the station the greater the *strippedness*. The tree that might hold its leaves almost through the winter in the valley, scatters them on the mountain-top at the first frost. There is, indeed, desolateness enough in advanced years without this. "It is one of the painful consequences of old age," said Chancellor Kent, when pronouncing a decree in a contested will case, "that it ceases to excite interest, and is apt to be left solitary and neglected. The control which the law gives to a man over the disposal of his property is one of the most efficient means which he has in a protracted life to command the attention due to his infirmities." It is, therefore, not *love*, but *money* that must be relied on to secure comfort in advanced years. But how wretched must be the heart when this conviction grows over it! Need we wonder at the utter faithlessness and bitterness by which extreme and powerful old age is so often marked; the corroding and corrosive suspiciousness of a Du Bois; the subtle treachery of an Alexander VI.; the luxuriant cruelty of a Tiberius?

Of this desolating influence of an old age of power we have a most striking illustration in the last days of Charles V. There are few men whom we would suppose more likely to rise above such an influence. In his youth and manhood he had been tolerant, if not generous. He respected Luther's safe conduct, though ecclesiastical authority was ready to pronounce it null. He granted liberty of conscience, under certain limits, to his Protestant subjects; and he afterwards maintained these grants inviolate. He made war on Rome, and even took the sovereign pontiff captive. Nor were his declining years without the softening influence of family affection. His two sisters, the dowager-queens of France and Portugal, accompanied him to his retirement and solaced him with their reverent love. His son, when accepting the crown, continued to bestow on the father who surrendered it to him, unabated filial affection. The dying emperor, also, had everything around him calculated to impress him with a sense of the immediate responsibility of death. The *Miserere* of the choir in the monastery of St. Justus swung across the nave of the chapel into the communicating windows of his own chamber. His coffin lay open by his side; yet, amid all these solemnizing and affecting associations, his mind became the more and more inflamed by a dark and malign bigotry. He knew not how to tolerate heretics any longer. He addressed, day after day, letters to his daughter, the Regent, urging fire and the sword as the punishment of those who would deny the dogmas of the Romish Church. Had he continued to have lived and reigned, he would have seamed the heart of Europe with a burning share. Well it was for the world that the shades of Estramaduros fell on him, and that the open coffin at last closed.

But if the grave ends the turbulence of the oppressor, much more does it bring rest to the oppressed.

"THERE THE WICKED CEASE FROM TROUBLING, AND THERE THE WEARY BE AT REST; THERE THE PRISONERS REST TOGETHER; THEY HEAR NOT THE VOICE OF THE OPPRESSOR. THE SMALL AND GREAT ARE THERE; AND THE SERVANT IS FREE FROM HIS MASTER."

§ 164. Death, however, does something more than close the wrongs of the oppressor and the sufferings of the oppressed. It is, after all, the great lesson that teaches us the insignificance of things material and sensual.

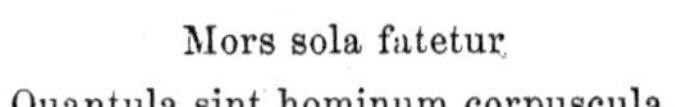

Mors sola fatetur
Quantula sint hominum corpuscula.

It is the magician who resolves the illusions of fancy and ambition. We may look forward to ourselves at one moment as crowned with the poet's laurels, but in the next moment the laurels drop and the shroud follows. Mr. Pitt stands one day overwhelmed with the adulations of place-men and would-be place-men, and walks austerely through the House of Commons in all the arrogance with which his natural haughtiness led him to wield his now undisputed sway. The next moment, a traveler passing by an almost deserted villa at Putney, enters an open door and sees lying unwatched on its bed the bódy of the just departed premier. Worship due only to God is paid to Louis XV. as he totters from the scenes of his debauch to the bed where the smallpox is soon to seize him! Contempt and loathing, such as would scarcely be visited on the meanest pauper, are his as he lies a weltering and putrid corpse. And even the good meet with the same oblivion. The right arm of Whitefield, which formed so important an agent in his wonderful eloquence, was lately filched from its grave at Newburyport and carried about Europe as a sight. Mr. Madison's grave is distinguished only by an unlettered stone. That of Marion is hidden beneath the undisturbed moss. And who is there who passes to and fro in the crowd of population by the Presbyterian burying-ground at Princeton, that takes time to consider that there lie, side by side, the remains of Jonathan Edwards and Aaron Burr?

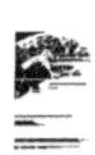

§ 165. But if death be a monitor to teach us the unworthiness of all things human, it is also an executioner to bring the probationer to account. The trial of life, when this dread officer of divine law arrives, is over. He who has been tried has had every opportunity given to him which Divine mercy can extend. There must be at some time a final account. The balance must be struck at some definite period, in order that the Judge may speak. Death, therefore, enters into the very essence of probation.

How far death is an element in intellectual progress, is

noticed in the following striking remarks:—"Perhaps it may seem to some of you as a startling paradox, but it is nevertheless a fact, that the shortness of human life is one of the most powerful elements of human progress. It would seem as if, as the human mind grows and develops, the philosophy and opinions which govern the conduct of life continue to be modified and moulded, until about the age of twenty-five or thirty, when the character becomes unchangeable, opinions become prejudices, and the whole mind, as it were, petrified. Further progress would be impossible, but that another generation, with minds still plastic, comes forward, takes up and carries on the work a few steps, and becomes petrified in its turn. There are certainly some noble exceptions to this rule—instances of minds which with their maturity retain the plasticity of youth—but the very rarity of the exception only proves the rule."*

b^3. *In its manner.*

a^4. *Its unexpectedness.*

§ 166. What would be the effect of an announcement of the period in which death is to occur, we may determine from a consideration of those cases in which such announcement was really supposed to be made. "The *apprehension,*" says Mr. Dendy, in his "Philosophy of Mystery," "of a misfortune or fatality, may prove its cause." Of this we have an illustration given in the case of Glaphyra, mentioned by Josephus, who believing herself warned by the spectre of a deceased husband of approaching death, gradually, as if in obedience to the command, prepared herself

* Report Smithsonian Institute, 1857, p. 124.

to die. Lord Lyttleton's death, now attributed to suicide after a similar supposed supernatural warning, brings us to the same conclusion. Take also the following case, which occurred some years ago in the neighborhood of Philadelphia. The cholera was at that time raging in the city, and a farmer in excellent health, by way of a practical joke, was accosted by a series of medical students, each with the information that he was showing symptoms of the epidemic. "You certainly ought to be careful." "You have the marks of the incipient disease." "Pardon me for interrupting you, but you ought at once to go home, and take immediate advice." The man went home, and was seized with the Asiatic cholera in its most unequivocal shape. To the same effect is the result of an experiment said to have been tried by Frederick William III. of Prussia. Six persons condemned to death were by royal permission selected as the objects of a medical experiment as to the contagiousness of cholera. Three of them were placed in beds of persons who had died of the disease, but without notice of the fact; three others were informed that they would be so exposed, but were placed in beds with no such supposed infection. Those who had warning were all attacked with the disease, and one of them, at least, fatally; the others escaped. Of a similar character are the cases, which are not rare, of persons who, in undergoing a mock execution, have really died of fright. And the only instances that Scripture gives us of a prophetic intimation of the time of death, are those of Saul and Sapphira; and in these, the effect was instantaneous. Saul, when he heard he was to be slain in the approaching battle, was "sore afraid," and fell paralyzed to

the ground. And though the fate of Sapphira was the result of a direct divine command, yet the accompaniment of the mere annunciation of this command was immediate death.

§ 167. Even were a destruction of the vital powers not to follow, there would be in almost every case a suspension of the nervous energies. Could Mr. Huskisson have seen the time and the circumstances of his own premature death on the railway, it is not likely that his powers, down to the last moment, would have been devoted to perfecting those beneficial schemes of economy, to one of which he fell a victim. The internal improvements of New York would scarcely have received from De Witt Clinton the powerful impulse that inaugurated them, had that capable and indefatigable statesman known that he was to be taken from the work almost in early manhood,—that the energies spent on it would, by his premature death, be unrequited, either to his family or himself, and that he was to be laying the corner-stone of those whom he regarded as his political adversaries. So it is in social life. The fool in the Scriptures would never have built his house and barn, if he had known that this was to be the signal of the awful message that that night his soul was to be demanded of him.

Perhaps we might rise from this to a still higher induction, and take the ground that ignorance of the future is essential to the healthy action of the individual man. In this the epicureanism of Horace unites with the asceticism of Milton. The one, in obedience merely to his gay yet shrewd love of ease, writes,—

> Tu ne quæsieris, scire nefas, quem mihi, quem tibi
> Finem Dii dederint.

And Milton, with his grander sweep, tells us,—

> Let no man seek
> Henceforth, to be foretold what shall befall
> Him or his children; evil, he may be sure,
> Which neither his foreknowing can prevent;
> And he the future evil shall, as less
> In apprehension than as substance, feel
> Grievous to bear.

On home this knowledge of the future would fall with a double oppressiveness. No man can deny this who, to take the suggestion of a recent impressive writer,* looks back upon his greatest personal sorrow, and inquires what would have been the effect had he all along known of its approach. The young child, who gives so much of the purest peace to its parents,—what would their feelings be if they were to see before them, from its very birth, the little waxen form stretched in its early coffin? The wife, whose comfort and pride it is to throw the delights of home around her husband,—how would her heart sink within her and her hand fail, if in the centre of that home in the decorating and refining of which for another's sake she had bestowed so much care, she were to see that other stretched on the bier, with his hands folded over his breast, and his face bound in the bandages of death? Would the mansion, whose erection has employed so much labor or has evolved and perpetuated so much architectural taste,—would it have reared its marble front, had its owner known that the first pageantry it was to witness was to be that of his own death?

* Rev. John Caird, Sermon on Solitariness of Christ's Sufferings.

Who would keep up the light of hope in the heart or the preparations of welcome in the home, if months or years in advance the wreck of the ship were seen in all its sublime horror? As it is, life lifts an unpenetrable screen before the grave, hiding the path of approach. It is thus we have freedom to hope, energy to undertake, calmness to execute.*

b^4. *Its shape.*

§ 168. *Sudden* death is in itself often a mercy. He who, when advised of his approaching death, turned to the wall and wept bitterly, saying, "I shall see man no more in the land of the living," recalls to us the instinctive feelings of our race when the probability of death is brought home to us at a period when the sensibilities are in health and vigor. Those who have witnessed the *breaking*, as it is called, of such news to persons under these circumstances, will recollect the terrible shock and the sharp recoil that follows. But in that Providence which regulates death as well as life these cases are but rare. Where sudden death does not come, the approach of the mortal hour is, in many cases, preceded by a deadening of the sensibilities; in others by a sort of mist, which, like the vapor of Indian Summer, throws a graceful halo over the scene. And, so far as the mere article of death is concerned, it may be questioned whether the pain connected with it is, under any circumstances, peculiarly great.

§ 169. Those who speak of it after a resuscitation generally concur on this point. The experience of Dr. Adam

* See on this point, Fleming's "Plea for the Ways of God," p. 91.

Clarke, one of the coolest of observers, is very remarkable on this point. In his life, by Dr. Lettsom, the latter thus gives us a sketch of a conversation in which the two were engaged:—

"Dr. Lettsom said, 'Of all that I have seen restored, or questioned afterwards, I never found one who had the smallest recollection of anything that passed, from the moment they went under water till the time in which they were restored to life and thought.' Dr. Clarke answered Dr. L.: 'I knew a case to the contrary.' 'Did you, indeed?' 'Yes, Dr. L.; and the case was my own. I was once drowned.' And then he related the circumstances, and, after a detailed account, said, 'Now, I aver, 1st. That in being drowned, I felt no pain. 2d. That I did not, for a single moment, lose my consciousness. 3d. I felt indescribably happy, and, though dead as to the total suspension of all the functions of life, yet I felt no pain in dying; and, I take for granted, from this circumstance, those who die by drowning feel no pain, and that probably it is the easiest of all deaths. 4th. That I felt no pain until once more exposed to the action of the atmospheric air, and then I felt great pain and anguish in returning to life, which anguish, had I continued under water, I should have never felt. 5th. That animation must have been totally suspended from the time I must have been under water, which time might be, in some measure, ascertained by the distance the mare was from the place of my submersion, which was at least half a mile, and she was not, when I first observed her, making any speed.'"

§ 170. Cowper, in those melancholy memoirs which bear

witness at once to so much misery and so much hope, speaks of an attempt at suicide, which was frustrated after he became insensible, in which he could not recollect any particular pain. Lord Bacon gives us an anecdote to the same effect; and Sir Benjamin Brodie adds the weight of his great experience and eminent sagacity.*

§ 171. Still more important than this is the gradual preparation of mind by sorrow and by old age. It is here that death, as well as pain, may be taken as the test by which the real value of religion is discovered. When death comes into the house purely human comforts are blasted, and turn with blackened face upon him who puts in them his trust. It is otherwise with religion, for then even the smoky chimney-wall becomes the panel on which are spread pictures which, be they myths or not, are fraught with the greatest loveliness and peace. It is under such influences, and in such scenery, that we best see the sweetness of the preparation by which the believer is made fit for death. Long illness, which, in our blindness, we cannot explain, but which tones the mind for the awful moment; old age, cutting away cord after cord binding the present to the past; affliction and sorrow, so subtly dividing the very sinews of the heart; the removal of objects of love to that home above where the eye of the dying man sees a treasure dearer than all below,—these things come to take from the parting moment nearly all its terror. For, says Lord Bacon, "death comes graciously to those who sit in darkness, or lie heavily bur-

---

* See *ante*, § 18.

dened with grief and irons,—to desolate widows, pensive prisoners, and deposed kings: to all such death is a redeemer, and the grave a place of retirement and rest." Or, as the same idea is expressed by a late thoughtful writer:—

I am footsore and very weary,
  But I travel to meet a friend.
The way is long and dreary,
  But I know that it soon must end.

He is traveling fast like the whirlwind,
  And though I creep slowly on,
We are drawing nearer, nearer,
  And the journey is almost done!

Through the heat of many summers,
  Through many a spring-time rain,
Through long autumns and weary winters
  I have hoped to meet him, in vain.

On the day of my birth he plighted
  His kingly word to me:—
I have seen him in dreams so often,
  That I know what his smile must be.

I have toiled through the sunny woodland,
  Through fields that basked in the light,
And through the lone paths in the forest
  I crept in the dead of night.

I will not fear at his coming,
  Although I must meet him alone;
He will look in my eyes so gently,
  And take my hand in his own.

Like a dream all my toil will vanish,
  When I lay my head on his breast;
But the journey is very weary,
  And he only can give me rest!

§ 172. Add to this a Christian hope, be it really true or be it not,—view this hope as a mere temporal alleviator,—and then see how still more the path brightens. And, in this view, take the following lines, not as Christian poetry, but as the type of a psychological phenomenon, and compare them with the expression, beautiful as that expression is, of merely the stoical submission which has been just described:—

One sweetly solemn thought
  Comes to me o'er and o'er—
I'm nearer home to-day
  Than I ever have been before.

Nearer my Father's house,
  Where the many mansions be;
Nearer the great white throne,
  Nearer the jasper sea;

Nearer the bound of life,
  Where we lay our burdens down;
Nearer leaving the cross,
  Nearer gaining the crown.

e^1. *They are the incidents of an intermediate stage in a series of progressive advances from chaos to final perfection.*

§ 173. Taking the whole scheme of geological history, we find that such a series of advances has been made from the earliest point to which that history goes back. The advance, it is true, has not been equal and regular, nor do its successive eras melt into each other as they move on, but rather, as in a panorama, landscape after landscape is separately unrolled, leaving a pause between each, so each of these grand periods of cosmical progress begins and terminates as a unit, leaving a pause to divide it from its successor. But while this is the case, the advance from period to period is unequivocal, though this advance is one not of development but of a specific new introduction. We have the period of inorganic matter. We have the period when a colorless and pulpy vegetation scarce laid claim to organic life under the mist-shroud that encompassed it. We have, separated from this by an appreciable parenthesis, the period of rich and juicy cone-bearing ferns, and of the tortoises and fish-monsters which crowded the adjacent friths and lagoons. We have the period of giant mammalia, such as compose the dynasty now found in Nebraska, hemmed in by impassable barriers at both its formation and its extinction. Suppose, as has already been asked, it should be inquired for what purpose does this vast and luxurious vegetation of the second of these periods exist? Is it not a positive excrescence, and is not the rapid succession of animal deposit by which death manures these immense growths, in itself a defect and an evil? Countless centuries afterwards, the iron forges, the coal mines, and the industrial interests, which time puts in motion, answer the question by saying that the world is moving on in a series of progressive advances, each of which is the base from which a successor of a higher grade takes its start. Such being the case, and the scheme heretofore having been unbroken,

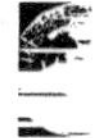

we find ourselves, in our present human history, occupying an intermediate stage in this grand onward progress. And this stage is one which involves the culture of a countless host of individual souls on probation for perfect bliss. It is, however, still an intermediate stage, and necessarily liable to the evils and imperfections belonging to such stage.*

* See this point very ably developed in Mr. Walker's "God in Creation." And see also *post*, § 277, etc.

CHAPTER II.

POSITIVISM.

a. IN WHAT POSITIVISM CONSISTS.

§ 174. AUGUST COMTE, to whose singleness of purpose no less than to whose intellectual power, the present popularity of Positivism is due, was born in the south of France, in 1788. Of noble descent, though utterly penniless, he was thrown into the turmoil of the French Revolution at a period of life when his acute and refined sensibilities and his high love of order and classification were the most likely to be increased by the reaction from the tumultuous chaos with which he was surrounded. Disgust, which a spirit so proud and so severe, would feel for the multitude of merely speculative theories which then floated across the political and social horizon, united with a strong attachment to inductive philosophy, led him, at the outset of his career, to seek to gather from the facts of history and nature the laws by which history and nature are governed. To this work he devoted a life, which, though broken in its centre by insanity, and toward its end by a domestic connection as injurious to his mental powers by its absurd sentimentalism, as it was to his moral character by its impurity, was at least intellectually pure and unsordid. He died in 1858.

The principal work through which M. Comte made known

his views is his "Cours de la Philosophie Positive." In the preparation of this work he had the advantages and disadvantages attending the delivery of a course of lectures. He began in 1826, and his lucid style, his extraordinary power of classification, and his fine mathematical parts, secured for him the attendance of some of the most eminent scientific men then collected at Paris, including Blainville, Poisson, and Humboldt. His course was hardly opened before he was attacked by a disease of the brain, which for three years incapacitated him for work. When his lectures were resumed, he found his audience increased by the addition of men such as Esquirol, Beriot, Broussais, and Fourier. The lecture-shape, into which his speculations were thrown, enabled him, as he proceeded, to avail himself of the counsels of others, and of the gradual development of his own acute and comprehensive mind. By this means he not only retained for a series of years the attention of the distinguished men by whom his lectures were attended, but he excited throughout all Europe that peculiar and curious interest which the serial form of publication is apt to evolve. Men of science, even among those most attached to orthodox Protestantism, were forward to recognize the wonderful combination of analysis and synthesis, and the severe and exact induction of the new philosopher. Sir David Brewster, as early as 1838, even transcended the limits of the present estimate of Comte's disciples, in recognizing "his simple yet powerful eloquence, his enthusiastic admiration of intellectual superiority, *his accuracy as a historian*, his honesty as a judge, and his absolute freedom from all personal and national feelings." "His views," says

Dr. Buchanan, "are expounded in a style singularly copious, clear, and forcible." And Dr. McCosh, even when exposing the arrogance as well as the baselessness of Comte's social and theological assumptions, declares that "every one is constrained to admire his penetrating intellect and clear style."

§ 175. In the loyalty and capacity of his disciples, Comte has been no less fortunate than in the candor of his adversaries. In England, his lectures, which in French fill six volumes, have been brought before the public in an abridged edition by Miss Harriet Martineau; and though in this translation he loses the freshness and naturalness incident to the productions of a mind that grows as it speaks, his text is purged of much redundancy of style, as well as from not a few philosophical positions which would have stood in the way of his acceptance.* To Mr. G. H. Lewes he is indebted not only for a still more condensed and more effective summary of his lectures,† but for a very skillful though incidental defence of their principles, in a work on the "History of Philosophy," whose speciousness and biographical interest will carry it to many points to which the severe style and the great bulk of the original course would keep the latter from penetrating.‡ In the present

* The Positive Philosophy of Aug. Comte. Freely translated and condensed, by Harriet Martineau. 2 vols. London, 1853. New York, 1 vol., Calvin Blanchard, 1855.

† Comte's Philosophy of the Sciences, being an Exposition of the Principles of the Cours de Philosophie Positive of August Comte. By G. H. Lewes. London, 1853.

‡ The Biographical History of Philosophy, from its Origin in

year, Mr. Henry Thomas Buckle, in a work whose elaborateness and plausibility to a superficial observer conceal its inaccuracy of statement and narrowness of induction, has produced a ponderous apology for the Positive Philosophy in a distinct historical treatise.* And in a work destined to a far more lasting reputation, Mr. J. S. Mill has brought to the indirect though potent defence of the same system his fine dialectic power and his remarkable philosophical research.†

§ 176. In this country, Comte's exponents though less able, have not been less numerous. In this direction, the late Mr. Horace Binney Wallace's acute critical, and metaphysical parts obliquely bore, though it is but just to say, with a uniform protest against those atheistic sequences which belong to Comte's original conception. In Mrs. Child's "Progress of Religious Ideas," the positive idea of religion is espoused with a coarseness of tone which may at least serve to put the careless reader on his guard against its essential godlessness of spirit.‡ To these may be added

---

Greece down to the Present Day. By George Henry Lewes. New York: Appletons, 1857.

* History of Civilization in England. By Henry Thomas Buckle. Vol i. From the second London edition, to which is added an Alphabetical Index. New York: D. Appleton & Co., 1858.

† A System of Logic, Ratiocination, and Induction, being a Connected View of the Principles of Evidence and the Methods of Scientific Investigation. By John Stuart Mill. New York: Harper & Brothers, 1858.

‡ The Progress of Religious Ideas through Successive Ages. By L. Maria Child. In three volumes. New York: C. S. Francis, 1855.

one or two minor publications in which the principles of the same philosophy are expounded if not defended.*

Comte's speculations fall into two classes—the first comprising his course of Positive Philosophy, completed by him in 1842; the other his scheme of religious belief, mainly contained in his Catechism, published ten years later.† In the first class his system was purely inductive, and, in one sense, destructive; in the second, deductive and constructive. In the first he ignored all facts except those ascertained by natural science, and from these facts alone he sought to draw laws to govern not merely the material, but the spiritual. In the latter he sought to construct not merely a polity, but a religion; his office was not merely that of the discoverer, whose duty it is to make known the secret principle by which our race is controlled, but that of a high priest, who, finding that after all there remains a vast residuum of the emotional and spiritual which a system of economical laws cannot regulate, seeks to establish for this purpose a religion. The former ignores the sentimental and the supernatural; the latter not only recognizes them, but establishes a special mechanism by which they are to be fed and governed.

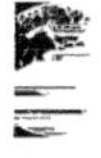

* The Positive's Calendar: an Exposition of the Positive Religion of Comte, by one of his Followers. New York. Philosophy of Mathematics, etc. By W. M. Gillespie. New York, 1851.

† Catéchism Positiviste, par August Comte, etc. Paris, 1852. The Catechism of Positive Religion. Translated from the French of August Comte, by Richard Congreve, M.A. London: John Chapman, 1858.

§ 177. As elucidating these two phases of Comte's philosophy, the remarkable circumstances of his life, falling as it does into two parallel periods, may be found of much value. His early history, and the natural reaction of his clear and exact intellect from the chaos of the French Revolution to a system of moral if not governmental absolutism, have been already noticed. From his eighteenth year till almost his forty-fifth, he was subjected to the severe discipline, and, at the same time, the withering blight, of circumstances not merely of penury, but of solitude and desolation. During far the greater period of the time he was engaged from six to eight hours a day in private tuition, from whence his income, owing perhaps to that want of flexibility of temper so essential to a successful teacher, was but scanty. In 1832 he was received into the faculty of the Polytechnic School, but only as a tutor of the lower grade. Here again the jealousy of those whose scientific and metaphysical dogmas he so ruthlessly attacked, aided by his own intolerance, led to his final dismissal. Once again he was obliged to betake himself to teaching, though under circumstances very different from those by which his earlier life was surrounded. His growing celebrity; the gradual recognition by the world of his genius; his integrity, and his indomitable energy, drew to him reverent and remunerative pupils. And a very singular connection framed by him with Madame Clotilde de Vaux—a connection partly sentimental, partly sensuous—opened to him a field of observation before entirely unknown. This remarkable woman, hereafter to be the chief priestess, or more properly, eternal mother of positive religion, was, or appeared to her lover to be, possessed of all the fascinations

of intellect, accomplishment, and manner. Soon the severe philosopher began to recognize a new force which had not been previously noticed by him among his dynamical phenomena. The name of love might have been that to which this agency would, under ordinary circumstances, have been entitled; but Comte subtilized it into emotions more refined. The veneration due to sanctity, the regard to loveliness, the tenderness to the closest of domestic relations, increased by the obedience to arise from the succeeding relations of child to parent,—these principles were to be apotheosized into a divine code. It so happened that Madame de Vaux was a Roman Catholic, so far at least as concerned a deep appreciation of the æsthetic and the supernatural. The æsthetic and the supernatural, he was, therefore, to introduce into the religion of which he was to be the founder; and he betook himself to construct an imposing ceremonial to touch the former, and a vast canonization to excite the latter. How this was done will be seen hereafter; but at present, it may be stated in brief, that while in the first period of his life his aim was to draw correct laws from actual phenomena; in the second period he fabricates false phenomena to support a factitious law.

§ 178. Let us now proceed to examine, at least in its theological relations, that scheme of positive philosophy which it was the business of the first part of Comte's life to construct, and on which his reputation mainly rests. The mission before him was noble, and well worthy of the years of poverty, of isolation, and of unremunerated toil which he devoted to it. It was, to give it in his own terms, to discover and state the conditions to be developed in modern society, so as (1) to restore health; and (2) to resolve the anarchy of opinion occasioning social disease. Such a task is well worthy the devotion of the highest intellect; and to Comte, with his exquisite perception of and controlling passion for order, passing, as he had just been, through the metaphysical and economical uproar of the French Revolution, the commission came with a dignity and weight sufficient to drive from his contemplation all selfish aims. His it was, he believed, not only to classify science, but to reconstruct humanity. His it was not only to prescribe to knowledge its boundaries and properties, but to open to society that causeway, for so long covered by the rubbish of prejudice and ignorance, by which it could reach truth and light. And here, at the outset, he took the bold and grand position—afterwards, it is true, occasionally forgotten, but in the first half of his career always before him—that the subordination of the intellect, and then of the heart, to the laws of morality, is a prerequisite of the wise reconstruction of society and of government. In this position his coincidence with the early Puritan leaders in America will at once be noticed. Each sought to prepare for a reanimation of society by the enunciation and enthronement of a code of moral and intellectual laws. Each thought that without such a basis government and society would be insecure and unjust. But here they differed, one failing in the recognition of the *natural*, the other of the *supernatural* element; the one ignorant that such a code would be imperfect and arbitrary without a harmonious development of that universal science of which it is but an incomplete part; the other forgetting that even this harmonious development of all deri-

vative knowledge is imperfect without the recognition of and the dependence on Him from whom this knowledge is derived. The one wanted *breadth;* the other *height.* Before each lay a fierce and unfordable river, like the Niagara below the falls. The one failed from lack of materials to reach the opposite side, and from want of compass of machinery; the other, because he forgot that to raise a pierless bridge that was to be eternal, its support must be derived from on high. The one relied on faith alone; the other only on reason; and each have left to a more divine, and, at the same time, a more liberal philosophy the grand work by which faith and reason are to be made one.

§ 179. It may also be premised that the term *positive* is used by Comte in a sense distinct from that accepted by prior philosophers. Bacon, Jonathan Edwards, and Kant, applied the term *positive* to those principles, which, underived from reasoning or observation, form the instinctive and undemonstrable basis on which all derivative truth must rest. Our own existence—the existence of a moral sense, the existence of matter—have in this sense been treated as *positive.* The positive laws of Comte, on the other hand, are the results of inductive experiment, and positivism is simply a digest of knowledge derived from phenomena. Observational science is hence the sole source of knowledge. The process is to be first one of *induction,* and then of *deduction.* The entire body of phenomena are to be colligated as the basis for a complete and profound induction. From these the general principles which regulate the universe are to be drawn, and when drawn, are to be classified so as to make a harmonious whole. The work thus assigned to himself by the great positive philosopher may, therefore, be illustrated by that of him who should undertake to collect from the reports of the English and American courts a philosophical exposition of the common law. Thousands of volumes of reports are to be gathered together, embracing hundreds of thousands of cases. From each the correct points are to be first extracted and then arranged, and then exhibited as a complete and philosophical whole. So it was that Comte attempted to extract from the book of physical nature the grand common law that regulates humanity.

§ 180. It is by use of this analogy that we are able to detect two of the main defects in Comte's basis of induction—defects which fatally affect his system of philosophy. Let it be supposed that in such pretended summary of the common law there should be an entire exclusion of: (1) all cases involving mental conditions, *e.g.* insanity in its relations to crime, to wills, and to contracts; and (2) all cases decided in a particular locality, though to this excluded locality such treatise afterwards is claimed to apply. However interesting a treatise thus constructed might be, it would neither be complete nor authoritative. And yet, these omissions are, in fact, made by Comte in the collection of his primary phenomena. He excludes entirely the result of all psychological observation. He abhors metaphysics. That vast mass of phenomena which are connected with our intellectual and moral natures form no part of the materials on which his induction acts. Objective conditions alone, he condescends to notice.

On the other hand, he formally excludes from the range

of his observation all social history except that of Europe. Thus he himself tells us that "we must study the development of the most advanced nations, not allowing our attention to be drawn off to other centres. * * It is the selectest part, the vanguard of the human race that we have to study; the greater part of the white race, or the European nations, even restricting ourselves to those of Western Europe."* And afterwards he specifies the countries to be thus examined, as follows: "It must be our rule to study the civilization, not of any nation, however important, but of the whole portion of mankind involved in the movement of Western Europe; that is, (specifying the nations once for all,) Italy, France, England, Germany, and Spain." It is observed, that this excludes Asia, the birth-place of civilization, North Africa, the theatre of her most luxuriant youthful growth, and America, the scene of her present greatest activity.

Having thus noticed the nature of the philosophy of Comte and the subject-matter from which his induction is drawn, let us proceed to consider what are the principles stated by him, so far, at least, as they concern the theistic argument. These principles converge to a single proposition, viz., *that the highest order of civilization, and the truest philosophy, lead to the establishment of a code of positive laws, susceptible of as definite ascertainment as the courses of the stars, which laws are capable, if obeyed, of producing the highest degree of happiness as well as*

---

* Pos. Phil. English ed., vol. i. p. 181; Am. ed., vol. i. p. 541; Martineau's translation.

*the greatest amount of morality, and to which laws, therefore, it is the duty of each individual to submit.**

b. BY WHAT IT IS SUSTAINED.

§ 181. The induction by which this proposition is sought to be proved, falls under three heads: (a^1) *historical*, or that drawn from the history of the countries selected for examination; (b^1) *personal*, or that drawn from individual history; and (c^1) *phrenological*, or that drawn from the structure of the human brain. These will be now briefly considered.

§ 182. a^1. *Historical.*

It is assumed by Comte that history, within the limits he prescribes to himself, shows three distinct stages of development: (*a*) the *theological*, which is the original, which is again divided into (a^1) *fetichism*, (b^1) *polytheism*, and (c^1) *monotheism;* (*b*) the *metaphysical*, or the period of doubt; and (*c*) the *positive*, or the period of definite law. These stages are treated by Comte substantially as follows:—

The savage, who is assumed to be the first form of

---

* Observe, in connection with Comte's classification, that of Schelling, as the contribution of one who, like Comte, is seeking the material for a skeptical philosophy, but who, with equal ability, occupies an independent stand-point. Schelling lays down three great periods: first, that of *fate*, when history exhibits the working of mere arbitrary dynamical energy; second, that of *nature*, which is one of equal but absolute development; third, that of *Providence*, when we are to recognize the Absolute and Universal, as an aggregate divinity. See Transcend. Idealismus, part iv. prop. 4. See also Morell's Hist. Phil., pp. 440–450.

humanity, looks with wondering awe upon the objects around him and pays to each a specific homage. This is Fetich-worship. The term, not very accurately, as will be presently shown, is taken by Comte from Mosheim, who, when examining the intellectual system of Cudworth, tells us that "the sacred animals of the Egyptians were originally Fetissos. This phrase, which the French language has converted into *Fetiches*, is Portuguese, and signifies a divine agent that communicates oracles. A Fetich is therefore matter, in some form or other, in which a God resides." Strictly speaking, however, the Fetich is regarded by Comte as worshiped, not as the embodiment of a Deity, but rather as in itself, from its own properties, the subject of a gross and dull adoration. In fact, Fetich-worship is held by Comte as requiring so small a degree of intelligence, that he announces that it is engaged in by the higher branches of the brute creation. "Several species of animals," he tells us, "afford clear evidence of speculative activity; and those which are endowed with it certainly attain a kind of gross fetichism as man does. The difference in the case is, that man has ability to raise himself out of this primitive darkness, and that the brutes have not; except some few select animals, in which a beginning to polytheism may be observed, obtained no doubt by association with man. If, for instance, we exhibit a watch to a child or a savage, on the one hand, and a dog or a monkey, on the other, there will be no great difference in their way of regarding the new object, further than their form of expression."* And,

* Pos. Phil., Eng. ed., vol. ii. p. 187; Am. ed., p. 546.

to make this still more plain, we are told, something in the style of Lord Monboddo, that it was reserved to subsequent eras to develop men, in this light, at least, from the condition of "monkeys."

§ 183. If this be true, Fetich-worship, in the Positive sense, is nothing more than a mere stupid gaze. This is followed, in gradual ascent, by Polytheism, in which certain members or heads of specific tribes are invested with supernatural attributes, and worshiped as such.

The mythology, both of the subtle Greek and the imperial Roman, may come next. The trees and the waters are represented by dryads and naiads, who are treated either as the divine embodiment of the entire classes, or as special supernatural agencies residing in individuals. With this may arise hero-worship; and these two elements, involving the adoration either of divinities residing in matter or brutes, or of divinities as the shades of departed great men, form *polytheism*. This, again, as human intellect develops, is narrowed into *monotheism*. Men become weary of worshiping gods who are either the ideal representations of brutes or stones, or at the best, of fellow-creatures with like passions with themselves. Hence arises the idea of a Jehovah, or supreme and single God. This idea, however, according to the Positive faith, is revealed neither by oracle nor instinct, but is a myth, for its own period beneficial enough, but at the same time the mere creature of human speculation. Soon, however, "the forces that caused this idea, dissipate it." Men begin to discover that organic creation is governed by certain eternal and inflexible laws. These laws enter so closely into the moral as well into the physical universe, that it is found as science progresses, that there is at each step less and less ground on which a voluntary special Providence can act. Still, however, there is a reluctance to give up the sublime thought that such a Providence exists, and between this belief and that of the prevalence of certain fixed laws—between, in other words, the conception of fixed laws and the conception of special providences—the human intellect is kept in a state of doubt and agitation during a period which is called the *Metaphysical.*

§ 184. The *metaphysical* period is mainly that of destruction. It falls, according to Comte, into three phases: (1) that of Protestantism, in which the theologic element, itself highly charged with metaphysics, divides into a series of controversial currents, each surging against and neutralizing the other; (2) that of Deism, in which Nature steps in and takes temporarily the throne of God, while the Deity Himself retires in austere seclusion or good-natured indifference from the affairs of a world which, by the aid of certain impulses with which He supplies it, succeeds pretty well in governing itself; and (3) that of *Atheism,* in which even the idea of a Deity on furlough is swept away, and the world is regarded as not only practically and temporarily, but eternally and primarily endued with self-government. By these three processes the mind is supposed to be cleared from all its theistic prejudices and metaphysical doubts, and to be prepared for the reception of the great final truth of the administration by Positive Law.

§ 185. *Positivism,* which is declared to be the last and perfect development of human society, as well as the only true basis of individual government, contents itself with the discovery and the harmonious arrangement of those natural laws by which the universe is governed. It rejects both the supernatural ordination and the metaphysical causation of the phenomena with which it deals, but treats them as isolated and causeless, contenting itself, by the application of a wide induction, with drawing from them the general principles or laws by which they can be harmonized. As, however, this method of discovery and classification varies with the degree to which the phenomena with which it deals are extricated from the confusion of metaphysical doubt, and as the several classes of these phenomena differ greatly among themselves in reference to their capacity for generalization, the sciences do not arise simultaneously from the heterogeneous chaos of the middle period, but struggle upward at long though unequal intervals. First comes Mathematics, that with the simplest of solvents, and the most soluble of phenomena. Next emerges Astronomy, impelled by the energy of her mathematical elements, and hurrying to enter upon the magnificent sweep of phenomena on which she is to act, but delayed by the medium of astrology through which she has to pass. Mechanical and cosmical philosophy comes next, and then Biology, which, compelled to separate from Psychology, on which she has heretofore, in the metaphysical era, mainly relied, now, in somewhat crippled isolation, crawls forth to inform us of the secret springs, not merely of the human body, but of the human soul. Last of all, but as yet with crest scarcely more than protruding above the mists of theological prejudice and metaphysical doubt, comes Sociology. To the extrication of the latter science, the genius of Positive Philosophy

mainly devotes itself. When this last task is consummated, we will obtain, we are told, the rules by adoption of which individual and social prosperity can be best promoted, virtue most highly exalted, vice most deeply depressed, and even religion, by being shorn of the supernatural and mystical, made for the first time businesslike and intelligent. In what way, however, the latter part of the programme has been carried out, will subsequently be seen when we come to examine the theology of Comte as developed in his later days.

Let us now proceed to consider the facts on which this remarkable series of theories rests,—a task that is made the more difficult from the fact that the positive philosophers cite no authorities for their historical statements.

a^1. *There is no evidence of primary Fetichism.*

§ 186. Schlegel, it is true, speaks of Fetich-worship as the lowest stage in heathen religions,* but Fetich-worship of the character to which he refers is very different from the mere monkeylike curiosity placed by Comte under this name. But a close examination of history shows that the sweeping together of all sensuous religionism under this common term, is both unphilosophical and inaccurate. The same year that gave to light Comte's complete course was marked by the publication, by Dr. Karl Eckerman, of the University of Göttingen, of an elaborate and exhaustive exposition of the religious history and mythology of the most prominent nations of antiquity; an exposition, written without reference to any theological theory

* Phil. of Hist., lect. vi.

whatever, but which presents a comprehensive and thorough digest of the recorded facts bearing on the particular issue.*

On the point before us, Dr. Eckerman thus writes:—"We turn to Hylozoism. Since the Deity intermarries with Nature, divine (spiritual) and physical life are entirely identified. Impregnation, procreation, growth, and blossom, coming into existence and dying, are regarded as the activities and passivities of the Deity. Nations which, of their own accord, and in various ways, are occupied with nature, and hence carry with them a sympathizing heart for it, are easily led to this system of religious belief. With them spring becomes the time of the divine happiness; winter the time of unhappiness and of death. Vivid contrasts are common in this system of theology, placing in opposition Life and Death, as in Dualism, Light and Darkness. Hylozoism is the mother of wild orgic dances, of cruel sacrifices, of painful tortures, scourgings, and mortifications. In this religion the images of "Begetting" and "Bringing Forth" are principally worshiped, because the sexual relation of the animal world is imputed to the Deity. Hence this creed presents, opposing one another, a productive male and receptive female Deity, a Father and Mother, on which account it has been called, not very wisely to be sure, hylozoistic Dualism.

* Lehrbuch der Religionsgeschichte und Mythologie der vorzuglichsten Völker des Alterthums, Nach der Anordnung K. O. Müllers. Für Lehrer, Studirende, und die obersten Klassen der Gymnasien verfasst, von Dr. Karl Eckerman, Assessor der philos. Facultät der Universität Göttingen. Halle, 1845. *Ibid.*, Bänd 3 and 4; Halle, 1847, 1848.

"This form of religion was, at an early period, received in the East and in the West, even in India itself, where it united itself with the emanation system. Babylonians, Assyrians, Phœnicians, Phrygians, and Egyptians, were servants and worshipers of nature, and it can hardly be denied that the worship of God among the Greeks and Romans may be traced back to the worship of nature, just as this assumed an ameliorated form. But the worship of Dionysos (Bacchus) has remained more barbarous and unchecked. On Grecian soil, more than anywhere else, Hylozoism united itself with anthromorphism, and hence the gods here appear much more human.

"*Out of Hylozoism arose, in Chaldea, Sabæanism or star-worship, in Egypt the worship of animals, which must be regarded only as specially developed phases of the same principle.* But it is not on that account to be supposed that the worship of animals was the basis of religion in Egypt, and still less that the adoration of animals considered sacred is based upon the observance of their apparent utility or mischievousness. The worship of animals depends much more upon the observation of the evident system of material law which these animals obey, or, in other words, on the unmistakable perception of their instincts. The dweller on the Nile sees in this a clear expression of Divine wisdom.

§ 187. "Another modification of Hylozoism is Fetichism. Fetichists are those who select as a deity some peculiar or distinctively striking material object. *Fetichism is the lowest grade of religious culture, and we do the Greeks undoubtedly great injustice if we, with Bortiger, B. Constant, (and now, also, with H. W. Bensen,) think to trace back their worship to Fetichism.* By separating individual examples from the whole, as the holy oak in Dodona, the sacred stone of Eros at Thespia, the Graces at Orchonenos, the thirty stones at Phasia, and other things of the kind, and examining these without reference to the connection, a form of religion is arrived at, the existence of which is apocryphal even in Africa. Men, in the course of time, forget the Divine Spirit and the meaning of the matter esteemed sacred, and cling stubbornly to the dead form. But who has investigated so accurately the condition of religion in the heart of Africa? Prejudice and pious Christian religious zeal misled the investigators. *The time will come when Fetichism will stand as the result of superficial critical observation.*"

§ 188. Equally significant, as relating to the old Chaldean worship, is the following statement by Mr. Layard:* "As I have more than once had occasion to observe, a marked distinction may be traced between the religion of the earliest and latest Assyrians. *It is probable that corruptions gradually crept into their theology.* Originally it was a pure Sabæanism, in which the heavenly bodies were worshiped as mere types of the power and attributes of the Supreme Deity. Of the great antiquity of this primitive worship there is abundant evidence; and that it originated among the inhabitants of the Assyrian plains, we have the united testimony of sacred and profane history. It obtained the epithet of perfect, and was believed to be the most ancient

---

* Nineveh and Babylon, vol. ii. p. 333.

religious system, having preceded even that of the Egyptians."

§ 189. Into these questions of fact, involving though they do the very foundation of his system, neither Comte nor his disciples have thought it necessary to enter. It may be that, if Fetich-worship existed at all, it was an exceptional form, which, like what we assume the image-worship of the most degraded and ignorant Roman Catholic to be, was not an original and substantive worship, but the perversion, by a gradual ignoring of the spiritual, of a religious culture whose first object was the spiritual clothed in a material attribute or dress. If this view be correct, the whole induction of Positivism falls. Instead, however, of examining the historical proof, Comte starts with the bold assertion, unsustained by any citations, that Fetichism was the original form of human religious culture. To this it may be sufficient, after the remarks which have just been made, to reply that history, so far as it goes, proves the contrary. It will be scarcely necessary to cite the traditions of a primeval golden age. Out of Scriptures they form the earliest putative records of our race. Their affirmative testimony to an early theism may be here passed. It is enough for the present argument to say, that whatever may be their worth, they give no basis for the assumption of a primary Fetich-worship.

§ 190. When we come to what is undisputed history the indications are still more hostile to Comte's theory. Take the Saxon stem, one selected by Comte himself. Of the early Germans, Tacitus says, "Their deities were not immured in temples, nor represented under any kind of resemblance to the heathen form. To do either were, in their opinion, to derogate from the majesty of superior beings." So the laws of Mena—the old Indian literature—are express in recognizing a worship in which the spiritual was ever the primary object, nor do they in any case recognize the mere matter-adoration of Fetichism. The following summary of the early orthodox Hindû writers is given by Mr. Archer Butler:* "We begin with the Supreme Being. The Uttara Mimansa, which is to theology what the Purva Mimansa is to works and their merit, which is the great depository of the Vedantine beliefs, and whose chief extant memorial is the *Brahmê Sutra*, attributed to Vyasa, (an avatara of Vishnou himself, the reputed author, also, of the Mahabharata, the great Hindû epic,)—this the high orthodox school of philosophy, declares from the Vedas themselves—of God—that He is the Supreme Eternal One, the Emanatory Cause (*i.e.* at once the efficient and material cause) of the universe. From Him all proceeds; into Him all is to be ultimately resolved; as a spider extends and retracts his thread, or (to use another common Hindû comparison) as the tortoise protrudes and then gathers back his lower limbs. It would not be easy to parallel the sublimity of the descriptions which the Vedas themselves contain of this All-creating Essence,—the whole riches of a most opulent language are exhausted upon the infinity of his perfections; and the very title of Godhead (Bhargas) is constructed of three monosyllabic verbs, which signify to shine, to delight, and to move. In both the Brahmin and Buddhist systems a trinity

* Lect. Anc. Phil., vol. i. p. 250.

of natures is discoverable; though upon the precise attributes of each divine personage there seem to be many varieties of opinion. In the ordinary expositions of the Vedantine theology they are declared to be Creator, Conservator, and Destroyer; among the atheistic followers of Capila a sort of natural trinity is professed, under the title of Goodness, Foulness, and Darkness; and, among the Buddhists of Népaul, (according to Mr. Hodgson's interesting account,) the same notion reappears under the names of Buddha, Dharma, and Sanga,—Intelligence, Matter, and Multitude. Such is the Deity of the Vedas. The Deity of the Sankhya of Patandjali seems to be of much the same character. But the Sankhya of Capila (to which I have just referred) denies the existence of a God altogether in any other sense than that of an intelligence issuing out of primitive nature and to be resolved hereafter into it. These sages urge that we can derive no proof of a Supreme Creator distinct from insensible nature, either from sense, reasoning, or revelation. All things are evolved out of an intelligence which was itself but a secondary formation. Were God detached from nature He could have no inducement for creation; were He fettered to nature He could have no ability for such a work. I need not remind you how completely these sophisms anticipate the more modern atheism of Europe. Of course, you may suppose the Capilists are obliged to exert some ingenuity in endeavoring to reconcile their views with the solemn Theism of the Vedas. They urge that passages in these sacred records really refer either to a liberated soul, or to some of the mythological deities; or, by some other such evasion, endeavor to escape the fate which drove the followers of Buddha out of the Indian peninsula. I suspect, from scattered intimations, that, while the Capilists attack the foundations of religion, the Buddhists originally were guilty of the darker crime of attacking the authority of the priesthood,—a difference which will sufficiently explain the difference of their fortunes. It is certain that, even to the present day, a genuine Buddhist, from the heights of his ascetic sanctity, is apt to despise the inferior aids of sacerdotal ministration, and is in fact more highly reverenced by the people; upon the same principle which gave to the mendicant saints of the Roman order an influence so far above that of the secular clergy.

§ 191. "The Vedanta philosophy does not *enlarge* upon nature as distinct from its great Author. But this deficiency is fully supplied by the copious dissertations of the Sankhya and *Vaiseschika* physics. I before stated that the Sankhya Capila constitutes twenty-five principles of the universe. At the head of the list stands the venerated name of Nature or Pracriti,—eternal matter undivided, without parts, not produced, but productive. The next title on this solemn bead-roll of the universal system is Intelligence, (Buddhi or Mahat,) first production of nature and prolific of all subsequent existence; and for the accommodation of religious associates, it would seem that this very intelligence divides into a triune Deity; thus conciliating (though awkwardly) the theistic and atheistic hypotheses. Third in the catalogue, comes the *Personal Conviction*, (Ahancara,) a singular element in a system of nature, but which seems to me to be internally connected with the theory of *Illusion*, (Maya,) which this school probably countenanced; and

which may seem to base physical existence itself on the transitory belief of it. The Capilist next enumerates five pure elements which themselves produce the grosser and perceptible elements of the external world. The organs of speech and motion are then named, and that *Manas* or *Mind*, which seems to discharge the same functions as the *communis sensus* of the old psychologists, with additional functions of activity. 'The external sense perceives, the internal examines, consciousness makes self-application, and intellect resolves.' Finally, is introduced that eternal essence which, though it may transmigrate through innumerable bodies, is made by wisdom capable of final liberation and perpetual repose,—the Purusha, or Soul. The treatise itself, (the Karica,) sums up the whole:—'Nature, root of all, is no production; seven principles, including the Great Intellect, are productions and productive; sixteen are productions unproductive; soul is neither production nor productive.'"

§ 192. Mr. Gladstone, in his Studies on Homer, touches with his usual subtlety and eloquence on this point. He marshals the classical evidence in favor of a primeval intercommunion between the one great God and the human race, and he shows that even the Homeric theistic philosophy rested on this assumption. The same propositions have been examined, with equal skill and far greater copiousness, by Vossius, in his work "De Theologia Gentili," and by Cudworth, in his "Intellectual System of the Universe." The difficulty about Mr. Gladstone's view—a difficulty growing from his tendency to persistent and earnest advocacy—is, that while Cudworth properly restricts himself to showing that the classic mythology (*e.g.* in the Homeric writings*) recognized one single superior Deity, Mr. Gladstone insists upon drawing from the same data, not only the revealed doctrine of the Trinity, but a very questionable theory as to the Virgin. There is a double difficulty in this. It leads sincere Christians to reject an important branch of theistic proof,—it tempts the critical inquirer to doubt the whole.

§ 193. So also, Larcher, in a note to Herodotus, states that the most ancient nations were not idol-worshipers, and adds: Lucian tells us that the ancient Egyptians had no statues in the temples. According to Eusebius, the Greeks were not worshipers of images before the time of Cecrops, who first of all erected statues to Minerva. And Plutarch tells us that Numa forbade the Romans to represent the Deity under the form of a man or an animal; and for seventy years this people had not in their temple any statue or painting of the Deity.

§ 194. b^2. *The character of the development of our race affords a strong presumption against the hypothesis of a primary Fetich-worship.*

This worship, according to Comte, was shared by the dog and the monkey, with whom as to intelligence, the human worshiper was about on a par. But do not the facts negative the supposition of so great an intellectual grade having been overcome by us as that which lies between the monkey and the man? In that portion of the duration of man which history records—say three thousand years—we

---

* See Cudworth, vol. i. p. 476, etc.

see no increase of the sentimental and æsthetical faculties, the very ones Comte relies on as the elements of religious culture. Homer, in the vivacity of his imagination and his keen appreciation of and capacity for the expression of beauty; Phidias, in his sculpture; the artists who reared the Pantheon, and the mechanists who constructed the machinery by which the Pyramids were raised,—have found no superiors among their successors. So far as the intellectual measurement of our race is concerned, the altitude we reach now is about the same as that we reached at the earliest periods to which history goes back. It is a parallelogram of great length, it is true, but of equal height. Where then can we find the intellectual depravation assigned by the Positivists to primeval man?

§ 195. c^2. *Fetich-worship, such as it claimed to be, exists at the present day among people with whom a polytheistic or perhaps a monotheistic religion once prevailed.*

It is enough, in order to meet Comte's position, to show that Fetich-worship exists in the present day. That it does, in the true sense in which the term should be used, is not a matter of doubt. Nowhere, in fact, in mythological history, do we find a sketch approximating so closely to that of Comte, as one lately given us by Captain Walter M. Gibson, whose remarkable adventures among the Dutch and Malays, have created so much recent interest. "I was informed," he tells us, in an address before the American Geographical and Statistical Society, in the City of New York, "by a fellow-prisoner at Welterveden, by one Captain Van Woorden, who had been four years commanding at the small post of Lahat, in the interior of Sumatra, and who had had frequent opportunities to observe the Orung Kooboos, both male and female, sit around a buluh batang, or species of bamboo, that attains to a great size, and would, all in concert, as many as could, strike their heads repeatedly against the trunk of the tree, and utter some rude, grunting ejaculations; this, he observed, took place whenever any one, or all the band got hurt, or received any special gratification, but mostly when injured. Now, it is well known that a large portion of the semi-civilized, semi-pagan Sumatrans, believe that in the enormous tufts of the buluh batang, as well as in the marringin-tree, there exists widadiri dowas and rakshashas, or good and evil supernatural beings; and, what is remarkable, that throughout Sumatra, all the beings of their pagan mythology are of the feminine gender. I have heard described by their orung menyanyee, or pantunverse-singers, some most ravishing pictures of the widadiri, or good wood-nymphs of the bulah batang."

§ 196. But beyond this, the history of Christianity indicates that there exists a tendency, varying, it is true, with climate and political relations, to overcrust the spiritual and vital with the material. To show this, it is not necessary to go further than to refer to the processes by which the reverence for saints became saint-worship, by which saint-worship became image-worship, by which, among the more ignorant, image-worship has, as in certain of the nominal Roman Catholic provinces in South America, become scarcely distinguishable from idolatry. Here is undoubtedly a great development, but it is in a direction the reverse from that announced by Positive Philosophy. So it has been with

Judaism. "The Jews," says an acute observer, "corrupted their pure monotheistic truths into what these writers (the followers of Comte) believe the fables, legends, miracles, and absurd dogmas of the Old Testament; and as if *that* were not enough, proceeded to bury them in the huge absurdities of the Rabbinical traditions."* Such is the view taken from the stand-point of Positivism. View the Jewish history from the stand-point of Christianity, as we are now entitled to do, and the retrograde movement from the pure Theism of the Old Testament, to a sensuous symbolism, from obedience to the decrees of God to submission to the commentaries of man, is equally manifest.†

§ 197. *d^2. The three stages of Theology, Metaphysics, and Positivism are often coincident.*

Nowhere is this more evident than in the present century and in the very countries which Comte has selected as the basis of his induction. Side by side we have Positivism, Metaphysics, and Theology, each struggling with an energy which would be strangely out of place in systems which succeed each other in a definite line of descent. The positive philosophers find the supposed predecessor, to whose funeral they so confidently issued invitations, arising from his grave, and contemptuously driving the intruders from the coveted domain. The profound research and the acute analysis of

* Eclipse of Faith, p. 144.

† Observe Coleridge's antithesis of the Quaker and the Romish doctrines of the sacrament:—"The one evaporated it into a myth; the other consolidated it into an idol." Here, in the latter alternative, God gives man a spiritual religion, which man carnalizes. The "development" is not from matter to spirit, but from spirit to matter.

Agassiz on the one side, the close logic and the comprehensive intellect of Sir William Hamilton on the other, have shown that science, physical as well as metaphysical, is able to maintain its own cause on its own ground against a purely phenomenal philosophy. Nor are the disciples of Kant at all disposed to yield the ground occupied by that great and bold thinker. They feel that toward Kant the course of Comte was unjust and ungenerous; that the French philosopher took from the German the system of classification which was the latter's own, but which the former perverted by applying it to an induction which, by excluding psychological phenomena and confining it to physical, tells that half truth, which is a whole falsehood,—and they are now proceeding with a strength greater than even that of their master, (for the present controversy shows to them the side on which his defences were left the most incomplete,) to prove that true philosophy involves not merely those truths which arise from phenomenal induction, but those also which come from subjective faith and reason. Nor, if we pass to the theological element, do we find it dying out. It will be enough, in order to meet this point, to call attention to the fact, that never, in the history of our race, was that evangelical faith which, of all phases of Christianity is the one least liable to the charge of symbolism, more active in the multiplication of its agencies, more potent in the effect produced. Were the question one of mere statistics, it would be at once decided. The same sagacity which recognizes in the Cherbourg dock and in the Parisian walls, in the increased discipline and multiplying numbers of the French armies, the growing energy of France, could not fail

to perceive a similar proof of the progress of positive Christianity in the birth as well as growth of foreign missions in the last fifty years, in the extraordinary cotemporaneous resuscitations of the Protestant churches of England and Germany, and in the power with which the press has acted in the same direction through the great publication agencies of Great Britain and America.

In public, and what may be called merely worldly opinion, we see no sign of the alleged decay of Christian vigor. In view of Comte's doctrine, as expounded by Mr. Buckle, "that more may be learned respecting the moral nature of man from statistical facts than from all the accumulated experience of ages," let us take, as an example, the attitude of the public men of the United States toward religion. It is not necessary here to go into the question of the actual degree of faith on the part of those whose names will be presently mentioned It is sufficient for the present purpose to take the proof at its lowest gauge, and to regard them merely as *representative* men, as men responding to and reiterating a definite public sentiment. And in this view let us take the remarkable contrast between the public men of the revolutionary era and those of the present era. Of the former, with the exception of Washington, Chief Justice Jay, and Richard Henry Lee, it is difficult to find one who was an unreserved believer in practical Christianity. Jefferson rejected the Pauline epistles entirely, discharged from the Gospel narratives all the miracles, and, discrediting the divine character of Christ, held only to certain of His precepts as forming a suitable moral code. John Adams, as the correspondence between the two in their latter years

shows, held to the same belief; nor did Franklin believe even as much. But when we pass farther down the line of history, a great change is observable. John Quincy Adams, with whom the second generation of American statesmen may be said to begin, was a Unitarian, it is true, but of a stamp very different from his father. A professed believer in the inspiration of the Scriptures, and a regular attendant at what in many instances was orthodox public worship, he held to a scheme of doctrine which Priestley or Middleton would have rejected as identical with orthodoxy. General Jackson was not only in the last few years of his life an earnest and devoted professor of religion, according to the usages of the Presbyterian Church, but during his whole career unreservedly avowed an intellectual belief. Mr. Polk, though with the qualifications which his greater reserve of character was likely to produce, took the same position. Mr. Clay, Mr. Webster, General Harrison, and Mr. Benton, not only professed a belief in Christianity as a Divine scheme, but, at the most solemn periods of their lives, announced their trust in the evangelical doctrines of grace.*

---

* With respect to Mr. Benton, whose rugged individuality led him to repel, almost fiercely, attempts on the part of others to enter within the precincts of the emotional in his very remarkable character, we have the following statement recently brought to light, being part of a letter from Dr. May, the attendant physician of the deceased statesman:—

"It may not be inappropriate for me here to state that although he never expressed to me any views upon the subject of religion, he did so freely after this to the Rev. Dr. Sunderland, his pastor and friend, as the following statement of Dr. Sunderland will show. He says:—

§ 198. Now, this change of sentiment may be viewed either as the expression of a subjective individual faith, or as a response to an altered public sentiment. It is enough for the present purpose, as has just been observed, if the latter be true. But it is hard to see how the former can, with any justice, be rejected. Most of the professions of faith made by those whose names have been mentioned, were repeated, and this in language the most passionate and unreserved, when they were on their dying beds, with nothing to gain from human applause, and everything to lose by that Divine displeasure which, even on the deist's principles, will visit hypocrisy and falsehood. Now, what interpretation does human judgment assign to declarations made under such circumstances in reference to other issues? "It is considered," says the common law, "that when an individual is in constant expectation of immediate death, all temptation to falsehood, either of interest, hope, or fear, will be removed, and the awful nature of his situation will be presumed to impress him as strongly with the necessity of a strict adherence to truth as the most solemn obligation of an oath administered in a court of justice. When every hope of this world is gone, when every motive to falsehood

---

During the last week of Col. Benton's life I had several interviews with him at his own request. Our conversation was mainly on the subject of religion, and in regard to his own views and exercises in the speedy prospect of death. In these conversations he most emphatically and distinctly renounced all self-reliance, and cast himself entirely on the mediation of the Lord Jesus Christ as the ground of his acceptance with God. His own words were, 'God's mercy in Jesus Christ is my sole reliance.'"

is silenced, and the mind is induced, by the most powerful considerations to speak the truth, a situation so solemn and awful is considered by the law as creating the most impressive of sanctions."* If we accept this standard, and believe that even among public men, a class which almost beyond all others is the most drawn away by worldly associations and by pride of opinion from the humbling doctrines of the cross, there is this gradual approach to a definite gospel faith, what becomes of the assumption that among the "select" *men* and leaders of human action theological belief is extinct? If we take the other alternative, (and both are probably true,) that these declarations of opinion are at least in part responsive to a prevailing public sentiment, what becomes of the position that the "select" *races* are passing through the same cycle?

§ 199. The difficulties which have just been mentioned in respect to the theological era apply with equal force to the metaphysical. There is no more evidence of metaphysics having been born at the burial of theology, than there is of theology having been buried at all. There is no more evidence of metaphysics passing from infancy to manhood, than there is of theology having passed from manhood to death. The fact is, psychology, in its fullest sense, has of all sciences been the most equal and the least susceptible of variation. We may hit upon a series of eras of metaphysical speculation, and find a difficulty in saying which is the most vigorous. Certainly if we take the present century there are no symptoms of a progress to decay. The Scottish school,

---

* See Wharton's Cr. Law, § 669.

including Reid, Dugald Stewart, Dr. Thomas Brown, Sir J. Mackintosh, Sir W. Hamilton; the German, including Fichte, Schelling, Hegel, Feuerbach, Kant; the English, including Whewell, Coleridge, Morell, and Archer Butler, present an array of intellectual splendor which is indicative of anything but a sunset. Nor as we go backward, does the brilliancy of the metaphysical orb vary. It would seem as if in that point of the intellectual firmament the speculative genius of men has always centered, and from thence diffused its most intense light. Let us go back to the beginning of the nineteenth century, and see whether in the period to which we then arrive we discover an approach to the opakeness and chaos of a merely preparatory era. Far otherwise; for even Comte himself bows in recognition of the almost inspired reason of Bacon, the acute analysis and philosophical generalization of Des Cartes, the rarefied and inexorable idealism of Spinoza, the exact sense of Locke, the extraordinary learning and felicitous ingenuity of Leibnitz, and the keen, though merely destructive speculativism of Hume. Nor, as we go still farther back, do we discover any diminution of the power with which the cotemporaneous intellectual energies of distinct periods bent themselves to this particular point, and diffused from it their greatest brightness. So it was in the period of the Schoolmen, the occasional frivolity of whose topics should never lead us to forget the uniform ingenuity of their speculations. So it was with that grand Grecian school which comprised Socrates, Plato, and Aristotle. So it was at the earliest period to which a technical intellectual history takes us, viz., that in which Hindû philosophy, at least eight hundred years before Christ, almost anticipated future generations in refined subtlety. According to Comte, the birth of the science of metaphysics was at this time more than a thousand years distant. According to Comte, this science, at the time of Locke, of Des Cartes, and of Bacon—of all its stages the exactest and most disciplined—was in a babbling and discursive infancy. And now, according to Comte, it is being carried to its grave. In point of fact, however, its proportions, almost at all times measured by the full standard of the human mind, have remained, as that mind has, at an altitude, which, though exhibiting undulations of surface, preserves now, so far as concerns its creative and speculative powers, the same general height that it did at the earliest period of its history.

§ 200. e^2. *In non-Christian countries, Fetichism, as it is called, instead of being the accompaniment of a barbaric infancy, is cotemporary with high metaphysical as well as artistic culture.*

Take, for instance, Egypt, when at the height of its æsthetic splendor, and observe the character of its worship. "Ancient Egypt," says Mr. Gross, a writer who is far from hostile to modern Positivism, "was a vast menagerie of sacred animals, whose ample roof was the vault of heaven; and from the confines of Thebes or Disopolis to the mouth of the Nile, at Canobus, the whole country teemed with hiero-animal life."* Thus the ram was worshiped at Thebes; the goat at Chemmis, Hermopolis, and Mendes; the dog at Cynopolis; the wolf at Lycopolis; the cat at

* Gross, on Heathen Religions, p. 185.

Bubastis; the crocodile at Tachompso. Besides these local deities, there were others to whom was reserved a catholic worship. Three holy bulls stood conspicuous among the latter. The first was Mnevis, with black and bristly hair; the second Onuphis, whose locks were shaggy and recurved; the third Apis, on whose forehead a ray of light from heaven had marked two white spots, one in the shape of a triangle, the other in that of a half-moon. To Apis supreme honors were assigned. When found—and the chances against a bull with such a combination of color and marks were, of course, great—the sacred animal was "conveyed in triumphal procession to a temporary abode, where, during the space of four months, he was attended and fed with the greatest care, in a building, the east side of which was uninclosed. At the expiration of this period, a festival was proclaimed, which began at the new moon. As soon as the solemnities were concluded, Apis was conducted to Heliopolis, where he had the honor to have every attention shown to him by the priests, during an interval of forty days. This time having elapsed, he was finally brought to Memphis, and duly installed in the Temple of Phthah, where his presence was recognized in clouds of precious incense and splendid offerings. If he died, or the time arrived when he had to make room for a successor—which happened at the termination of the Apis-period, or the lunar cycle of twenty-five civil years—there was universal mourning throughout Egypt until another Apis was found: the dead one was either publicly entombed in the Temple of Serapis, or elsewhere privately interred. Apis was the symbol of Osiris, considered as the sun, as the Nile, and as the principle of fructification; and in consequence of the connection of Osiris thus defined with Isis, Apis also symbolized this goddess, regarded as the moon, the fertile earth, and material nature."*

§ 201. Now, if the positive theory be correct, Egypt, at the time it was "this vast menagerie of sacred animals," must have been swaddled in the grossest ignorance. The positive philosopher, if taken to those shores where the cat, the dog, and the crocodile were worshiped, would say, "Here, at least, I will find the rudeness of semi-idiotic infancy. Here I will see the human Fetich-worshiper uniting in a common religious brotherhood with animals—*e.g.* the dog and the monkey—from whom in moral and intellectual attributes he is hardly distinguishable."

But how was it in fact? The memorials of the artistic skill and of the economical energy and endurance of these Fetich-worshipers—the only class in ancient history, in fact, who are deserving of this name—will rival any that we could suppose modern Europe, with all the advantages of present civilization, to exhibit. "It is evident to me," says Champollion, "as it must be to all who have thoroughly examined Egypt, or have an accurate knowledge of the Egyptian monuments existing in Europe, that the arts commenced in Greece by a servile imitation of the arts of Egypt, much more advanced than is vulgarly believed, at the period at which the first Egyptian colonies came in contact with the savage inhabitants of Attica and the Peloponnesus. Without Egypt, Greece would probably never have become

* Gross, on Heathen Religions, p. 188.

the classical land of the fine arts. Such is my entire belief in this great problem. I write these lines almost in presence of bas-reliefs which the Egyptians executed, with the most elegant delicacy of workmanship, nineteen hundred years before the Christian era."* No less emphatic is Belzoni's testimony, after having, with a battering-ram, burst his way at Goornau into these halls of "fabulous splendor," then for the first time opened in three thousand years, and found surrounded by the most elaborate sculpture, and the most vivid paintings, in a mausoleum which even that of the Escurial cannot rival, the alabaster sarcophagi of kings who were themselves high priests of Fetichism.

§ 202 The same high artistic culture is exhibited in the memorials we have of the cotemporaneous domestic life. "The civilization of families," says a very recent observer of these cemeteries, "must have been equal to the best days of Rome. Articles of luxury, gold and silver ornaments, fine colors and embroideries, all abounded, and it appears evident that the splendor of life among the wealthy in Egypt, at the time of the captivity, was never surpassed, even in the days of Cleopatra." "The period of Remesis Sesostris has well been styled the Augustan era of Egypt. The Nile valley was a continuous row of prosperous cities, magnificent temples, and royal palaces. The arms of the country were everywhere triumphant; the arts were cultivated, and adorned the cities, houses, and most of all the tombs; nor is there at this remote age an article of household luxury, a fauteuil or a cooking utensil, a harp or a

* Champollion's Fifteenth Letter, dated Thebes.

set of toys, that does not seem to have its counterpart in the splendid tomb of this monarch, now lying open at Thebes."*

Nor were the industrial interests of the nation neglected. Splendid ships, themselves identified with the public worship as symbols, rode the Nile. A canal, one thousand stadia long, joined the Red Sea with the Mediterranean. Mining was conducted on a scale far transcending that of modern times, for mountains were dug down to get at the ore, and rivers turned from their channel to wash it out.

b[1]. *Personal experience.*

a[2]. *Psychological.*

§ 203. According to positivism, the experience of all men, or, at all events, that of the higher and more cultivated individuals, begins with theology and ends either with atheism, or, at least, with the recognition of government by a system of fixed and arbitrary law.

The experience of all men, we apprehend, is just the other way. There are few who, on turning back to the earliest period of thought to which their memory can take them, but will agree to the position that such period was godless. The infant, it is said, is a Fetich-worshiper, and, as it stretches out its hands to the fire or the moon, does but imitate the Sabæanism of the Chaldean shepherds. But at this early stage of infancy this supposed act of worship can be regarded as a mere gesture of pleasure or of acquisitiveness. This view is strengthened by running the parallel still farther. Do we see in childhood the progress from Fetichism through polytheism to monotheism? Comte's

* Prime's Boat-life in Egypt, etc., pp. 476–7.

own detachment from society, and his domestic isolation (until the later period of his life) combined with the natural rigor and coldness which distinguished his earlier days, in leading him to estimate the innocent simplicity and faith of childhood at a pitch in which few will acquiesce. For most of those who go back to even a religiously educated infancy will recollect what confused meaning was assigned to the theological formulas, *e.g.* catechisms or hymns, with which the early memory was charged, and how the eye associated with the pulpit and the pulpit cushion, the pew, and the chancel, anything but religious thoughts.

§ 204. But we have other tests than that of individual retrospection,—tests not unlike those by which, through a cavity produced by disease or wounds, Harvey was able to verify his theory of the circulation of the blood. Take children, whom blindness and a loss of hearing and of speech have sealed up from religious culture, and then, when by the humane agencies of modern art, an avenue is at last opened to their understanding, observe how utterly ignorant they are of the first idea of worship. And so, also, with those who have been brought up—as late English parliamentary inquiries show us is not rarely the case even in that enlightened country—in a social ignorance, perhaps even more profound than that of a deprivation of the senses.

§ 205. If we measure the condition of the religious element by its moral results we are led to the same conclusion. A child's heart gives no indication of any intuitive religious ascendency. Dr. Arnold, than whom there have been few who have united a wider field of observation with healthier discerning faculties, and whose theological bias was not such as to lead him to an exaggerated view of innate corruption, told the boys at Rugby, in one of his sermons, that the four great characteristics of childhood were "teachableness, ignorance, selfishness, and living only for the present."* "In the last three of these, the perfect man should put away childish things."† "Our path" (that of those in whom religious principle has made a settlement) "is not *backwards*, but *onwards* * * * * When we compare a boy's state after his first half year, or year, at school, with what it is afterwards; when we see the clouds again clearing off; when we find coarseness succeeded again by delicacy; hardness and selfishness again broken up, and giving place to affection and benevolence; murmuring and self-will exchanged for humility and self-denial; and the profane or impure, or false tongue uttering again only the words of truth and purity; and when we see that all these good things are now, by God's grace, rooted in the character; that they have been tried, and grown up amidst the trial; that the know-

* It was in reference to the first of these that Arnold considered our Lord to speak, when He declared that to enter into the kingdom of heaven it was necessary to "become as little children." It should be recollected that these words were uttered as part of a rebuke of the ambition of the disciples. They desired to know "who should be greatest in the kingdom of heaven." They had, in their personal assumption, even endeavored to hinder "little children" from coming to Him. His answer was such as to show them that those who were to enter into the kingdom of heaven were to be stripped of all earthly distinctions. They were, in this light, to go back to infancy, and, in the second birth, to proceed as naked to the world above as in the first birth to the world below.

† Arnold's Christian Life, its Course, Hindrances, etc., p. 68, etc.

ledge of evil has made them hate it the more, and be the more aware of it,—then we can look upon our calling with patience, and even with thankfulness." In this view the loss of the mere superficial and ignorant simplicity and ignorance of childhood is not to be mourned over, when followed by the real humility of Christian experience :—

Grieve not for these: nor dare lament
 That thus from childhood's thoughts we roam:
Not backward are our glances bent,
 But forward to our Father's home.
Eternal growth has no such fears,
 But, freshening still with seasons past,
The old man clogs its earlier years,
 *And simple childhood comes the last.**

§ 206. The experience of the man of the world will coincide with that of the Christian on this point. There are few who will not recollect periods, both in themselves and in children who have come under their observation, in which the duty of speaking truth, and of respecting the property and regarding the feelings of others, was regarded with far greater laxity than it came to be under the influence of worldly culture, if not of religious experience.†

* Burbridge's Poems, p. 309, quoted by Dr. Arnold in a note in which he introduces the extract by saying, "This thought," (that in the text) "is expressed very beautifully in lines as wise and true as they are poetical."

† Mr. Thackeray thus speaks on this point:—"The *Simplicity of Youth.*—Nevertheless, as we have hinted, the lad was by no means the artless stripling he seemed to be. He was knowing enough, with

b[2]. *Statistical.*

§ 207. Let us turn, however, to "statistics," which are assumed by positivism to be of so much higher value than

---

all his blushing cheeks; perhaps more wily and wary than he grew to be in after years. Sure, a shrewd and generous man (who has led an honest life and has no secret blushes for his conscience) grows simpler as he grows older; arrives at his sum of right by more rapid processes of calculation; learns to eliminate false arguments more readily, and hits the mark of truth with less previous trouble of aiming and disturbance of mind Or is it only a servile delusion, that some of our vanities are cured with our growing years, and that we become more just in our perceptions of our own and our neighbor's shortcomings? I would humbly suggest that young people, though they look prettier, have larger eyes, and not near so many wrinkles about their eyelids, are often as artful as some of their elders. What little monsters of cunning your frank schoolboys are! How they cheat mamma! how they hoodwink papa! how they humbug the housekeeper! how they cringe to the big boy for whom they fag at school! what a long lie and five years' hypocrisy and flattering is their conduct to Dr. Birch! And the little boys' sisters! are they any better, and is it only after they come out in the world that the little darlings learn a trick or two?"—*The Virginians*, No. 6.

Montaigne, as we are reminded by Dr. Buchanan,* "speaks of an error maintained by Plato, 'that children and old people were most susceptible of religion, as if it sprung and derived its credit from our weakness.' And we find M. Comte himself complaining, somewhat bitterly, that his *quondam* friend, the celebrated St. Simon, had exhibited, as he advanced in years, (cette tendance banale vers une vague religiosité) a tendency toward something like religion."† The same retrograde motion has been exhibited, though in a march still

---

* Faith in God, etc., vol. i. p. 488.

† 1 Buchanan, on Faith, etc., p. 488.

psychological observation. And here the statement may be safely ventured, that where we find one case of religious infancy maturing in a skeptical old age, we find twenty of the contrary. The Christian will remember the youth of John Bunyan, in its strange alternations of roystering debauch and awful remorse, and that of John Newton, in its fierce abandonment; nor will the philosopher fail to recall that of Robert Hall, pure indeed, but giving its first intellectual adhesion to rationalism, and passing through Socinianism to evangelical Christianity, and those of Southey, Coleridge, and Wordsworth, in which Comte's order was reversed, positivism coming first and theology last. Certainly among those speaking the English tongue, the cases, even in this supposed age of metaphysical doubt, if not of positive skepticism, are very rare where men of eminence in any department have distinguished their maturer years by avowed atheism. Mr. Buckle has thought proper to dispose of the splendid exception afforded by Mr. Burke to the pretended course of positive development, by announcing that that eminent statesman and gorgeous rhetorician was "deranged." But, so far as *intellectual* assent to the truth of Christianity

---

more extraordinary for the short period in which it united the extremest points, by Mr. O. A. Brownson, the sociology of whose youth has developed into ultramontane Romanism. And lastly, the great founder of positivism himself, who was in his own person to have exhibited the inexorable progress of phenomenal truth, turns out to have yielded to the seductions of superstition, and in his old age, as will be presently shown, to have succumbed to a "vague religiosity" which made up for its disbelief in whatever *was* revealed, by its faith in whatever was *not*.

is concerned—and that is the only test which positivism admits—Mr. Burke, among modern statesmen, is far from standing alone. Since the subsidence of the French Revolution, at which period the positive era is supposed to begin, it is difficult to find a public man either in England or this country, who has not avowed at least such intellectual belief. And not a few, as has just been observed, have marked the declining years so specially relied on as the period of "positive" belief, by an emphatic Christian confession.

Even among the leaders in inductive science—those whose supposed progression toward atheism is the ground-work of positive philosophy—there will be found few who do not recognize, not merely a definite theism, but the divine legation of Christianity itself. "Here," says Dr. Hitchcock, speaking on this point, "we reckon the princes of the intellectual world, such as Newton, Kepler, Galileo, Pascal, Boyle, Copernicus, Linnæus, Black, Boerhaave, and Dalton; and among the living such men as Herschel, Brewster, Whewell, Sedgwick, Owen, and a multitude of others. The very same argumentation that leads such original discoverers to derive the principles of science from facts in nature, carries them irresistibly backward to a First Cause; and, indeed, the inductive principle, as developed by Bacon, forms the true basis on which to build the whole fabric of natural religion; and he who fully admits the truth of natural religion, is in a state of preparation for receiving revealed truth to supply its deficiencies. So that, upon the whole, the inductive sciences are, of all others, most favorable to religion, and the most intimately connected with it."*

---

* Religious Truth Illustrated from Science, p. 31.

The educational history of the United States gives no support to M. Comte's theory. Take, for instance, the colleges at the era immediately succeeding the Revolution. In Yale College, the number of communicants, immediately before the accession of President Dwight, was not over ten; and once, when the Lord's Supper was administered, about that time, only one undergraduate was present. In 1797 the tide turned. In 1802, of two hundred and fifty then in college, one-third were professed and earnest Christians, and of these one-half became clergymen. At present, the proportion of church members is much larger.

In Bowdoin College, from 1802 to 1806, and afterwards in 1811, there was not a single professed Christian among the undergraduates. In 1825, a reaction began so remarkable as to justify the remark of Professor Stowe, that "if the religious character of the college gains as much from the year 1850 to 1875, as it did from 1825 to 1850, it will be all that the most ardent friends of the Lord Jesus can reasonably hope for before the millennium."

In eleven New England colleges in 1853, out of 2163 students, 745 were professors of religion, and 343 candidates for the ministry. At present, 1859, the number of professors of religion may be rated as two-thirds of the aggregate. In the educational institutions of Europe, the progress has been in the same direction. Tholuck tells us that, with the exception of Wurtemberg, there were, thirty years ago, among the German teachers of divinity, "not more than three or four that might be called evangelical." Knapp himself, timid in his course, if not indistinct in his conceptions, was the only believer in a real Christianity in the

University of Halle, which contained no less than nine hundred divinity students; and he stated at this time, that out of one thousand students in general, he knew but one real Christian, and he was a Moravian. Neander began the battle nearly single-handed, though Schleiermacher walked totteringly by his side in his earlier steps, giving an impulse even where he was unable to confess a principle. The Prussian Evangelical Union of 1817, though patriotic rather than religious, registered a marked advance. Then came Hengstenberg, resolutely and even defiantly vindicating the inspiration of Holy Writ; and Tholuck and Olshausen, the one bringing a most pathetic and persuasive eloquence, the other an inexhaustible fund of thought, and both unswerving loyalty, to the work of exposition. Then followed Nitzsch, Julius Müller, Dorner, Lange, Ullman, Rothe, Stier, Hagenbach, Herzog, Twesten, eminent for their literary gifts, turning back the current of skeptical culture that was almost submerging Germany, and with them Wicheru in all the loveliness of his comprehensive Christian tenderness. Thirty years ago, there was scarcely an orthodox minister to be found. At the *Kirchentag* held in Berlin in 1853, there were two thousand, and these all representative-men. In Berlin, we have in the theological chairs, Hengstenberg, Tholuck, Twesten, and Nitzsch, and in the pulpits, Krümmacher, Hoffman, Arndt, and Büchsel. In Göttingen, positive orthodoxy is taught by Dorner and Ehrenfeuchter. Leipsic, once the seat of a resolute skepticism, now has its theological faculty controlled by Linder, Ahlfeld, and Kahnis, all holding a high Lutheranism, and the latter, as those familiar with his essay on German Protestantism will bear witness, maintaining an almost uncompromising altitudinarianism. In Tübingen, Beck, Landerer, Palmer, and Oehler, all of them "without exception decidedly Christian and evangelical scholars,"* follow Strauss, Vischer, and Baur.

I can see no facts in England on which the induction of Comte, or of Mr. Buckle, who follows him in this respect, can be based. The revival of the Anglican Church at the close of the last century is notorious. The funds contributed toward foreign missions form a test of this. From 1769 to 1788, they averaged at £4114. In 1835 they were about £100,000. In 1856 they were £250,000. The increase has been equal and gradual. In education the movement has certainly not been in the contrary direction. "The tone of young men at the University," said Dr. Maberly, head-master at Winchester, speaking of thirty years back, "whether they came from Winchester, Eton, Rugby, Harrow, or wherever else, was universally irreligious. A religious undergraduate was very rare." But speaking of fifteen years after, the same authority says, "Dr. Arnold's pupils were thoughtful, manly-minded, conscious of duty and obligations when they first came to college."

c^1. *Organic structure.*

§ 208. "The scientific principle," says Comte,† "involved in the phrenological view, is that the functions, affective

* Schaff's Germany and its Universities, p. 101, from which a part of the sketch in the text is reduced.

† Pos. Phil., Martineau's trans., Appleton's edition, p. 388.

and intellectual, are more elevated, more human, if you will, and at the same time less energetic, in proportion to the exclusiveness with which they belong to the higher part of the zoological series, their positions being in portions of the brain more and more restricted in extent, and further removed from its immediate origin,—according to the anatomical decision that the skull is simply a prolongation of the vertebral column, which is the primitive centre of the nervous system. Thus, the least developed and anterior part of the brain is appropriated to the characteristic faculties of humanity; and the most voluminous and hindmost part to those which constitute the basis of the whole of the animal kingdom. Here we have a new and confirmatory instance of the rule which we have had to follow in every science; that it is necessary to proceed from the most general to the more special attributes, in the order of their diminishing generality."

From this general position the conclusion is reached that, as arising upward from the vertebral column, we come first to the animal properties, next to the sentimental, and then to the intellectual, so human life will fall into three parallel divisions. To this it may be remarked:—

§ 209. a^2. It rests on a theory which in itself is not much more than a mere hypothesis, and which, in its present application, is negatived by the fact that the supposed organs in the cranium have been removed without affecting the corresponding attributes.

§ 210. b^2. Life does not show that the sensual, the sentimental, and the intellectual, separate into distinct grades. On the contrary, they coexist in so large a number of cases as to defeat any reliable generalization. "Lusty minds give lusty morals," we have been told; and the cases of Mirabeau, of Burns, of Byron, are sad illustrations of this truth.

§ 211. c^2. If we extend the proposition over history, we find an insuperable difficulty from the argument proving too much. If each of the three compartments of the brain is to have its group of centuries, each of the minor lobes is to have its *decade*. If we are to have a *final* period for the intellectual, we must have that period subdivided, as is the front of the brain, so that each of the intellectual, or semi-intellectual faculties—causality, comparison, music, form—can have its specific era. It is not necessary to pause here to say that this assumption is as hostile to present experience as is the hypothesis of the general stages to past history.

c. General considerations by which the positivist philosophy is to be met.

a^1. *The pushing back of first causes strengthens rather than weakens the theistic argument.*

§ 212. The falling of water may be so governed as to move the hands of a twenty-four hour clock, but to make a clock that will wind itself in periodic succession requires the highest degree of human skill,—to so construct it that it will renew itself indefinitely, requires a skill which is divine. If we trace marks of contrivance in that law of adaptation which would place a hundred water-clocks in harmonious action, should we not trace such marks still more strongly in a mechanism capable itself of making and governing such clocks in an infinite succession?

The hand-car on a railroad, also, as it glides before us under the immediate action of the human hand, leaves no doubt on our minds as to the spontaneity and purpose with which it moves. Is this conviction diminished when we find this specific impulse, caught up with an infinite series of others, and united in a vast consistent plan; when we see hundreds of locomotives—some with freight, some with passengers, each governed by its own law which substitutes mechanical for human strength—traversing, in obedience to a preordained programme, a road several hundred miles long, and this with almost perfect regularity as to distances and hours? That the development of a system of general and harmonious laws is looked upon by the positivist as hostile to theism, is not disputed; and it is equally clear that the positive philosophers have striven to make this impression both general and deep. Undoubtedly the code which they have endeavored to extract from the phenomena of the universe is destructive of all faith in Providence, but the objection lies, not to their seeking to establish the general laws by which the world is governed, but to the very erroneous induction by which the laws they announce have been obtained. The existence of a comprehensive and beneficent system of law, in fact, is the strongest evidence of the existence of a Divine lawmaker and judge.

b^1. *No materials exist from which a system of positive laws, as forming a Divine rule of government, may be inferred.*

§ 213. There is a vital distinction between a *causal* law, *i.e.* one that rules the genesis of events, and an *empirical* law, one that merely registers their occurrence. There is a vital distinction, for instance, between the time-tables issued from period to period by the officers of an extended railroad and the systematized observation of running by even a long and accurate series of travelers. The records of the latter are open to error: (1) from the imperfectness of observation; (2) from occasional disturbances of time at specific points, which may be compensated for in the long run; (3) and—which is the main consideration—from a variation in the hours of departure of the trains which the time-table itself may indicate as to take place at a specific period, but which prior observations will not denote. Now, let a traveler rely on the latter, and he will find that though in a mere statistical point of view the results, like empirical laws in general, are interesting as helps to the memory, and useful as the base for business tables, they are in themselves of no permanent and absolute value as indications of the future. What is more, supposing, as geology teaches us, that there are certain cycles of interruption in the process of the universe itself, these empirical results lead to positive error. A man who relies on a superseded table of hours of departure is worse off than he who goes to the depot and waits.

It would be out of place to show here that the mere mnemonic tables of phenomenal observation are, from their nature, subject to certain periodic interruptions, whose secret mere human induction cannot reach, but which destroy their continuous value. Mr. Babbage, in that remarkable treatise known as the "Ninth Bridgewater Treatise," has shown that in a very long series of events such periodic variations, *i.e.* alterations by the Grand Engineer of the universe, of the time-table by which events proceed, are mathematically certain. The geologic record gives proof that such alterations and readjustments have from time to time occurred.

§ 214. The results of empirical observation are, therefore, incapable of becoming permanent laws for the future.

In this connection the following remarks, by Archbishop Whately, may be well studied :—"There is no more fruitful source of confusion of thought than that ambiguity of the language employed on these subjects, (logical and physical sequence,) which tends to confound together these two things so entirely distinct in their nature. There is hardly any argumentative writer on subjects involving a discussion of the Causes or Effects of anything, who has clearly perceived and steadily kept in view the distinction I have been speaking of, or who has escaped the errors and perplexities thence resulting. The wide extent accordingly, and the importance of the mistakes and difficulties arising out of the ambiguity complained of, is incalculable. Of all the 'Idola Fori,'* none is perhaps more important in its results. To dilate upon this point as fully as might be done with advantage, would exceed my present limits; but it will not be irrelevant to offer some remarks on the origin of the ambiguity complained of, and on the cautions to be used in guarding against being misled by it.

"The Premise by which anything is proved is not necessarily the Cause of the fact's *being* such as it is, but it is the cause of our *knowing*, or being convinced that it is so; *e.g.* the wetness of the earth is not the cause of rain, but it

* Bacon.

is the cause of our knowing that it has rained. These two things—the Premise which produces *our conviction*, and the Cause which produces that *of which* we are convinced—are the more likely to be confounded together, in the looseness of colloquial language, from the circumstance that (as has been above remarked) they frequently coincide; as, *e.g.* when we *infer* that the ground will be wet from the fall of rain which *produces* that wetness. And hence it is that the same words have come to be applied, in common, to each kind of Sequence; *e.g.* an Effect is said to 'follow' from a Cause, and a Conclusion to 'follow' from the Premises; the words 'Cause' and 'Reason,' are each applied indifferently, both to a Cause properly so called, and to the Premise of an Argument; though 'Reason,' in strictness of speaking, should be confined to the latter. 'Therefore,' 'hence,' 'consequently,' etc., and also 'since,' 'because,' and 'why,' have, likewise, a corresponding ambiguity.

§ 215. "The multitude of words which bear this double meaning (and that in all languages) greatly increases our liability to be misled by it; since thus the very means men resort to for ascertaining the sense of any expression are infected with the very same ambiguity; *e.g.* if we inquire what is meant by a 'Cause,' we shall be told that it is that from which something 'follows;' or, which is indicated by the words 'therefore,' 'consequently,' etc., all of which expressions are as equivocal and uncertain in their signification as the original one. It is in vain to attempt ascertaining by the balance the true amount of any commodity if uncertain weights are placed in the opposite scale. Hence it is that so many writers, in investigating the Cause to which any fact or phenomenon is to be attributed, have assigned that which is not a *Cause*, but only a *Proof* that the fact is so; and have thus been led into an endless train of errors and perplexities."*

c^1. *The subordination of human conduct to absolute law is destructive of individuality.*

§ 216. The influence of positive philosophy on merely intellectual progress it may not be out of place here briefly to consider.† *Metaphysical* speculation it is the avowed object of positivism to extinguish. What would be the result of this is stated by Sir W. Hamilton in the following brilliant passage:—

---

* Whately's Rhet., part i. chap. ii. § 3.

† This is shown in science itself. Positivism, as adjusted by Comte, is to be a finality beyond which discovery is not to go. Even the astronomer, according to the positivist chief, is to be admonished lest he push his investigations too far.

"We subjectively, then, condense all astronomical theories round our globe as a centre; and we absolutely reject all theories which, as disconnected with our globe, are by that fact at once mere idle questions, even granting them to be within our reach. This leads us finally to eliminate, not merely the so-called sidereal astronomy, but all planetary studies which concern stars invisible to the naked eye, and which have, consequently, no real influence on the earth. The true domain of astronomy will now, as at the beginning of things, be limited to the five planets which have always been known, together with the sun, equally the centre of their movements as of the earth's and the moon, our only satellite in the heavens. * * * * *

"We put aside all inquiries, as absurd as they are idle, as to the temperature of the stars or their internal constitution. * * *

"Biology may be led to lay too much stress on insignificant beings or acts."

"Nor would such a result have been desirable, had the one exclusive opinion been true, as it was false—innocent, as it was corruptive. If the accomplishment of philosophy imply a cessation of discussion—if the result of speculation be a paralysis of itself; the consummation of knowledge is the condition of intellectual barbarism. Plato has profoundly defined man, 'the hunter of *truth;*' for in this chase, as in others, the *pursuit* is all in all, the *success* comparatively nothing. 'Did the Almighty,' says Lessing, 'holding in His right hand *Truth*, and in His left *Search after Truth*, deign to proffer me the one I might prefer;—in all humility, but without hesitation, I should request—*Search after Truth.*' We *exist* only as we energize; *pleasure* is the reflex of unimpeded energy; energy is the *mean* by which our faculties are developed; and a higher energy the *end* which their development proposes. In *action* is thus contained the existence, happiness, improvement, and perfection of our being; and knowledge is only precious as it may afford a stimulus to the exercise of our powers, and the condition of their more complete activity. Speculative truth is, therefore, subordinate to speculation itself; and its value is directly measured by the quantity of energy which it occasions — immediately in its discovery — mediately through its consequences. Life to Endymion was not preferable to death; aloof from practice, a waking error is better than a sleeping truth. Neither, in point of fact, is there found any proportion between the *possession* of truths and the *development* of the mind in which they are deposited. Every *learner* in science is now familiar with more truths than Aristotle or Plato ever dreamt of know-

ing; yet, compared with the Stagirite or the Athenian, how few among our *masters* of modern science rank higher than intellectual barbarians! Ancient Greece and modern Europe prove, indeed, that 'the march of intellect' is no inseparable concomitant of 'the march of science;'—that the cultivation of the individual is not to be rashly confounded with the progress of the species.

"But if the possession of theoretical facts be not convertible with mental improvement; and if the former be important only as subservient to the latter; it follows that the comparative utility of a study is not to be *principally* estimated by the complement of truths which it may communicate, but by the degree in which it determines our higher capacities to action. But though this be the standard by which the different methods, the different branches, and the different masters of philosophy *ought* to be *principally* (and it is the only criterion by which they *can all* be *satisfactorily*) tried; it is nevertheless a standard by which neither methods, nor sciences, nor philosophers have ever yet been even inadequately appreciated. The critical history of philosophy, in this spirit, has still to be written; and when written, how opposite will be the rank, which on the higher and more certain standard, it will frequently adjudge—to the various branches of knowledge, and the various modes of their cultivation—to different ages, and countries, and individuals, from that which has been hitherto partially awarded, on the vacillating authority of the lower!

"On this ground (which we have not been able to state, far less adequately to illustrate,) we rest the pre-eminent utility of metaphysical speculations. That they comprehend all the sublimest objects of our theoretical and moral interest; that every (natural) conclusion concerning God, the soul, the present worth and the future destiny of man, is exclusively metaphysical, will be at once admitted. But we do not found the importance, on the paramount dignity, of the pursuit. It is as the best *gymnastic of the mind*—as a mean, principally, and almost exclusively conducive to the highest education of our noblest powers, that we would vindicate to these speculations the necessity which has too frequently been denied them. By no other intellectual application (and least of all by physical pursuits) is the soul thus reflected on itself, and its faculties concentred in such independent, vigorous, unwonted, and continued energy; by none, therefore, are its best capacities so variously and intensely evolved. 'Where there is most life, there is the victory.*' "

§ 217. Without accepting all the positions laid down in the remarkable passage which is given above, it is enough for the present purpose to call attention to the truth of the main position Sir W. Hamilton establishes, viz., that it is essential to intellectual life, as well as to spiritual, that there should be a continued striving toward the infinite, a gradual growth and strengthening by an approximation to the centre of Truth and Grace.

§ 218. So much for freedom of thought. As to the influence of positivism on freedom of action, there is still less room to doubt. Individual liberty, as a factor, did not enter into the calculations of the great founder of

---

* Sir W. Hamilton's Discussions, p. 46; Harper's edition.

positivism. Everything, by his philosophy, as will be presently more fully shown, is to be done by a splendid and exhaustive centralization. By this are to be ordained rites and ceremonies, creeds and beliefs, natural affection and supernatural awe, occupations and pursuits, labor and relaxation, manners and usages. Throughout the whole of the comprehensive and elaborate scheme which Comte has developed as the digest of past experience and the law of future action, we meet with no reference to the liberty of choice on the part of the individual man. Everything is prescribed by him down to the minutest detail. All power is taken from the individual and vested in the government which is to execute this complex code. Of course, in such a scheme a representative government is out of the question. Hence it is that the central authority proposed by Comte is essentially autocratic. It is to act, it is true, in conformity with "the positive laws of nature," so far as they are discovered; but as it executes, so it interprets these laws, and, when they do not apply, ordains new laws for the special purpose. It is no wonder, therefore, that Comte hailed with rapture the resuscitation of the Napoleonic system which marked his later days, and declared the usurpation of December 2, 1850, by which Louis Napoleon, in violation of his oath, destroyed the French constitution, and assumed dictatorial powers, to be "the fortunate crisis which has lately set aside the parliamentary regimen, and instituted a dictatorial republic." So it is also that the Emperor Nicholas is eulogized as one "who, while he gives the immense empire of Russia all the progress *compatible with its actual condition, preserves it by his energy and* *prudence from useless ferment.*" To positivism representative government is peculiarly inauspicious. "The actual form of dictatorial power," says Comte, speaking of France, "already permits the direct propagation of all thought that has a tendency to reconstruction. For it has at last (Napoleon III.'s destruction of the Republic) broken the power, which could lead to no good, of mere talkers. * * * During the last four years the reason of the people has suffered profoundly from the unfortunate exercise of universal suffrage. * * A blind spirit of pride has been developed in our proletaires, and they have been led to think that they could settle the highest social questions without any serious study. The southern population of Western Europe have been much less tainted by evil. The resistance of Catholicism has sheltered them against the metaphysical influence of Protestantism and Deism. But reading negative books begins to spread the spirit even there."

§ 219. One remedy alone exists, and that is the creation of a dictator, who, armed with a positive law of inexorable precision and universal application, controls not merely society, but thought. This scheme, it is hardly necessary to say, is as fatal to intellectual growth as it is to moral agency and civil freedom. We may, then, well pause to apply to the genius of positivism that magnificent reply, which Schiller gives us, as addressed by the Marquis von Posa to Philip II. :—

PHILIP. (*Something in the way in which Comte complacently turns to the south of Europe.*) Look
Upon my Spain. Do you not see that here
Blooms happiness beneath unclouded peace?
This rest to Flanders I would now extend.

MARQUIS.

A churchyard's rest! And you yet would hope
To end what you have now begun; you hope
To check the upward growth of Christendom,
The universal spring-tide to restrain
That all the world would freshen! You would stand
Alone in Europe; you would cast yourself
Under the wheel of that sublime decree
That orders all things onward; you would seize
With human arm upon its spokes!
* * But no!
Nature herself forbids it! She is built
On freedom, and from it her opulence
Is drawn.
And He, the world's great Architect,
Rather than see man's liberty destroyed,
Permits the hosts of sin awhile to rage.
Grandly He sits behind vice-regent laws,—
He, the great Master-workman; and those laws,
But not Himself, the blinded skeptic sees,
And cries "O laws, be our divinity!"
And see! This skeptic's blasphemy speaks more
To His great praise than e'en the Christian's psalm.*

---

* Schiller, Don Carlos, act ii., scene x. I have given in the text rather a paraphrase than a translation. The original stands thus;—

PHILIP.

Sehet
In meinem Spanien euch um. Hier blüht

It is in this that we may see the inconsistency of positivism with human liberty and progress.

d[1]. *The religious sanctions of positivism are inadequate.*

a[2]. *In what these sanctions consist.*

§ 220. In his "Catéchisme de la Religion Positive,"* a

Des Bürgers Glück in nie bewölktem Frieden;
Und *diese* Ruhe gönn' ich den Flamändern.

MARQUIS, (schnell.)

Die Ruhe eines Kirchhofs! Und Sie hoffen
Zu endigen, was sie begannen; hoffen
Der Christenheit gezeitigte Verwandlung,
Den allgemeinem Frühling aufzuhalten,
Der die Gestatt der welt verjungt? Sie wollen
Allein in ganz Europa; sich dem Rade
Des Weltverhängnisses, das unaufhaltsam
In vollem Laufe vollt, engegen werfen?
Mit menschenarm in seine Speichen fallen?
Sie werden nicht! * * *
Sehen Sie sich um
In seiner herrlichen Natur! Auf Freiheit
Ist se gegründet—und wie reich ist sie
Durch Freiheit! * * *
Er—der Freiheit
Entzückende Erscheinung nicht zu stören—
Er lässt des Uebels grauenvolles Herr
In seinem Welt all lieber toben—ihn
Den Küntzler, wird man nicht gewahr, bescheiden
Verhüllt er sich in ewige Gesetze;
Die sieht der Freigeist, doch nicht ihn. Wozu
Ein Gott? sagt er; die Welt ist sich genug!
Und keines Christen Andacht hat ihn mehr
Als dieses Freigeists Lästerung gepriesen.

* The translation used in the text is by Mr. Congreve. London: John Chapman, 1858.

work not published by him until his maturer years, Comte brings before us a system of religion which he considers as a requisite appendage to the code of economical law he previously promulged. His position, when he conceived this scheme, was greatly changed from what it was when his lectures were planned. Then he was poor, friendless, obscure, and solitary. Now he has affluence at his command; he has many friends who are capable both of appreciating and of rewarding his services; he is at the head of a numerous school of enthusiastic disciples; his genius is acknowledged even where his doctrines are the most condemned; and he has established a home of his own, at the head of which stands a lady who, however unreconcilable with Christian ethics may have been her connection with him, devotes powers of fascination, almost unrivaled, to the object of making that home happy.* The

* Comte has made his relations to Madame Clotilde de Vaux public property by introducing them into the mythology of which he is the centre. The most devout worshiper of the Olympian gods could not speak of their domestic alliances with a more delicate reverence than does the founder of positivism when speaking of her, who, though entering for a time into his home, passed from thence to the throne before which all men are to bow. Greater himself than Numa Pompilius, inasmuch as the laws which regulate mind are higher than those which regulate matter, she, "the holy Clotilde," the companion of his solitude and reinvigorator of his philosophy, rises above the nymph Egeria, and unites the three anomalous attributes of being "his objective daughter," "his subjective mother," and "the best personification of the Supreme Being." Mormonism cannot surpass this in its grotesque sacrilegiousness; Mormonism, in its spiritual wifedoms, scarcely gives us anything worse than the rela-

austere philosopher, under this soothing influence, found a new sphere open to him which required a new code of laws for its government. Sensibility to the beautiful and the re-

---

tions which are covered with this mythological veil. Of this "angelic impulse that commanded his second life," this "incomparable angel," as he thinks proper to call her, we know but little more than that she was a married woman and a novelist, and that by some process which is not defined, she had, when she met Comte, got rid of her husband, and attained what the philosopher calls an "irreproachable moral freedom." Comte, who had previously formed a marriage of convenience, the object of which was to rescue him from immediate want, and having now, not very generously, when his circumstances made him independent, also got rid of his wife, is circulating through the community in the like "irreproachable moral freedom," when he encounters Madame de Vaux. Disengaged as each is, and attracted by "the sad conformity of their domestic relations," the philosopher and the sentimentalist find that the one is the complement of the other, and that the two, by the necessities of nature, form but one. They unite, enter together into "a holy home," maintaining what he calls an objective union, until, by an interchange of elements, he learns love and she positivism; he becomes sentimental and she strong-minded. After this union of a year she dies, or rather, to speak the language of positivism, passes to "her glorious subjective eternity" from "her sad objective existence." Now, all this would be as irrelevant here as it appears at first sight inconsistent with so grave a topic, were it not that Comte makes these relations the basis of the theology of positivism as much as were the relations of Jupiter, of Juno, and of Venus, made the basis of the mythology which directed the foundation of ancient Rome. The future Æneas of positivism, who seeks to colonize it on an inhospitable shore, will have to rely on the softening influence of this high priestess of love to modify the sterner influences and principles fined; reverence for the sublime; affection for the lovely,—these he discovered to be conservative as well as recuperative elements which it was desirable to organize and cultivate. There must be an ecclesiasticism erected to form the trellis to train up one class of sentiments; there is to be a system of family sacraments in like manner to train another class. This training, it is true, was not to be for *heaven*, but for *earth*. The plants which it is to cultivate are to be serial, not perennial; they are to bloom for this life alone, and then to be forever buried in the grave. But it is no small tribute to the importance of religion, and to the universal craving of man for an object of worship, that the chief apostle of modern atheism should find it necessary to his system to create an imitation god in order to supply this craving and satisfy these orphaned affections. Women who have become deranged from the loss of their offspring, we have been lately told, have found solace, under the skillful management of the psychological physician, in infants belonging to others which have been placed in their arms. In this we have proof of a mother's love, and of her sense of loss of the thing loved. The great reconstructer of society in our own time has borne witness to analogous truths in his attempts to substitute a sham for a real divinity. He

---

which, before that time, controlled the great Chief Priest of humanity. Comte himself confesses this in one of his addresses to his disciples. "I have just completed," he says, "the principal part of my religious structure, and the decisive little work *in which the subjective participation of my holy, eternal companion is already unanimously recognized.* * * * *It is for this reason that I shall always repudiate the stupid material economy which would deprive me of a powerful spiritual assistance.*"

has thus attested not only man's craving for, but his orphanage from God.

The new faith, which is to form the theology of positivism, and which is set forth in the catechism before us, involves the denial of the existence both of God and of the human soul. In order, however, to develop the qualities of reverence and subordination to the Infinite and Absolute—qualities which Comte now discovers to be important to the healthy growth of the race—certain fictions are to be presented to the inquirer, not as real food, but as corals with which to promote philosophical dentition. The articles in this creed are somewhat as follows:—

A "Great Spirit," which is the aggregate of all humanity, being an absorption of "the continuous succession of generations." Each "true servant of humanity" (of the fate of others not falling under the bounds of positive fidelity we are not informed) "has two forms of existence." The first of these is that of conscious individuality, which is what precedes death. The second begins after death, and is a state of entire unconsciousness. The soul survives only in the "heart and intellect of others." It is no longer, however, an "entity" as to itself, but is only a memory retained by society. It is a shadow without a substance. It forms, however, in connection with its associates, the "Great Spirit," which is the aggregation of the memories of the great dead as marshaled in the perceptions of the living. It is here that we are to find at once the object of supreme worship and the motive for an earnest probation.

But in what way is this worship to be conducted and this probation to be made available? The answer is given with a detailed and inexorable precision, which leaves to the disciple of positivism not even ritual discretion. There are to be two forms of worship, the public and the private. Of these, the latter is the chief, and is to be "addressed to women;" the former the subordinate, and is to be addressed "to humanity." "The affective sex"—for it is in this light, and not that of strong-mindedness, that woman is placed in order to become the object of positivist worship—"is naturally the most perfect representation of humanity, and at the same time her principal minister." "The mother, the wife, the daughter, must in our worship * * * develop in us respectively—the mother, veneration; the wife, attachment; the daughter, kindness." Women are to reciprocate this worship by adding to it that of their husbands and sons.

§ 221. Among the ordinances thus established, were nine social sacraments. These are:—

"Presentation," an equivalent to baptism.

"Initiation," commemorating the passage of the child from his mother's hands to those of the "priesthood," in whom is vested the charge over public education.

"Admission," by which the disciple "is authorized to serve humanity," though as to what this means we have no further information.

"Destination," which is fixed at the age of twenty-eight, until which period the particular line of duty of the candidate is to remain undetermined, a system which we apprehend would not be very acceptable among our American pioneers.

"Marriage," which men cannot enter into until they are twenty-eight, nor women until they are twenty-one.

"Maturity," which is to indicate and solemnize the arrival of a full intellectual and physical development, and which is fixed at forty-two.

"Retirement," which is placed at sixty-three, when the pupil, for such he always remains, being but an automaton member of this vast and remorseless social mechanism, is to go into a seclusion similar to that of the monastery, surrendering his property, except what is enough for his mere personal wants.

"Transformation," which is a substitute for the Romish extreme unction, in which the positivist "Priesthood mingles the regrets of society with the tears of the family of the deceased, and shows that it has a just appreciation of the life that is ended. It first secures, when possible, compensation for errors committed, and then it generally holds out the hope of subjective incorporation."

"Incorporation," which represents the Romish canonization, and which takes place seven years after death, when "a solemn judgment, *an idea*," (not a reality, for immortality is a mere fiction,) "*which, in its germ, sociocracy borrows from theocracy, finally decides the lot of each.*"

In the positivist ritual, everything in the shape of the old calendar is to be uprooted, with the exception of the days of the week, whose names are to be retained rather as indicating the servitude of the past than of conciliating its prejudices. There are to be thirteen monthly festivals, each of which commemorates either the supreme humanity itself, or some of its component items, including "women, or the moral Providence of the race;" "the conjugal union," which is to be personified as a sub-god; and the "collective dead," or at least such of them as have been incorporated in the essence of humanity. Not only are the services of the monthly festivals thus prescribed, but in those of each week the topics of contemplation and adoration are arbitrarily and finally determined. And even as to the gestures to be used in repeating the formulas of faith, there is to be no discretion. When this is done, the worshiper is to "place the hands in succession on the three chief organs—those of love, order, and progress."

So with regard to ecclesiastical architecture and symbolism. Modern philosophy will never be able to taunt Christian ecclesiasticism with finicalness, when the directory of the great founder of positivism is kept in view. Entertaining no doubt that the Romish Church would gradually pass into his school, Comte, in condescension to the inconvenience which would arise from erecting a large number of new temples after his peculiar plan, agreed that the "old churches, in proportion as they fall into disuse," should be accepted and employed by the positivist priesthood. This, however, ought not to be long. The earliest practical time should be chosen to erect new temples, concerning which certain positive directions were laid down. They must "orientate," if a term may be borrowed from modern ecclesiology, toward Paris, which is the metropolis of humanity, and which, therefore, as humanity with the positivist is God, is the heaven toward which the worshiper should turn. A "sacred wood" is to surround the temples, and in each there is to be placed, as "the symbol of our goddess," "a woman of thirty, with her son in her arms." Even the trappings of the religious processions are regulated. Banners are to be carried, on the "white sides of which" "will be the holy image;" "on their green, the sacred formula of positivism."

The positivist priesthood is endowed with power greater than even Hildebrand claimed for the pontifical hierarchy. The priests, of whom for the western world there are to be twenty thousand, are, each in his special sphere, though in subordination to the central high priest, to control the education, to administer the sacraments, and to promulgate the ethics, by which the minds of their particular parishioners are to be influenced and their conduct controlled. The priests are to have the government of the public treasury, disbursing it as they think fit. Marriage with the priest is obligatory, though like all other positivists, he cannot marry before twenty-eight, and then only once. The ultimate control of this enormous and absolute sacerdotalism is a high priest, whose see is to be Paris.

But while this vast authority is thus vested in the positivist hierarchy, the founder of the system did not let it pass from his hands until he had prescribed what course was to be taken in respect to every contingency that fell within his contemplation. Even the method of study was regulated by a standard which was to be universally applied to the dull as well as to the brilliant, to the poet as well as the philosopher. The boy, after receiving the sacrament of initiation, is to go to the "school adjoining the Temple of Humanity, there to hear from the priesthood perhaps one or two lectures on the doctrine of positivism." He is then to undergo a novitiate of seven years, each of which is to have its specific topic, following, it seems, from "geometry up to morals," "the objective ascent which it took humanity so many centuries to accomplish." And then with one of those arbitrary dicta which more than anything else show at once the sublime self-reliance and the profound psychological ignorance which marked the founder of positivism, we have it announced, "during this scientific preparation the learner will be monotheistic"—in adolescence pantheistic, in maturity atheistic. Never did Philip II. with the Moriscoes, or Louis XIV. with the Huguenots, ever attempt so arbitrary a decree. The disciple is not to *become* a believer; he *is* one. The initiation of an unconscious infant into the positive Church is to work upon him effects which the most extreme Christian sacramentarian never ascribed to baptism. The infant is declared not merely to be hypothetically and ecclesiastically a believer of the views which positivism prescribes for him, but to be so actually and potentially. He is not expected to be converted to them; the supreme and infallible authority pronounces him to hold them without the choice of conversion. If he do not, he is either in an abnormal condition, requiring medical treatment, or in a state of moral treason, requiring penal discipline.

b^2. Their inadequacy.

a^3. In destroying human liberty.

§ 222. No diversity of tastes or talents is permitted. Watt would not begin the study of mechanics until his eighteenth year, and must leave it finally six months after for poetry; Shakspeare, after six months at poetry, must be for six years absorbed in the exact sciences.

Nor could there be *belief*, as there could be no *faith.* The positivist creed is not propounded to be studied and accepted; it is declared to be a part of the constitution of all men, as to which there can be no inquiry.* In the sciences, as well as in trade, there will be no competition, and hence no progress. Men will move forward, not in the eager race of a free rivalry, but as shackled slaves, with down-cast faces and sluggish limbs, each treading to the same beat. No explorer would press ahead of his fellows to the centre of the Arctic ice; no adventurer push singly forward among untrodden wastes or barbarous realms; no mechanic concentrate the life-energies of an acute and sagacious intellect to the consideration of a single point, which, however minute, might be necessary to the perfection of some great and essential improvement.

§ 223. b^3. *They substitute for a faith which, if false, is believed to be real, one which, if real, is believed to be false.*

It substitutes, in other words, for a believed truth, a confessed sham. What effect can playing at church have when all know the thing is but play, unless to impress the earnest with a mocking and indignant contempt, and the light with a withering skepticism? What can produce a more profound sense of unreality than the consciousness that we are worshiping a Deity who is nothing but our own memory of the dead; who is avowedly a mere doll-providence, made and dressed for us by the priest, and handed to us to be

---

* See here Sir W. Hamilton's remarks, quoted *ante*, § 216.

pressed to the breast and nursed, in order to satisfy the agonizing craving for the Infinitely Lovely and Great, for which the bereaved soul pants with such tremendous reality? What can so sicken and crush the heart, way-sore and sighing for a peace to come in an eternal home where there will be no more worldliness, to be turned to gaze, not at the calm heights and sanctified hosts of Jerusalem the sacred, but to the labyrinths and intrigues of Paris the vain?

c³. They dwarf the human by degrading the divine.

§ 224. The prisoner, cramped for years in a cell where his arms cannot be raised or his frame stretched, finds his muscles shrunk and his stature lessened. The soul expands or contracts with the object of its worship. Let that object be declared perfect, immutable, omnipotent, and the soul rises upward to it by an infinitude of steps. As it ascends, and finds the infinitude before it undiminished by the infinitude it has passed, it becomes humbler as it becomes greater, more reverent and loving as it becomes more sublime. But the positivist's divinity claims no such infinite and soul-elevating attributes. It is not a reality, but a memory. It is but a blurred and faded picture of a procession of such of our fellow-mortals as the priesthood permits to be commemorated.

d³. They establish an absolute hierarchy, of all forms of government the most injurious.

§ 225. Nothing, we may now be well permitted to assume, is so open to corruption, is so likely to reach and embitter even the most secret fountains of human happiness, and to trample on the conscience as well as the body, as a priesthood invested with unchecked powers. That such powers, beyond any precedent, are vested in the positivist hierarchy, will be seen on noticing the following points:—

They have an arbitrary control over the treasury.

They are the sole expounders of a law which claims to reach all points of conduct, and which pretends, not merely to be a statute, to be obeyed when announced, but to be a part of each man's internal constitution, obedience to which, announced or unannounced, is to be exacted under the severest penalties.

They create, by consecrating the dead, at once the God to be worshiped, and the heaven to be sought.

They are the sole educators of the people, and the supreme task-masters who are to determine at what, where, and how each man is to work.

d. Positivism as modified by Mr. Buckle.

§ 226. Mr. Buckle, so far as we can draw his views as a system from the very remarkable volume which is now the only avowed product of his pen,* accepts and teaches Comte's theory of positive law with the following modifications:—

Comte, at least in his late writings, insists that ecclesiastical authority and a derivative creed, are essential to complete social development. Mr. Buckle considers the first always mischievous, and declares that no religion is of value that is not the spontaneous product of the believer's intel-

---

* History of Civilization in England. By Henry Thomas Buckle. Vol. i. From the second London edition. New York: D. Appleton & Co., 1858.

lect. The former makes the sanction of religion external and prescriptive; the latter makes it subjective and voluntary. Each is strongly tinged by his national ties—the first admiring France and Roman Catholicism, the latter England and Protestantism, as the better types of political and ecclesiastical development. Each rejects a divine revelation, but they differ in their proposed substitute—the one providing a creed to be announced by an absolute hierarchy, the latter a sentiment to be evolved by the believer himself.

Comte recognizes a variety of agencies by which antecedents are connected with sequences; Mr. Buckle but one, intellect; though in this respect, as will presently be seen, his incidental teaching differs widely from his direct.

Comte's basis for induction includes almost every branch of human knowledge, except metaphysics and psychology, which he rejects; Mr. Buckle avowedly, at least, confines himself to statistics.

Mr. Buckle's argument, when analyzed, falls into the following positions:—

The actions of men are produced, not by their volitions, but by their antecedents.

These antecedents, which in this sense may be treated as law, are to be collected from statistics.

The philosophical office of history, therefore, is to classify these statistics so as to be able to announce these laws.

These points may be considered in the above order, taking *first* that which treats human action as dependent, not on volition, but on antecedents.

Now here we must not confound Mr. Buckle's position with that of the necessitarians, in the controversy just noticed.* The last-mentioned thinkers consider the necessity acting on man to be *moral*, not *material*. The forces that bear on him, they hold to be very different from those which bear on matter. To man there always remains *choice*. He yields, often, it is true, as an inferior to his superior's influence, but always voluntarily. On the other hand, Mr. Buckle makes mind the subject of law in the same sense as is matter. Freedom of will he utterly and vehemently rejects. The position that consciousness proves this freedom, he meets by denying the competency of consciousness to speak on the subject at all. He admits, it is true, that consciousness thus speaks, but he declares that consciousness is not trustworthy. But is not this objection untenable from its very generality, in the same way that a similar objection to a witness in a common law court would at once be overruled by the judge on the ground that it indicates no specific disability? "I object to consciousness as a witness," says Mr. Buckle, "because it is liable to err." But as this is an objection to *all* testimony, it is an objection to *no* testimony. The unimpeached testimony of concurrent consciousness can no more be rejected on this ground than can the unimpeached testimony of concurrent by-standers, on the ground of a similar liability to error.

Again, the fallacy of this position may be demonstrated through its consequences. If law acts on mind as on matter, why is the man who shoots another with a gun any more culpable than the gun itself? The Duke of Wellington

* See *ante*, § 114.

once told a story, as illustrating the distinction between moral and physical courage, of a soldier who was trembling on the battle-field. "You are afraid," said one of his comrades. "If you were half as much so," was the reply, "you would long since have run away." The more wary of the positivist philosophers, as they stand trembling over this very danger, might well apply the same remark to the dashing young volunteer who prances so gaily up to a mine so fatal. Did he know as much, he would be as timid as themselves in attempting to reconcile morality with positivism. But he does not, and he achieves the result by throwing morality overboard altogether. It is of no account, he substantially tells us; it is only a superannuated agency, incapable of moving itself, and therefore of moving others. Mankind in the aggregate, he announces, are not in the least affected by moral principles; why then trouble ourselves about them? Morals are stationary; and hence, like a fort which when once passed by an invading fleet, only wastes its powder by firing its guns; morality may be permitted to discharge the slow thunder of its oracles without exciting more than the smiles of that philosophy which has passed out of its reach. *Intellect* is now the only motive power of the human race; *morals* have long since been laid on one side.

§ 227. Now in one sense, Mr. Buckle is right in his position, though it is a sense fatal to his whole theory. Morals, it is true, are stationary; but they are stationary in the same way as the water-tanks which are placed along a railway. They are, it is true, permanent, and are supplied by one and the same element. They nevertheless are essential to the motive energy of the train. Intellect is in this sense the mere conduit of morals. It resorts to them for a force, and at its best serves merely as the agent, or acts as the conductor, by which that force is applied. Hence it is that the fact that morals are "stationary," is no reason why they do not influence mankind. For they are the eternal and immutable principles of right and wrong, applying themselves to each juncture with specific and appropriate energy, pronouncing their decision on each new combination of circumstances in the same way that the common law, while its dogmas remain the same, gives its impulse to, and pronounces its judgment on, each contingency that arises. Thus the common law, from its stationary base, supplies the energies by which at one time the watchfulness of the sailor is sharpened, at another the skill of the ship-builder refined, at another the zeal of the mechanic stimulated. It says to the capitalist, "You I hold responsible for your employees' negligence;" to the machinist, "you for your machine's defects." So it is with morals. While stationary, they pronounce from time to time decrees on each issue that arises in the educationary advance of our race. Thus toleration of the opinions of others is an eternal principle of morals, and is written in the New Testament; and yet its application to the successive stages of human history has been from time to time delayed, until those stages require its action. First, it is limited to mere oral divergencies, guaranteeing, in all matters not touching the peace of civil society, freedom of speech. Then, as the printing-press is introduced, it imposes on the printer a range of duties specially belonging to his office, and it imposes on government another range. So it is with the precept to love our neighbor as ourselves, which develops a series of progressive duties as our relations expand; giving us one class of obligations to the family, and others to each near social or political interest that may from time to time spring up; *e.g.* children over-worked in factories, the outcasts of a large city, the victims of pestilence or oppression in a foreign land. Then again these duties are pushed on, as obstacles arising from ignorance cease to exist, giving us, for instance, the successive ameliorations of the penal code, arising from the removal of the once prevalent conviction of the political necessity of severe punishments. So with regard to imprisonment for debt.*

Now in cases such as these, the fact that "morality is stationary," does not diminish either the energy of its motive power, or the precision with which it decides each issue that successively advances. So it is with the doctrinal truths of the New Testament. They are absolute and immutable. They cannot "develop." They act on the human character, however, with a power wonderfully expansive and adaptative. They may be listened to a thousand times without making any impression. Then often suddenly and without any assignable cause, they become illuminated with an awful and alarming meaning. The soul is agitated to its centre by this strange phenomenon,—truths at once stationary and yet so inexorably aggressive. Then comes conviction, and then, in God's pleasure, conversion. But the process does not stop here. The work of sanctification is progressive. The Christian discovers new beauties each

---

* See *ante*, § 100.

day in those stationary truths.* Perhaps his last breath may testify that even his dying hour revealed in them a new depth and fullness. For the oracles of God, immutable and perfect as they be, speak not in one complete burst of symphony, at a single swell possessing and entrancing the soul with their entire melody, but in a series of notes, unequal,

---

* Dean Trench illustrates this point very beautifully in his "Hulsean Lecture on the Development of Scripture." Take the following extract:—"Truth, once given, has only gradually revealed itself; how the history of the Church, the difficulties, the trials, the struggles, the temptations in which it has been involved, have interpreted it to its own records, brought out their latent significance, and caused it to discover all which in them it had; how there was much written for it there as in sympathetic ink, invisible for a season, yet ready to flash out in lines and characters of light, whenever the appointed day and hour had arrived. So that in this way the Scripture has been to the Church as their garments to the children of Israel, which, during all the years of their pilgrimage in the desert, waxed not old, yea, according to rabbinical tradition, kept pace and measure with their bodies, growing with their growth, fitting the man as they had fitted the child, and this, until the forty years of their sojourn in the wilderness had expired. Or, to use another comparison which may help to illustrate our meaning: Holy Scripture thus progressively unfolding what it contains, might be likened fitly to some magnificent landscape on which the sun is gradually rising, and ever as it rises is bringing out one headland into light and prominence, and then another; anon kindling the glory-smitten summit of some far mountain, and presently lighting up the recesses of some near valley which had hitherto abided in gloom, and so traveling on till nothing remains in shadow, no nook nor corner hid from the light and heat of it, but the whole prospect stands out in the clearness and splendor of the brightest noon."

sometimes almost inarticulate, often not interpreted till long after, not till perhaps some great sorrow or trial required their aid. In this view, morality, as well as religion, may be likened to an engine stationed at a mountain-top to draw up a train from below. Progress is *through* it, *to* it. The traveler in the valley at first sees it not, as he finds himself gliding upward on the inclined plane. Gradually, however, as he approaches, and as trees and rocks are passed, the motive power grows into view. So it is with stationary truths of religion and ethics. They draw us to themselves, and as they draw, they unfold, not because they come nearer to us, but because we get nearer to them.

§ 228. The second position on which Mr. Buckle relies is, that general laws governing human volition are to be discovered from statistical observation.

This may be illustrated as follows:—In a particular city there were twenty burglaries year before last; there were twenty-one last year; there will be twenty-two the next. If a man, therefore, is brought up charged with this crime, we ought to say to him, "My friend, I am sorry that the lot happened to fall on you, though as it was necessary it should fall on some one in order to make up our requisite number of burglars, you are not to blame yourself."

Now it is enough for the present, to notice one fatal flaw in this theory of the power of statistics to resolve the contingencies of the future. It rests upon what is popularly called the doctrine of chances; and it assumes that as such a crime must necessarily occur, the event overrules, when it does occur, the free will of the agent. Now it will require but a moment's glance to show the absurdity of this. One hundred balls are placed in a bag. One is white, the others black. Now when the bag is shaken so that a particular ball drops out, the result is not chance, but the peculiar combination of forces on the ball that drops. If the balls be replaced in exactly the same position, and the bag be shaken exactly in the same way, then precisely the same ball will be thrown out again. There is no "chance" at all that any given ball, unacted on by such special impulses, will be thrown out once in a given number of times. So there is no "chance" that one out of a given number of innocent men will commit the above-mentioned burglary. The one who commits it will be he who is guided to the act by the forces of his own will.

Take also the position that each burglary that is committed diminishes the probability of a second, there being a less number thus required to make up the requisite average. Now it is true, that if out of the bag we take ten of the black balls, the "chances" against the white are now eighty-nine to one, instead of, as before, ninety-nine to one. When the whole of the ninety-nine black balls are taken out, then we may be sure that the white ball will come next. But if we keep the proportions of the balls the same, by returning to the bag those drawn out, then we may draw black balls forever, without increasing the probability of drawing the white. So when the number of white balls is indefinite, then no calculation can be made at all. Yet it is on such a calculation that Mr. Buckle rests when he makes the conduct of one individual to be governed by the question, whether or no by the conduct of others the requisite annual quota of crime has been contributed by the community at large.

Mr. Buckle's last point is drawn from the two former, and is that which more particularly concerns his credit as a historian. The philosophical office of history, he holds, is so to classify the objective phenomena which make up human conduct as to be able to exhibit the laws by which moral agency is governed. No history is trustworthy which introduces other factors than this into its calculation.

Now I may remark that this destroys Mr. Buckle's own sources of information. All prior historians, he tells us, are in error, because they mixed up *volition* with *phenomena*. And yet, as Mr. Buckle's very copious notes abundantly show, it is from these prior historians that he derives almost his whole material. But, after all, *phenomena*—in other words, what a man *does*—form a very imperfect index to human character. Let us take that period, for instance, in Louis Napoleon's life, in which he landed at Boulogne, with a small squad of amateur soldiers and a tame eagle, which was to light upon the banner of the expectant emperor in such a way as to excite the superstition and awaken the enthusiasm of the French. Suppose death had followed this adventure, would not the phenomenal historian pronounce this most reticent, subtle, and profound of statesmen, to be a weak and babbling charlatan?

One of the results of this erroneous and low method of generalization has been already noticed.* It substitutes the memoranda of passengers, as to the time of arriving of

* See *ante*, § 213.

particular trains, for the time-table issued by the supreme hand that directs the motive power. The former are framed from loose notes drawn by memory from data which an accident or detention would overthrow; the latter controls the results rather than is controlled by them, and approaches to perfection as the authority that promulgates it approaches constancy and omnipotence. Now Mr. Buckle, in making up his philosophy, not only confines himself to the merely observational sources of information, but among these he rejects all that are psychological, or are based on personal experience, and takes merely those that arise from outside human calculation. How unreliable his conclusions become, we can judge by taking a proposition which he exhibits with the greatest complacency, as forming one of the most important of the discoveries of the new philosophy: "The number of marriages annually contracted," he tells us, "is determined, *not by the temper and wishes of individuals*, but by large general facts, over which individuals can exercise no authority. * * *Instead of having any connection with personal feelings*, they are simply regulated by the average earnings of the great mass of the people: so that this immense social and religious institution *is not only swayed, but is completely controlled, by the price of food and by the rate of wages.*"* Here he leaves out, (1) Divine appointment, and (2) human inclination; the latter involving the most potent of passions — affection, love, sexual instinct, desire for home, and hope of offspring.

The specific blunders of Mr. Buckle on questions of fact,

* Buckle's Hist. of Civ., vol. i. p. 23; Appleton's ed.

are almost numberless. Ordinarily speaking, such errors might be passed by with but a slight notice. With him, however, mistakes of "statistics" become perversions of principle. He relies for his laws on his facts. How careless he is in collecting the latter, will be seen from the following instances:—

*a*¹. "All the great sculptors come from Spain and Italy."* Now except Canova, no great sculptors came from Italy, and Spain is destitute of this kind of genius. Thorwaldsen, Chantrey, Crawford, Powers, Danneker, are of northern blood.

*b*¹. The French Calvinistic ministers "were insignificant priests." Mr. Buckle can find no one of them entitled to historical notice. So, however, do not think the historians of France. Among these "priests" we find some of the most potent intellects of the age, *e.g.* Daniel Chamier, whose discussion with Father Cotton, before Henry IV., is still a master-piece of controversial skill; and Samuel Bochart, of whom Bayle (good authority with Mr. Buckle) says: "He was one of the most learned men in the world. But his knowledge, vast as it was, was not his principal quality; he had a modesty infinitely more estimable than all his science. So he enjoyed his glory in complete tranquillity." With these rank Pierre Dumoulin, Andrew Rivet, David Blondel, Drelincourt, Daillé, P. du Bosc, Ancillon, and Claude, and in later days Vinet, Monod, and D'Aubigné. With equal narrowness of information, Mr. Buckle excludes from the lead-

* This is used as a main support of a law of climate.

ing minds of Scotland, in the present century, Chalmers, Reid, and Campbell.

c[1]. Sir Thomas Brown began, according to Mr. Buckle, who finds in this another "law," a believer in witches and "developed" into a disbeliever. In point of fact, the truth is just the reverse.

d[1]. Owen is ranked with "Chillingworth and Hales," and "Hobbes and Glanville," as enforcing the same contempt for tradition, and the same resolution to scorn the High-Church yoke. This is a most remarkable jumble. Owen was an intolerant Calvinist; Hales the loosest of Armenians. Hales was promoted by Laud; Owen ejected by Laud's successors. In one thing, however, they would unite, and that is an indignant surprise at being placed in the same category with "Hobbes and Glanville."

e[1]. This century is declared to have presented nothing in "the English tongue, in any department of theological scholarship, which is of value, and makes a mark on the age." For this, Theodore Parker is cited, as the "high authority;" thus disposing of Chalmers, Coleridge, Campbell, Whately, McCosh, Buchanan, Trench, Arnold, Stuart, Hodge, and Dwight. Then comes a dashing assertion as to the general increase of skepticism, for which assertion, so far as concerns the United States, we have the single authority of "Combe's Notes on the United States."*

f[1]. "The historical value of the writings of Moses is abandoned by all enlightened men, even among the clergy themselves." To support this absurdly erroneous assertion, we

---

* As to the incorrectness of this, see *ante*, § 206, 209, 210.

are pointed to two cases: Dr. Arnold, who reconsidered the whole question before the close of his life, and Mr. Baden Powell, who, latitudinarian though he be, is an accredited professor in Oxford, and has prepared for the Cyclopedia of Dr. Kitto (himself irreproachably orthodox) a series of papers for the purpose of accommodating the Mosaic record to the present condition of science. That he has done this with a sufficient regard to the plenary inspiration of the text, is not pretended. And yet Mr. Powell, even in the approach he makes to Mr. Buckle's views, is repudiated by almost the entire Christian Church. It may be safely said that among the many thousand clergy of orthodox creeds, there will not be one who confesses an acquiescence in Mr. Buckle's views.

*g*¹. "That the system of morals propounded in the New Testament contained no maxim which had not been previously enunciated, and that some of the most beautiful passages in the apostolic writings are quotations from Pagan authors, is well known to every scholar. * * To assert that Christianity communicated to man moral truths previously unknown, argues, on the part of the asserter, either *gross ignorance or wilful fraud.*" Now here is a fair specimen of Mr. Buckle's accuracy and temper. The only quotations in the apostolic writings from "Pagan authors," are Acts xvii. 28, "For we are also his offspring;" 1 Cor. xv. 33, "Evil communications corrupt good manners;" and Tit. i. 12, "The Cretians are always liars." Now each of these quotations was used by St. Paul as an *argumentum ad hominem*, for the purpose of showing that even his adversaries would concede a preliminary point in his argument, and neither is distinguished by any particular literary beauty. Mr. Buckle may excuse his blunder in this respect by his want of biblical knowledge, but this certainly will not excuse the temper with which he denounces those who do not agree with him.

h^1. "Not only Necker, but also Rousseau, were born in Geneva, and drew their earliest ideas from that great nursery of the Calvinistic theology." Necker, we are told, was "notoriously a rigid Calvinist," and so, we are to presume, was Rousseau. Now the ideas which Necker drew from Geneva were anything but rigidly Calvinistic; and Geneva, instead of then being the "nursery" of Calvinism, was its grave. Mr. Buckle is fond of quoting from D'Alembert, and cites him profusely. Had D'Alembert been consulted on this occasion, Mr. Buckle would have learned, from no less accessible and obvious an article than that on Geneva in the French Encyclopédie, that "all the religion that many of the ministers of Geneva have is a complete Socinianism, rejecting everything called mystery, and supposing that the first principle of a true religion is to propose nothing to be received as a matter of faith which strikes against reason." Necker was born in 1732. The Encyclopédie was prepared in 1745–52, at the very time Necker was drawing his "earliest ideas." The "company of pastors," by whom vacancies in the pastoral charges were filled, then avowedly made their appointments from rationalists. Voltaire tells us that in Geneva, at this time, he did not know a single Calvinist. Yet the "rigid Calvinism" of Geneva, at this time, is a "fact" which is an essential item in the calculations by which one of Mr. Buckle's most important laws is educed.

CHAPTER III.

FATALISM.

§ 229. THIS topic, in its general bearings, is a natural sequence of that just considered, as well as of those to be presently noticed. If we are controlled by a system of positive law, general as well as specific, such as holds the follower of Comte; if we are but constituent members in one great aggregate total of cosmical life, without the capacity of motion except in obedience to the common impulse, as holds the pantheist; if we are the mere evolutions or scintillations of an organic growth, as hold the advocates of physiological development, then we are the subjects of an arbitrary code, natural or supernatural, which excludes the agency of either special providence or individual will. It is proposed, however, in the present chapter, to consider fatalism as a distinct scheme of unbelief, separate from the several theories in which it is involved. In this view, let us notice,—

a. THE *a priori* PROBABILITY THAT THE SYSTEM WHICH AN ALL-WISE AND ALL-POWERFUL GOVERNOR WOULD ADOPT FOR THE MORAL EDUCATION OF CREATURES UNDER PROBATION WOULD BE A MIXED ONE OF GENERAL LAWS AND OF SPECIAL ADAPTATIONS.

§ 230. Let us take in view the given factors of a wise

and Divine Ruler on the one hand, and of man, in his present state, as a subject of probation, on the other. Let us imagine ourselves about to lay down a system of government for a colony of creatures, constructed like ourselves, on some distant planet. We see on the one hand, that it is important to cultivate in them habits of fixed industry, of patience, of energy, of social and domestic affection, of individual integrity. We see on the other hand, that it is equally important to generate in them submission under unexpected casualties,—hopefulness which a foreknowledge on their part of disappointments to come would destroy,—close dependence on and affection for the government that provides for them, so that the graces of humanity and of faith, might grow. How would we provide for this? The answer is, by a system of general laws; *e.g.* those of the seasons, which wheel round in their unvarying cycles, broken by special adaptations, such as those which particular rains, freshets, and tides, bring to bear on the husbandman's art.

Suppose that we had a system of general laws only, and those foreannounced. Not only the seasons, let us suppose, move on in their recognized order, but every rain by which a crop is to be washed away, every freshet by which a village is to be inundated, every season of peculiar benignity and fruitfulness, every blight which would render labor useless, is known beforehand. Where would we find that hardy industry which, in providing against the contingencies of disaster, and facing its reality, does so much to the development of the courage, the endurance, the self-reliance, the energy of our race? In those climates where we find the uniformity of the seasons most marked, either by a cold and rigid torpor, or by a regular and prodigal fructification, we shall observe the greatest lethargy and the most entire subordination of the spiritual and intellectual to the animal. But if in addition to this, misfortunes should move toward us equally heralded in advance, would not the paralysis be almost complete? Greatly indeed would present happiness be abridged, and present energy cramped, and present sorrow intensified, if the future were known. Who, in looking back at any of the great calamities which have struck him,—let him take the sharpest and most stunning shock of his life,—but will say, "had I known this, I never would have prepared that home; I never would have opened its door; I never would have entered at all on that train of business; I never could have enjoyed, even for a moment, sweet intercourse with that friend, had I seen the hearse that stood outside." Yet it is to this discipline that the heart owes its best training for immortality. If then, we are, even with our limited capacity, planning a training school for moral agents, conditioned as ourselves, would we rest the government of that school on a system of arbitrary, universal, all-penetrating, all-directing laws, and those laws to be preannounced?

§ 231. On the other hand, let us suppose that a government should be established in which no general laws are laid down, but in which each case is determined as it arises. Take, for instance, the *unexpectedness* of the action of such government, resulting in the inability of the subject to understand what measures to take to provide against the future. As an illustration of this, notice the condition of Rome under Tiberius, one scene in which is thus sketched by De Quincey :—

"At midnight an elderly gentleman suddenly sends round a message to a select party of noblemen, rouses them out of bed, and summons them instantly to his palace. Trembling for their lives from the suddenness of the summons, and from the unseasonable hour, and scarcely doubting that by some anonymous *delator* they have been implicated as parties to a conspiracy, they hurry to the palace—are received in portentous silence by the ushers and pages in attendance —are conducted to a saloon, where (as in everywhere else) the silence of night prevails, united with the silence of fear and whispering expectation. All are seated, all look at each other in ominous anxiety. Which is accuser? Which the accused? On whom shall their suspicion settle,—on whom their pity? All are silent—almost speechless—and even the current of their thoughts is frost-bound by fear. Suddenly the sound of a fiddle or a viol is caught from a distance—it swells upon the ear—the steps approach—and in another moment in rushes the elderly gentleman, grave and gloomy as his audience, but capering about in a frenzy of excitement. For half an hour he continues to perform all possible evolutions of caprioles, pirouettes, and other extravagant feats of activity, accompanying himself on the fiddle; and, at length, not having once looked at his guests, the elderly gentleman whirls out of the room in the same transport of emotion with which he entered it; the panic-struck visitors are requested by a slave to consider themselves as dismissed: they retire; resume their couches :—the nocturnal pageant has 'dislimned' and vanished; and on the following morning, were it not for their concurring testimonies, all would be disposed to take this interruption of their sleep for one of its most fantastic dreams. The elderly gentleman who figured in this delirious *pas seul*—who was he? He was Tiberius Cæsar, king of kings, and lord of the terraqueous globe."*

§ 232. Now what we would call for, *a priori*, to meet both these difficulties, is a government with laws enough in it to invoke energy and foresight, and with enough special direction in it to produce watchfulness and a sense of dependence on its Divine Head.†

Let us see, then, how far we find this system of government—this combination of general laws with special providences—carried out in the moral discipline of man. As to this point, there is, I apprehend, no difficulty. Upon the distant and general horizon the machinery of general laws moves like clock-work; *e.g.* the movements of the stars, the waxing and waning of the moon, with its consequent influence on the tides, the aggregate of rain falling in each year. But as we approach man, we become conscious of an atmosphere through which general laws cannot penetrate. It would seem as if moral agency was thus coated with an armor which defies the action of that inexorable code by which all the physical universe is enthralled. The nearer these general laws approach man, the more are they re-

---

* De Quincey's Cæsars, p. 129.

† See this question ably discussed in Bishop Potter's Sermon on the Immutability of Natural Laws; Phil. Lectures on Evidences, p. 127.

fracted and repelled. We cannot tell when any particular tide will rise to inundate the city docks, nor when a freshet will lift the river over the levee, nor when a premature frost will blight the crop. The closer we come to man, the more does the absolute yield to the fortuitous; *i.e.* to the *special* as distinguished from the *general* direction of God.*

§ 233. It would seem, therefore, that the government of the world is a mixed one of general laws and special adaptations.† The existence of the first element needs no proof. Skepticism almost uniformly asserts it, and Christianity finds no reason to meet it with a denial. The *second* proposition, however, that of a special providence, is met by the naturalist with a fierce hostility, and by the nominal Christian with practical unbelief. The following points may be noticed as serving to prove its existence.

§ 234. a^1. *God's constancy and dignity.*

If God cared enough for the world to create it, is it consistent with His infinite goodness and grandeur to suppose that when created He would desert it, and retire, like *le bon Dieu* of the French drama, to listen from the stage-box of an otiose and philosophic ease to the ceaseless wails of His own creatures struggling in agony before Him—seeking in their blindness the Infinite, and as they seek, falling, blinded as they are by a supernal malignant power, gashed and

---

* See *ante*, § 89, 129; *post*, § 241.

† Observe in this the remarkable analogy with the distinction between the common law and equity systems. "*Equity*," says Grotius, "*is the correction of that wherein the common law, by reason of its universality, is deficient.*"

wounded to the earth? "Can it be degrading for Him to act on that, however insignificant, which it did not degrade Him to create."*

§ 235. b^1. *His fatherhood.*

Heathen and Christian devotion unite in seeing in Him not merely the God, but the Father. Can we, in conformity with this conception, suppose Him to desert the home of His watchful care and love? "We ask of a father regard, in the first place, to the moral welfare of his children; we ask a rule and regimen which will contribute to form character, to ennoble sentiment, to develop self-control, and nerve with spiritual power. And we feel that this needs not only law, but the administration of law; not only rules, but influences; and not only these, too, but such changes, from time to time,

---

* Young's Mysteries of Good and Evil, p. 63.

"That which God has deigned to make, He will condescend to care for; and that which He has made in all its minutest details, He may, without derogation from His infinite majesty, continue to sustain and govern even in its least members and motions. The instance chosen by our Lord is among the most light and impalpable of all objects connected with the human frame. Yet, under the glass of the microscopic anatomist, the single hair presents wonders of structure and adaptation which no human hand can reproduce or imitate. Indeed, the further down we go into the interior recesses of nature, all invisible to the naked eye, the more amazing becomes the revelations of power, and skill, and goodness. So that the very antennæ of the fly that annoys our slumber, the dust of the downy fruit, and the volatile pollen of the lily or the rose, awaken new adoration of Him who is *maximus in minimis*, greatest in that which seems least." (*Alexander's Discourses*, p. 75; New York, 1858.)

that those rules can adapt themselves to emergencies created by the child himself in the use or in the abuse of his moral liberty."*

§ 236. c^1. *Man's universal sense.*

Where is prayer unrecognized? And yet does not prayer rest on the assumption, that He who is supplicated can answer? To the same effect speaks every temple, whatever may be its rites, wherever its site, or whenever it may have existed. These places of worship—from the cathedral to the Sunday-school room, from the Parthenon to the mound on which the Indian looks up to God, so universal that, wherever man is, there are they—attest the equal universality of the belief in a special providence. And in this conviction even the philosopher shares, whenever, as in every great crisis in the affairs of men, philosophy fails.†

---

* Bishop Potter, Phil. Lectures on Evidences, p. 133.

† "On this point let Dr. Franklin answer. No one will accuse him of superstition or of an undue regard of the supernatural. All will admit, that few men ever surpassed him as a shrewd observer of life and of human affairs, or as a profound inquirer after the causes and principles that lie at the bottom of great events. And what was his language in the Convention that sat in Philadelphia in 1787 to frame our Federal Constitution, when he rose to support his motion for daily prayers in that body?

"It must be remembered that weeks had elapsed without the Convention's having accomplished any part of its all-important work, and that irreconcilable differences seemed likely to defeat its purposes altogether. It was under these circumstances that Dr. Franklin introduced his resolution, and made the following remarks:—'In the beginning of the contest with Britain,' said he, '*when we were sensible*

d^1. The analogy of answer to prayer, which may be taken as an extreme case of special providence, with other agencies by which, humanly speaking, the course of events is altered.

§ 237. "I cannot believe," says the objector, "that the course of the world can be altered by the prayer of a feeble

---

of danger, we had daily prayers in this room for the Divine protection. Our prayers, sir, were heard, and they were graciously answered. All of us who were engaged in the struggle must have observed frequent instances of a superintending Providence in our favor. To that kind Providence we owe *this* happy opportunity of consulting in peace on the means of establishing our *future* national felicity. And have we now forgotten this powerful friend? or do we imagine that we no longer need His assistance? *I have lived, sir, a long time,* (*eighty-one years,*) *and the longer I live, the more convincing proofs I see of this truth, that God governs in the affairs of man.* And, if a sparrow cannot fall to the ground without His notice, is it probable that an empire can rise without His aid? We have been assured, sir, in the sacred writings, "that except the Lord build the house, they labor in vain that build it." I firmly believe this; and I also believe, that without His concurring aid, we shall succeed in this political building no better than the builders of Babel; we shall be divided by our little partial local interests, our projects will be confounded, and we ourselves shall become a reproach and a by-word down to future ages. And, what is worse, mankind may hereafter, from this unfortunate instance, despair of establishing government by human wisdom, and leave it to chance, war, or conquest. I therefore beg leave to move that, henceforth, prayers, imploring the assistance of Heaven and its blessing on our deliberations, be held in this assembly every morning before we proceed to business; and that one or more of the clergy of this city be requested to officiate in that service.'" (*Potter's Lectures on the Evidences, etc.*, p. 143.)

child, or an ignorant old woman." No one is more rigid in asserting the constancy of rational laws, in this respect, than Mr. Hume, when teaching metaphysics, and yet no one is more fertile in declaring the existence and effect of just such agencies than Mr. Hume, when writing history. An ignorant fisherman defeated the Spanish Armada by a trick. Another trick on the part of the Spanish Court led to the long subsequent introduction into the French marriage treaty of Charles I., of a clause which, by giving up the royal issue to their mothers' care during their childhood, consigned them to papacy and exile. The casual appearance at court of George Villiers, led to an ascendency which reduced James I. to vassalage, and brought Charles I. to the block. The unexpected presence of Mary in the chamber where Rizzio was slain, left on her then unborn son a taint which followed him through life, and which worked in him a degree of irresolution, if not cowardice, which degraded royalty in England, and sacrificed Protestantism in Bohemia. Such are the threads which the subtle finger of the historian delights to follow, when showing how the slightest influences may apparently move the law that controls human affairs. But if this be true, and if God be that supreme motive power, all philosophical objections to the efficacy of prayer are destroyed.

*e^1. Hypotheses on which a special providence can be explained.**

---

* See as to use of Hypothesis in Theol., 2 Chalm. Nat. Theol., Const. ed., 314.

§ 238. a^2. *By the assumption of a law based on angelic agency.**

It may be assumed that, as in conformity with the divine scheme, creatures, lower in the scale of life than man, are employed in ministering to him, so, in equal subordination to God's law, creatures, higher than man may be so employed.

Putting aside the testimony of Scripture, the analogy of nature leads us to suppose that as *below* man there is a descending scale reaching down to the atom, so *above* man there is an ascending scale reaching forward to the absolute. "We have no reason to suppose that the gradation is suddenly arrested just at the point where the animal and the spiritual are combined."† If so, in what office can such existences be better employed than in occupying toward the Divine Head, the same offices as the "fire and hail, snows and vapors, wind and storm, fulfilling His word?" So thought Milton:—

> "His state is kingly,
> Thousands at his bidding speed,
> And post o'er land and ocean, without rest."

If, however, these beings are thus employed, the analogy may be extended by supposing that they are employed in serving men. Archbishop Whately, the least sentimental of philosophers, draws this inference from the fact, that "as relates to the things of *this world*, we know that it is the ap-

---

* See these points enumerated in 2 Buch. on Faith, p. 176.

† *Ibid.*, p. 185.

pointment of Providence that men should be dependent on their fellow-men for various good offices, and, in many instances, for life itself. To minister to the distressed and afflicted, and to perform various other acts of kindness to our brethren, is among the duties most earnestly inculcated by our Lord and his apostles."* Or, to take the same analogy, as stated in the following lines, not the less impressive from the exquisite delicacy of their diction :—

"I have seen mourners by the sick one's pillow;
Theirs was the soft tone and the soundless tread,—
When smitten hearts were drooping like the willow,
They stood between the living and the dead.

"And if my sight, by earthly dimness hindered,
Beheld no hovering cherubim in air,
I doubted not—for spirits know their kindred,—
They smiled upon the viewless watches there.

"There have been angels in the gloomy prison,
In crowded halls, by the lone widow's hearth,
And where they passed, the fallen have uprisen—
The giddy paused,—the mourner's hope had birth."

There is no more reason why we should refuse to recognize the services of angels, for fear of angel-worship, than we should the services of the winds and storms, for fear of Fetichism. As created beings the members of neither are the subjects of worship.†

---

* Whately's Good and Evil Angels, p. 26.

† The scriptural prohibition is also absolute. See the argument forcibly stated in Whately's Good and Evil Angels, pp. 16, 17.

On the subject of the special guardianship by angels much more

b^2. *By the pre-arrangement of the laws of nature, so that in harmony with and subordination to them, prayer may be answered.*

§ 239. Prayer becomes in this way a general causal power,

---

difficulty exists. Mr. Alford, in his cumbrous though elaborate and instructive commentary, has lately brought before the church, with peculiar positiveness, the doctrine, that to each individual there is assigned a specific guardian angel. This he mainly rests upon Matt. xviii. 10, where our blessed Lord tells us, "Take heed that ye despise not one of these little ones; for I say unto you that in heaven their angels do always behold the face of my Father which is in heaven." And he goes so far as to intimate that we have ground to believe from Acts xii. 15, (where the disciples speak of Peter's "angel,") that guardian angels sometimes appear in the likeness of the individual himself. So far is this theory carried by the Romanists, that authority not devoid of respectability has been found to countenance the superstition, that on occasions of peculiar solemnity, the guardian angels may assume the bodies of those over whom they watch, and give warning of some great impending calamity. Romish hagiology is full of cases, where the bodies of saints appear to their own sleeping vision, or to that of others, to give notice of approaching death. And the fathers, even the earliest and best of them, so far countenanced the doctrine as to occupy no small portion of their writings with expositions of the way in which these substitutionary appearances occur.

Mr. Alford is not the only Protestant writer who espouses the same view. Dr. Chalmers, though only hypothetically, intimated, as is stated in the text, that there might be angelic messengers employed in the work of giving effect to prayer, though he refers rather to a general influence of the whole angelic body, than to a specific guardianship.

Mr. Kingsley introduces to us angels, as engaged in conveying to with its particular results foreordained. It receives an answer, because it is a part of the Divine pre-arranged polity that it should. This, it may be said, is fatalism, but the

---

us all the minor happinesses with which life is blessed—a sort of Kriss-Kringles or Brother Cheerybles of the skies.

And in Stiers's "Words of the Lord Jesus," the author declares that not only is a guardian angel assigned to each child on its birth, but that when grieved away by sin, the angel is re-commissioned to attend the sinner on his regeneration. How deeply this feeling is wrought into the popular mind, Mercy's dream in the Pilgrim's Progress, and Retsch's great picture of Satan playing chess with the young man for his soul, may testify.

Now let us pass from the poetry of interpretation to its sense. Calvin, whom, whatever we may think of his views on the great controversy which bears his name, we may agree with Hooker in holding as the gravest and wisest of commentators whom the Church, down to his own day, had known, when speaking of Matt. xviii. 10, says: "The view taken by some of this passage, as if it ascribed to each believer his own peculiar angel, is without support. For the words of Christ do not import, that one angel is in perpetuity attached to this person or that, and the notion is at variance with the whole teaching of Scripture, which testifies that angels encamp round about the righteous, and not to one angel alone, but to many has it been commanded, to protect every one of the faithful." (See Fairbairn's Hermeneutical Manual, p. 222.) This is almost in the same language repeated by Whitby, in a commentary, which, incorporated with those of Patrick and Lowth, has received the peculiar recommendation of that section of our Church to whom Calvin's distinctive views are the most distasteful. "I think," says this acute critic, "that neither of these opinions (those imputing guardian angels, first to children, and then to the just,) hath any good foundation in the holy Scriptures; certain it is, that in this place Christ saith not their '*angel*,' but their

same objection holds good to every action in which moral agency is involved. If it be an objection to prayer that there is no use in offering it, since its answer is already

---

'*angels*' behold the face of God; nor says He, that these angels belong to all, but only to 'these little ones;' nor that they always do attend upon their persons, but that they 'stand before the face of God,' ready to receive His commands, either to help them in their exigencies, or punish those who injure them; hence then it follows, not that they have always an angel present with them, but only that angels in general are 'ministering spirits to them.'"

It is not necessary to add anything in the way of critical commentary to these remarks. We may be permitted, however, assuming as we do with the great body of orthodox Anglican interpreters, that the theory of guardian angels is not called for by the text, to show how in two respects it is liable to perversion.

These are—1st. The diminution of the mediatorial glory of Christ, and of the work of the Holy Spirit; and, 2d. The danger of angel-worship. In the Romish Church both of these consequences have followed, and not illogically. For either the angels are involuntary mechanisms, or they are not. If the former, they can have no tutelary functions. If the latter, and if specially assigned to individuals as their spiritual companions and guides, it is impossible for the yearning and sad heart of man, always craving comfort from above, not to seek to enter into their converse. If this does not end in Romanism, it will lead to Spiritualism.

It should be observed, also, that "little ones" does not, as the sentimentalists of our day suppose, refer to *children*, but to the *disciples* of our Lord; and secondly, "behold the face of my Father," etc., involves no intercessory power. It signifies, in oriental phrase, only a supremacy in the court of heaven. "I am Gabriel," says that angel, "who stands before God;" and this in a case where it was a *message* alone that was delivered. So the Queen of Sheba speaks of Solomon's retinue: "Blessed are thy servants who stand always before thee."

secured by Divine ordination, it is equally an objection to sowing grain or plowing a field, that the crop will come without the effort. By this reasoning, petitions would be prevented, not only to an earthly potentate, but to an earthly friend. Nor does the multitudinous variety and human fluctuating weakness of prayer deprive it of the aid of the same energy. "When men are the askers and men also are the givers, He can, amid all the caprices of human appetite and fancy, still uphold the regularities both of a moral and a natural economy."* Why not, then, in a system in which He is GIVER as well as HEARER ?†

c^2. By a special connection between prayer and result as between cause and effect.

§ 240. "The doctrine of the efficacy of prayer," says Dr. Chalmers, "but introduces a new sequence to the notice of the mind—whereas it seems to be quarreled with by philosophy, on the ground that it disturbs and distempers the regularity of all sequences. It may add another law of nature to those which have been formerly observed—but this surely may be done without invasion on the constancy of nature." Thus magnetism does not disturb the laws of

---

* 2 Chal. Nat. Theol., p. 329.

† It may be said, in order to reach the charge of fatalism, that *foreknowledge* is, in this sense, but back history, and that human liberty and the contingency resulting from choice, are no more affected by history written *before* this event than they would be by history written *afterwards*. In this view, while fatalism *causes* the event, foreknowledge is *caused by it;* the fact exists, not because it is predetermined,—it is foreseen because it exists. This point has already been noticed. See *ante*, § 129–131.

nature; it only opens them to let itself in as an independent, but equally authorized and legitimate agency.

d^2. By pushing up the principle which governs the results of prayer, until it passes above the boundary by which human observation is limited.

§ 241. That there is such a boundary, may be shown both *a priori* and by induction.

A priori, what course would we suppose a Divine and all-merciful Father, having in view the shortness of human life, would take, in order to enable that life to be most economically and judiciously employed so as to subserve the object of probation?

We can answer this by inquiring what would be the policy of a judicious colonial secretary in drawing up a system of government for a colony about to settle in and improve a distant, and, as yet, unoccupied territory. "You are going," he would say, "to prepare farms to benefit yourselves, as well as to improve the soil. You are to get crops ready for a market, as well as to accommodate, if not to prepare a market for the crops. For this purpose, I give you all the practical information you will really need. You have here a statement of the stock and staples best suited to your particular climate, and of the kind of culture by which the soil may be most effectually used. You have here a topographical survey of the district in which you are particularly placed. It shows you how you can get your produce to the great river which runs a few miles off, and from that river to the sea. But it does *not* show you where that river finds its remotest source, nor does it indicate what are the influences, terrestrial and sidereal, by which that ocean is moved. If you are surprised at this, I can give you a very good reason for it. You are here for a practical purpose, and you have no more than enough time than is necessary to enable that purpose to be achieved. You are therefore furnished with a pocket-map and an emigrant's manual, both in small compass. Were I to undertake to give you a chart of the entire universe, it would be too large to be carried, and if studied, would leave no room for the duties of farming, to perform which you are sent. Yours is a specific work,—the reclamation of a wasted land, and the restoration to yourselves, whose infirmities, if not whose crimes, have made you the subjects of penal law, of those habits of industry and energy which form the most important safeguards to virtue and purity."

§ 242. Analogous to this is the information man requires in his earthly probation. "I do not care to know about the *causes* of sin," said John Newton, "since I am told how to *escape* from it." We are given, as it were, a topographical survey of the scene of our labors. That survey must end somewhere. If infinite, the great body of it would be not only useless for the immediate work we are sent to perform, but would be cumbrous and distracting. Even were it only to remind us what our specific duties are, it must, so far at least as its details are concerned, have its limits. There must be, therefore, if this analogy be correct, some line above which human observation cannot pass. Below this line we may expect to find such knowledge as is practical and pertinent to the discharge of our actual duties; above it, such knowledge as is purely speculative, and, for our present purposes, useless.

The *inductive* proof of this proposition is equally strong. *Material* agencies are governed by open and universal laws; *moral* enter upon the sea of life with sealed letters, the contents of which the subordinate only knows by the result. The *stars* are moved by a mechanism whose long strokes and revolutions we can see, as they approach, at a century's distance; God Almighty moves human destiny by His own finger, but conceals that finger behind an impenetrable cloud.

§ 243. Science itself bears witness to these truths with an emphasis which increases as it searches more closely into the nervous and psychical centres. "If statistics are true, when applied to size and quantity," says an eminent French physician, "they are no longer so, when relating to life and strength."* And M. Brierre de Boismont, in his work on Hallucinations,† declares that this presses on us the more strongly as "we advance in the consideration of the nervous system." Even Carlyle says: "The same uncertainty, in estimating present things and men, holds more or less in all times; for in all times, even in those which seem most trivial, and open to research, *human society rests on inscrutably deep foundations; which he is, of all others the most mistaken, who fancies he has explored to the bottom.*"‡ And Hegel, and this from a pantheistic stand-point, declares that, here at least, in the springs of human action, is an element which nothing but a Divine cause can explain.

---

* M. Max Simon, L'Opinion Reine du Mond; Union Médicale, 2 Août, 1851.

† Phil. ed., p. 195.

‡ Carlyle, Rev. on Voltaire, For. Quar. Rev., 1829.

When we go into an examination of the incidents which make up individual history, the same principle is established. Take, for instance, the remarkable fact, that so large and undue a proportion of deaths occurs about daydawn.*

* A late writer in the *London Quarterly Review* tells us, that out of two thousand eight hundred and eighty deaths which occurred within a given period, there was a division as to the hour too marked to be the result of what might be considered chance. If the proportion of deaths to hours were equal, one hundred and twenty deaths would occur in each hour. This, however, was by no means the case. "There were two hours in which the proportion was remarkably below this; two minima, in fact—namely, from midnight to one o'clock, when the deaths were eighty-three per cent. below. From three to six o'clock in the morning, inclusive, and from three to seven o'clock in the afternoon, there is a gradual increase in the former of twenty-three and a half per cent. above the average, in the latter of five and a half per cent. The maximum of deaths is from five to six o'clock in the morning, when it is forty per cent. above the average; the next during the hour before midnight, when it is twenty-four per cent. in excess; a third hour of excess is that from nine to ten o'clock in the morning, being eighteen and a half per cent. above. From ten in the morning to three in the afternoon the deaths are less numerous, being sixteen and a half per cent. below the average, the hour before noon being the most fatal. From three o'clock in the afternoon to nine the deaths rise to five and a half per cent. above the average, then fall, from that hour to eleven P.M., averaging six and a half per cent. below the mean. During the hours from nine to eleven o'clock in the evening, there is a minimum of six and a half per cent. below the average. Thus the least mortality is during the mid-day hours—namely, from ten to three o'clock; the greatest during early morning hours, from three to six o'clock.

§ 244. Now there may be a law on this point, so far as a collection of results may be entitled to that name, but we neither discover the principle on which the law is based, nor the cases to which it applies. So also with regard to the causes of death. Here is a topic to which science has devoted its peculiar scrutiny both to affect results and to collect information. Where, however, can we find any class of events which so entirely resist the inductive process? So far as respects sanitary and moral influences, we learn enough to say that any violation of cleanliness or temperance, will be productive of injury to life. But when we come to examine the issues of life and death themselves, we will find that their threads are held by an unseen hand. Observe, as an illustration of this, the contrast between *war*, the most efficient human means of destroying life, and *cholera*, the greatest Divine scourge. In twenty-two years of war, as returned by the London Board of Health, there were 19,796 killed, being a yearly average of 899. In 1848–9, there were no less than 72,180 persons killed by cholera in England and Wales alone. And yet of all agencies of death, war is that in which, in a human sense,

---

About one-third of the total deaths were children under five years of age, and they show the influence of the latter more strikingly. At all hours, from ten o'clock in the morning until midnight, the deaths are at or below the mean; the hours from four to five in the afternoon, and from nine to ten in the evening, being minima, but the hours after midnight being the lowest maximum; at all the hours from two to ten in the morning the deaths are above the mean, attaining their maximum at from five to six o'clock in the morning, when it is forty-five and a half per cent. above."

the notion of law is the most completely developed, while the cause and conditions of cholera have defied all attempts at discovery. So it is with individual agencies. A frost, the first of the kind for fifty years, caused the destruction of the French army in Russia, and the overthrow of the empire of Napoleon I. A slight pebble on the road caused the death of William III. of England. An iceberg, floated by a casual current out of its path, destroys one steamer, the tooth of a rat another, the momentary negligence of an engineer a third; a building falls and hundreds are crushed to death; a vessel carried by mistake out of her course, introduces into a northern city a fever that kills thousands. Death, in a human sense the most important of events, is that, of all others, whose causes most defy systematization.

Or, take the facts so exultingly classified by Mr. Buckle, that the average number of undirected, of misdirected, and of missigned letters, runs upward with the advance of population. Here is a "law," undoubtedly, but it does not impinge on the freedom of the individual man.* The aggregate of misdirected letters may be calculated, but we cannot say who it will be by whom the next misdirected letter will be sent. Probation is incased in a coat of mail so impenetrable and so polished, that the shafts of general laws bound off from it without effecting a lodgment.

From the reasoning which has just been given, we may conclude that the Almighty governs the moral universe in

* See *ante*, § 216–19.

person, sitting in the darkness of His own council-chamber, while He directs the physical universe through the agency of fixed and published law. This view, if correct, relieves the doctrine of special providence of all real difficulty.*

§ 245. The structure of the mind gives an additional strength to the view just stated. We judge from the short legs and heavy frame of one animal, that it was shaped to browse on the rich and continuous meadow, or to wallow in the reedy lagoon. We judge from the slight figure and delicate, though sinewy limbs of another, that it was designed for mountain heights. Such are the conclusions we draw from the fragments of the rhinoceros or the gemsbok that we find in a cabinet of fossils. How is it with man? Can we not judge of the limits of the field over which his mind is permitted to range from the structure of that mind itself?

Now on this point I know no higher psychological authority than Locke; a great and candid thinker, whose claims, for a time set aside under the brilliant though unsafe guidance of Cousin,† are now regaining even more than

---

* See this question examined in connection with that of the origin of evil, *ante*, § 129–131. See also § 88.

† It is one of the worst features of the eclecticism of this writer, that thinking rather rhetorically than philosophically, he gives us, not a harmonious reconciliation, but a scenic grouping of the conspicuous points of the preceding schools. It is a French psychological drama, in which, with due regard to the unities of time and place, the personifications of prior speculations are brought together in such attitudes as to produce the greatest sensation. In such a company the homely bearing and russet sense of Locke scarcely fit him to play a part.

their former authority. "Men have reason," he says, "to be well satisfied with what God has thought fit for them, since he has given them, as St. Peter says, παντα προς ζωην καὶ εὐσεβειαν, whatsoever is necessary for the convenience of life and the information of virtue; and has put within the reach of their discovery the comfortable provision for this life, and the way that leads to a better. How short soever their knowledge may be of a universal or perfect comprehension of whatever is, it yet secures their great concernments, that they have light enough to lead them to the knowledge of their Maker and *the sight of their own duties.* Men may find matter sufficiently to busy their heads and employ their hands with variety, delight, and satisfaction, if they will not boldly quarrel with their own constitutions, and throw away the blessings their hands are filled with because they are not big enough to grasp everything. * * * It will be no excuse to an idle and untoward servant, who would not attend his business by candlelight, to plead that he had not broad sunshine. *The candle that is set up within us shines bright enough for all purposes.*"

§ 246. It has been reserved, however, for Sir William Hamilton to demonstrate, with an unrivaled power both of analysis and of explication, the studiousness of that care with which the great Artificer of the human mind confines it to the limited, the relative, and the conditioned, and excludes it from the infinite, the absolute, and the unconditioned. The Philosophy of Common Sense, as expounded by this last and greatest of its teachers, bears so important a part in the development of a sound theism, that I may be permitted to give it here more than a passing notice.*

§ 247. Certain primary beliefs, according to Sir William Hamilton, lie at the basis of all truth. These are the objects of consciousness, and derive their force from the fact that they are necessarily true. Their value, therefore, depends on the veracity of consciousness. To doubt this "is to doubt the actuality of the fact of consciousness, and consequently to doubt the doubt itself, which is a contradiction, and subverts itself." Mr. Hume, in fact, whose authority is so often quoted on the other side, concedes this, in a passage which diverts from the renditions of consciousness the whole force of his subtle skepticism. "Should it

* To those who have not the time or the opportunity for the study of Sir W. Hamilton's entire works, scattered as they are over so wide a margin, I would recommend Mr. Samuel Tyler's "Progress of Philosophy," Phila., J. B. Lippincott & Co., 1858, a work which gives a succinct, perspicuous, and reliable statement of the positions of the great Scotch philosopher. It is greatly to be regretted that Sir William Hamilton died before he was able to place his views in the form of a comprehensive treatise. As now existing in their original shape, they are mainly to be found in his foot-notes and his supplementary dissertations to Reid, and in his "Discussions on Philosophy and Literature," first published by him as distinct articles in the "Edinburgh Review," and afterwards collected by him in a separate volume. The latter has been republished in this country, New York, Harper & Brothers, 1856. Of the entire material, a valuable analytical compendium, presenting many of the advantages of a distinct treatise, has been issued in this country by Mr. O. W. Wight. Fourth edition, New York, Appleton & Co., 1857.

be here asked me," he says, in the "Treatise on Human Nature," which his adversaries as well as his followers unite in appealing to as giving the ablest and most mature exhibition of his system, "whether I sincerely assent to this argument which I seem to take such pains to inculcate, and whether I be really one of those skeptics who hold that all is uncertain, and that our judgment is not in *any* thing possessed of *any* measures of truth and falsehood, I should reply that this question is entirely superfluous, *and that neither I nor any other person was ever sincerely and constantly of that opinion.* Nature, by an absolute and uncontrollable necessity, has determined us to judge as well as to breathe and feel; nor can we any more forbear viewing certain objects in a stronger and fuller light upon account of their customary connection with a present impression, than we can hinder ourselves from thinking as long as we are awake, or seeing the surrounding bodies when we turn our eyes toward them in broad sunshine. Whoever has taken pains to refute the cavils of this *total* skepticism, has really disputed without an antagonist, and endeavored by arguments to establish a faculty *which Nature has antecedently implanted in the mind and rendered unavoidable.* * * * If belief were a simple act of the thought, without any peculiar manner of conception, or the addition of force and vivacity, it must infallibly destroy itself, and in every case terminate in a total suspension of judgment. But as experience will sufficiently convince any one, that although he finds no error in my arguments, yet he still continues to believe and think and reason as usual, he may safely conclude that his reasoning and belief is some sensation or peculiar manner of conception, which it is impossible for mere ideas and reflections to destroy."*

Now here we have the assertion, not only of the existence of these primary beliefs, but of their necessity, (they are "unavoidable,") of their veracity, (they are likened to the impression on the eye of "bodies in broad sunshine,") and of their universality, ("neither I nor any other person was ever sincerely and constantly of that [the skeptical] opinion.") The PHILOSOPHY OF COMMON SENSE, as taught by Sir William Hamilton, takes these primary beliefs as the basis, and makes subordination to and agreement with them a test of all disputed propositions.

§ 248. So far as this system bears upon the question now before us, it may be summed up in a single principle. Our knowledge is limited by the condition of relativity. We can have no knowledge of the absolute. Hence it is that while the Hegelian school assumed to itself the title of the Philosophy of the Absolute, that of which Sir William Hamilton is the exponent, takes that of the Philosophy of the Conditioned. How these are distinguished is thus stated by Sir William Hamilton himself:—

"The philosophy of the Conditioned is the express converse of the philosophy of the Absolute—at least as this system has been latterly evolved in Germany. For this asserts to man a knowledge of the Unconditioned—of the Absolute and Infinite; while that denies to him a knowledge of either, and maintains, all which we immediately know, or can know, to be only the Conditioned, the Relative, the

* Essay on Human Nature, part iv. § 1.

Phenomenal, the Finite. The one, supposing knowledge to be only of existence in itself, and existence in itself to be apprehended, and even understood, proclaims—'Understand that you may believe' (Intellige ut credas;) the other, supposing that existence in itself is unknown, that apprehension is only a phenomena, and that these are received only upon trust, as incomprehensibly revealed facts, proclaims, with the prophet—'Believe that ye may understand,' (Crede ut intelligas. Is. vii. 9, sec. lxx.) But extremes meet. In one respect, both coincide, for both agree, that the knowledge of Nothing is the principle or result of all true philosophy.

"'*Scire nihil*—studium, quo nos lætamur utrique.' But the one doctrine, openly maintaining that the Nothing must yield everything, is a philosophic omniscience; whereas the other, holding that Nothing can yield nothing, is a philosophic nescience. In other words, the doctrine of the Unconditioned is a philosophy confessing relative ignorance, but professing absolute knowledge; while the doctrine of the Conditioned is a philosophy professing relative knowledge, but confessing absolute ignorance. Thus, touching the absolute: the watchword of the one is,—'Noscendo cognoscitur, ignorando ignoratur;' the watchword of the other is,—'Noscendo ignoratur, ignorando cognoscitur.'

"But which is true? To answer this, we need only examine our own consciousness; there shall we recognize the limited 'extent of our tether.'

"'Tecum habita, et nôris quam sit tibi curta supellex.' But this one requisite is fulfilled (alas!) by few; and the same philosophic poet has to lament:—

Ut nemo in sese tentat descendere,—nemo;
Sed præcedenti spectatur mantica tergo!"

§ 249. Our inability, therefore, to reconcile the two great primary beliefs of human consciousness—God's sovereignty and man's responsibility—arises from our own impotence, itself a proof of the proposition that the sphere from which the human intellect is thus excluded, is one which is enveloped in the mystery of the Divine counsels. In what way this relieves us from the fatalistic side of the necessitarian theory, is thus stated by Sir W. Hamilton :—

"There is no ground for inferring a certain fact to be impossible, merely from *our inability to conceive it possible.* At the same time, if the causal judgment be not an express affirmation of mind, but only an incapacity of thinking the opposite; it follows that such a negative judgment cannot counterbalance the express affirmative, the unconditional testimony, of consciousness,—that we are, though we know not how, the true and responsible authors of our actions, not merely the worthless links in an adamantine series of effects and causes. It appears to me, that it is only on such a doctrine that we can philosophically vindicate the liberty of the human will,—that we can rationally assert to man—'fatis avolsa voluntas.' *How* the will can possibly be free, must remain to us, under the present limitation of our faculties, wholly incomprehensible. We are unable to conceive an absolute commencement; we cannot, therefore, conceive a free volition. A determination, by motives, cannot, to our understanding, escape from necessitation. Nay, were we even to admit as true, what we cannot think as possible, still the doctrine of a motiveless volition would be only casualism; and the free acts of an indifferent are, morally and rationally, as worthless as the preordered passions of a determined will.

How, therefore, I repeat, moral liberty is possible in man or God, we are utterly unable speculatively to understand. But practically, the *fact*, that we are free, is given to us in the consciousness of an uncompromising law of duty, in the consciousness of our moral accountability; and this fact of liberty cannot be redargued on the ground that it is incomprehensible, for the philosophy of the conditioned proves, against the necessitarian, that things there are, which *may*, *nay*, *must* be, true, of which the understanding is wholly unable to construe to itself the possibility."

But does not this stop with the vindication of moral liberty, as *possible* though *inconceivable*, and does it not, on the other hand, give the fatalistic necessitarian scheme the advantage of being *conceivable* as well as possible? Does it not, therefore, bring us back once more to Fatalism, as, of the two schemes, the one beset with the less difficulty? This is answered by Sir W. Hamilton with exquisite subtlety and conclusive effect: "This philosophy is not only competent to defend the fact of our moral liberty, possible though inconceivable, against the assault of the fatalist; it retorts against himself the very objection of incomprehensibility by which the fatalist had thought to triumph over the libertarian. It shows that the scheme of freedom is not more inconceivable than the scheme of necessity. For while fatalism is a recoil from the more obtrusive inconceivability of an absolute commencement, on the fact of which commencement the doctrine of liberty proceeds, the fatalist is shown to overlook the equal, but less obtrusive inconceivability of an infinite non-commencement, on the assertion of which non-commencement his own doctrine of necessity must ultimately rest. As equally unthinkable, the two counter, the two one-sided schemes are thus theoretically balanced. But practically, our consciousness of the moral law, which, without a moral liberty in man, would be a mendacious imperative, gives a decisive preponderance to the doctrine of freedom over the doctrine of fate. We are free in act, if we are accountable for our actions.

"Such (φωνᾶντα συνετοῖσιν) are the hints of an undeveloped philosophy, which, I am confident, is founded upon truth. To this confidence I have come, not merely through the convictions of my own consciousness, but by finding in this system a centre and conciliation for the most opposite of philosophical opinions. Above all, however, I am confirmed in my belief, by the harmony between the doctrines of this philosophy, and those of revealed truth. 'Credo equidem, nec vana fides.' The philosophy of the conditioned is indeed pre-eminently a discipline of humility; a 'learned ignorance,' directly opposed to the false 'knowledge which puffeth up.' I may, indeed, say with St. Chrysostom:—'The foundation of our philosophy is humility.'* For it is professedly a scientific demonstration of the impossibility of that 'wisdom in high matters' which the Apostle prohibits us even to attempt; and it proposes, from the limitation of the human powers, from our impotence to comprehend what, however, we must admit, to show articulately why the 'secret things of God' cannot but be to man 'past finding out.' Humility thus becomes the cardinal virtue not only of revelation, but of reason. This

* Homil. de Perf. Evang.

scheme proves, moreover, that no difficulty emerges in theology which had not previously emerged in philosophy; that in fact, if the divine do not transcend what it has pleased the Deity to reveal, and willfully identify the doctrine of God's word with some arrogant extreme of human speculation, philosophy will be found the most useful auxiliary of theology. * * * * * * * *

"It is here shown to be as irrational as irreligious, on the ground of human understanding, to deny, either on the one hand, the foreknowledge, predestination, and free grace of God, or, on the other, the free will of man; that we should believe both, and both in unison, though unable to comprehend either even apart. This philosophy proclaims with *St. Augustin*, and Augustin in his maturest writings:—'If there be not free grace in God, how can He save the world; and if there be not free will in man, how can the world by God be judged?'* Or, as the same doctrine is perhaps expressed even better by *St. Bernard:*—'Abolish free will, and there is nothing to be saved; abolish free grace, and there is nothing wherewithal to save.'"†

---

* Ad Valentinum, Epist. 214.

† De Gratiâ et Libero Arbitrio, c. i. See this question considered in relation to the origin of evil, *ante*, § 113–131.

CHAPTER IV.

PANTHEISM.

a. In what it consists.

a[1]. *Material.*

§ 250. *Hylozoism*, as has already been incidentally noticed, holds that all matter is the seat of divine energy and is thus entitled to worship. When the entire personality of God is thus distributed, leaving no residuum behind, this doctrine becomes equivalent to material pantheism. The whole universe, psychical as well as physical, is material. Intellect is but an attribute of body. Deity itself has no spiritual personality, but comprehends and is bounded by the physical universe, itself self-existent and eternal. Nor is the view of those who hold that some portion of the divine energy remains undistributed, materially different in its consequences from that just stated. Though there be a divine spiritual residue remaining after the divinity of the universe is carved out, such residue is remanded to a condition of comatose insensibility, that of a Divinity on furlough, merely to be occasionally recognized by a complimentary adoration, and then to be passed practically by as possessed of no real power.*

* Of this class is the pantheism of worldliness, which makes the

b[1]. *Ideal.*

§ 251. In this scheme the *objective* does not exist, all material nature being resolved into the conception entertained of it by the intellect. Existence and thought, in this view, are identical, and the individual EGO is but an item in the ABSOLUTE GOD. There is no matter,—we are all god,—form the two fundamental articles in ideal pantheism.

It is among the German transcendental philosophers that this species of pantheism finds its chief exponents. State the doctrine philosophically, and it narrows itself to a denial of the distinct existence of any spiritual agency except God. There is no dualism in the universe. The soul is but a phenomenon of God, as the wave is but a phenomenon of the sea. Sometimes we hear the terms "Son" and "Spirit" used, and we suppose from this a recognition of even a divine distinction of persons. This, however, is far from the case. The "Son" is the universe; the "Spirit," the property which binds the Absolute and the universe together. Cousin tells us that the Trinity consists of, "at the

---

world, *e.g.* society, supreme, recognizing, it is true, the Divine Being as existing, but as in a state of retirement, and entitled only to nominal homage. Mr. Rogers thus illustrates this in his "Table-Talk." An English duchess was, one Sunday morning, too late for church, and found the door closed. "Never mind, Georgiana," said she to one of her daughters, as she turned away, "anyhow, we have done the civil thing." It was the "civil thing" done by the world to a superannuated God. But what an awful reverse to the picture have we when we contemplate that God, august, tremendous, present, patient, waiting the day of His power.

same time, God, Nature, and Humanity."* This well deserves a rebuke which is all the more severe from the fact that it comes from Mr. Morell: "Much as we admire Cousin, while he keeps within his proper limits, and much as we are disposed to maintain the truth of his philosophy, in most of its principal features, we cannot but repudiate, with all our energy, his attempts to intrude upon the sacred province of the Christian revelation. If he will stand up as a theologian, and fight the battle upon its proper grounds, let him do so, and there are plenty to take up the gauntlet he throws down; but it is not the part, which his own philosophy would dictate, to raise a new theory of revelation to supersede all the rest, without considering the facts and the evidences which the Christian revelation can display."†

It is not within my limit to examine the several phases which this doctrine assumes with the transcendental and eclectic philosophers. With Schelling it is termed *Identitätslehre,* or the doctrine of Identity. Hegel mounts above this, and tells us that the "World-Spirit" (Weltgeist) has freed himself from all incumbrances, and is able to conceive himself as Absolute and all-engrossing Intelligence, (absolute Geist.) According to this system, history is the mere autobiography of God; the world is but the flesh, ever changing yet eternal, in which His divine essence is embodied; He himself, as the all-comprehending personality, embraces all spiritual as well as material existence; to Him the world is necessary, as an inalienable property of

* See Morell's Hist. Phil., p. 655.

† *Ibid.* p. 661.

His own life; sin, like pain, is a form of good, and a necessary evolution of the Absolute; philosophy is the highest form of religion. In these views the transcendental writers, both in Germany and in this country, in the main agree. Even Cousin, in his History of Philosophy, does not, I conceive, vary much from this stand-point.* Sir W. Hamilton, indeed, declares that Cousin "is a disciple, though by no means a servile disciple" of Schelling. On the other hand, Mr. Lewes, in his History of Philosophy, tells us that "Cousin's system is but an awkward imitation of Hegel."† Both critics are in this correct. In Cousin's earlier papers, he undoubtedly followed more closely the Hegelian lead, while in his History of Philosophy he attaches himself more particularly to that of Schelling. In the practical maintenance of Ideal Pantheism, in fact, Schelling and Hegel agree, though they divide in their way of reaching the result. It is the result in which Cousin followed both. The "science of the unconditioned" at both eras found him among its disciples. In his later writings, however, while not expressly receding from this philosophy, he has with great solemnity declared, that so far as it is inconsistent with a true Theism, it was no longer held by him.‡

---

* See his Hist. of Mod. Phil, trans. by Mr. O. W. Wight, vol. i. p. 83.

† Appleton's ed., 1857, p. 738.

‡ I cannot but feel, however, that the leading philosophical critics of all schools agree as to the pantheistic tendency of Cousin's eclecticism. So far as concerns the Philosophy of the Absolute, Hegel, as is well known, claimed him as an adherent, and in reviewing Cousin's earlier writings, gladly welcomed his aid. Mr. Lewes, who

b. Objections to Pantheism.

§ 252. a^1. *Its hopelessness.*

It has no future. This wonderful "sea-change" of nature—this perpetuity of the world, in all its waning and waxing loveliness, only, however, to wane and wax again—this is the best hope that the pantheist can nourish. The soul is ever and ever to swing backward and forward from

---

may be well considered as representing positivism, and Sir W. Hamilton, as representing the Philosophy of Common Sense, speak for themselves in the text. The opinion of orthodox Christian theologians may be gathered from Dr. Chalmers, who declares Cousin's idealism to have a pantheistic leaning, and from Mr. Pearson,* who says,—"For the last twenty-five years, Cousin, the eloquent 'apostle of Rationalism in France,' and others of the eclectic school, have been inculcating, in the Ecole Normale, at Paris, a system much more favorable to pantheism than to the Christian revelation; and have raised up not a few instructors to disseminate the same throughout the country." To this we may add the remarks of Mr. Morell, a critic whose position, so far as religion is concerned, is of the extremest latitudinarianism. "Cousin's view of the Divine Nature," he says, "is confessedly somewhat recondite and indistinct. While on the one hand, he altogether repudiates the charge of pantheism, yet on the other hand, it is difficult to say how his opinions, as above described, can be altogether vindicated from it."† This element in Cousin's philosophy has been assailed with great power by Maret, in his "Essai sur le Panthéisme;" by Bautain, in his "Psychologie Expérimentale," and by the "Princeton Review," in 1839 and 1856. Dr. Henry, in his introduction to Cousin's Psychology, gives us, on the other hand, an elaborate reply to these attacks.

---

* Infidelity, etc., Carter's ed., pp. 67, 564.

† Morell, Hist. Phil., Cart. ed., p. 655. See *post*, § 256,

decay to resurrection, and then, not from resurrection to ascension, but from resurrection to decay. It is the tolling of the bell over the wrecked steamer :—

Tolling, tolling, tolling,
  The bell by billows rung;
Night and day, and day and night,
  Speaking with mournful tongue;
Toll for the queenly boat
  Wreck'd on yon rocky shore,
Sea-weed is in her palace halls,
  She rides the surge no more.

Nor can ideal pantheism hold a higher hope. Already its disciples declare :—" The currents of the Universal Being circulate through me. I am part or particle of God."* There is nothing for him to rise to, for he holds to no personal God to whom he may hereafter mount. And, at the best, all he can look forward to is, when the earthly house is dissolved, to be returned, as the air in the broken bottle, into undistinguished, unconscious space.

§ 253. b^1. *Its comfortlessness.*

It knows no providence to look up to, no heart, human enough to feel and divine enough to help, on which to repose. Its orphanage is infinite, for in all the weakness and dependence of perpetual pupilage, it stands in the isolation of the One Eternal and Supreme himself. So it is on its own showing; but, how much more awful is its state when it witnesses—and of this it must admit there is some chance—the shadow over it of a Father disowning because disowned!

* Emerson, Essays, etc.

§ 254. c^1. *Its repugnancy to common sense, denying individuality.*

Consciousness demonstrates to us *self*, observation *others*. Pantheism denies both. "We are each other, others are ourselves, all is God." But common sense comes in and declares, "I am myself, thou art thyself, and God is above and around us all."*

§ 255. d^1. *It destroys belief, not merely in a God, but in the practical sequences of nature, and generates, therefore, habits, not of energy and perseverance, but of dreamy mysticism and inaction.*

This is illustrated by the social working of pantheism as distinguished from that of even the sternest monotheism. Take, as an instance of the latter, even when in the shape which, to the philosopher, appears of all others the most rugged,—that of the Huguenots, the Scotch covenanters, the English Puritans, and the Dutch and German adherents of Calvin. No one can deny the industrial energy of these religionists. They were charged with so exalting God's sovereignty as to destroy human responsibility. Their conduct did not show this. Nowhere were to be found workmen who united in such an eminent degree patience with industry, and ingenuity with social purity and honesty. When they were driven from the south of France the looms stopped; when they were driven from the Palatinate the fields were deserted. But how has it been with pantheism? In the few cases where it has exercised any influence it has

* As to the way this point is met by the philosophy of common sense, see *ante*, § 247.

generated a dreamy imbecility which has repelled labor, and, by so doing, has left the energies open to the approach of sentimentalism or sensualism. So we find by examining the history of the Phalanxes and Brooke Farms, where the experiment of practical transcendentalism has been tried.* Nor, when we take the principle of the two schools, do we see any reason to be surprised at this. The former inculcates, in connection with reverence and love to God, the discharge of a series of severe specific duties, prominent among which are industry and an energetic practical benevolence. The latter leaves its disciples to simmer in complacent self-contemplation, or to evaporate into an inane because indefinite and universal sympathy.

§ 256. e^1. *It apotheosizes vice as well as virtue.*

Of all the pantheistic schemes, that of eclecticism makes the nearest approach to a true theism, and most vehemently repudiates the usual pantheistic corollaries. Yet the theory of Cousin, the founder of modern eclecticism, and its most brilliant advocate, involves the entire absorption of the individual purpose in the Divine. Mr. Morell, whose capacity as a critic all admit, and whose fairness cannot be doubted at least by those who have the benefit of his philosophical sympathies, tells us that "if we admit that the Deity of Cousin possesses a conscious personality, yet still it is one which contains in itself the infinite personality and consciousness of every subordinate mind. God is the ocean —we are but the waves; the ocean may be one individuality,

---

* See, as a very powerful delineation of the working of the latter system, Hawthorne's fine tale of the Blythedale Romance.

and each wave another; but still they are *essentially* one and the same. We see not how Cousin's Theism can possibly be consistent with any idea of moral evil; neither do we see how, starting from such a dogma, he can ever vindicate and uphold his own theory of human liberty. On such theistic principles all sin must be simply *defect*, and all defect must be absolutely fatuitous."* Such, in fact, is the position practically taken by Cousin himself. "History," he tells us in one place, "is the manifestation of God's supervision of humanity; *the judgments of history are the judgments of God himself.*"† Let us take, as an illustration of this, the way he claims war as a Divine evolution. "Wars and battles are, first, inevitable; secondly, beneficial." "The hazards of war and of the diverse fortunes of combats are spoken of without cessation; for my part, I think there is very little chance in war; the dice are loaded, it seems, for I defy any one to cite me a single game lost by humanity." "What is glory? The judgment of humanity upon one of its members; and humanity is always right."‡

"Humanity is always right," and this not because, like an infallible church, humanity is charged as a *corporation* with divine wisdom, but because the individuals who make up humanity bear the same relation to the Divine centre of truth as do the waves to the sea. War is right because it is a movement of these individuals, who are themselves the emanations of God. All other crimes lose their stain from the same reason.

---

* Morell's Hist. Phil., p. 660. See *ante*, § 249.

† Hist. Phil., trans. by Wight, p. 159.

‡ *Ibid.*, pp. 186–189.

If these results flow from eclecticism, a philosophy in which the Hegelian system is held in check by being placed in juxtaposition with Scotch orthodox psychology, *a fortiori* do they follow from those systems of which the "Absolute Idealism" of Hegel is the centre.

§ 257. It is no answer to this position that writers of this class express themselves in abhorrence of crime in general, and more particularly of such special offences as are most in the way of a sublimated transcendentalism. But this is in the same way that we speak of the pale hue of one planet and the lurid hue of another. It is a matter of opinion on our part, involving no charge of culpability on the planet. In fact, it is the Divine absorbent that has some of its outer evolutions thus tinged: it is not the planets individually. So with sin. It is dark or light,—it is lenient or heinous,—still the human perpetrator is not to be charged with it, but the Absolute ocean itself, of which man is a mere ripple.

§ 258. "But," it may be said, "is not this very much the same view as that which results from necessitarianism, a system considered an open one by the great body of Christian orthodox theologians?" The reply to this is decisive. The necessitarian, whenever, at least, he accepts the Christian orthodox formulas, recognizes the individuality and responsibility of the human will. It may be that this is inconsistent with the doctrine of necessity on any other hypothesis than that of the philosophy of Common Sense. Be this as it may, the Christian necessitarian makes the fullness of human responsibility one of the two great facts of his system. He never contemplates man's extinction or absorption. According to him the human soul is invested with the two sublimest of properties. The first of these is that of becoming a co-worker with God on earth and a co-heir with Christ in heaven. The second, almost equally sublime though inexpressibly awful, is that of being a persistent and continuous rebel against the Most High. This most decisive proof of an insoluble and repellent individuality, necessitarianism emphatically recognizes. It pictures before itself this insurrectionary will, eternally rearing its crest not only against the Almighty himself, but against its own peace and comfort. In this awful spectacle the Christian necessitarian shudderingly gazes as it were on a rock like that of St. Helena, in which a captive, confined in his island bounds, maintains in fierce, unsubdued isolation, a defiant and mocking rebellion. There is a tragic grandeur in this which shadows forth to us the individuality of the soul with a rugged sternness which even the pictures of bliss do not equal, just in the same way as the black and portentous cloud on the summer horizon is more readily traced than the sunlight fleece that is hardly distinguishable from the splendid infinite above. It ill becomes those who absorb the individual in the absolute to claim that they alone understand the dignity of human nature, and the sublimity of its mission. Nowhere are that dignity and sublimity asserted with such austere and yet such inspiring precision,—nowhere is a voice so warning and yet so cheering,—nowhere with accompaniments so august,—as by him who asserts the self-responsibility of man in making up his eternity of bliss or woe.

§ 259. *f^1. It is inconsistent with the marks of purpose and contrivance which we meet with throughout the universe.*

On this point I can do no more than refer to the first book in the present volume, as giving a summary of the argument from design.

§ 260. *g*¹. *It involves the absurdity and the self-contradiction of intelligence generated by matter; and brings us back again to a first cause, which differs from that of the theist in that while the one makes God create matter, the other makes matter create God.*

God, or the Absolute Intelligence of the Pantheist, is inseparable from nature. In the primeval stages of creation, therefore, when there was no organized life, God was matter—matter unlighted by any ray of intelligence. In the days of the sea-anemone, and of the beach-fern, the divine intelligence was purely vegetable. In future stages that intelligence would not arise above that of the insensate crustaceans that sprawled over the soft mud of the paleozoic lagoons, or the gigantic and ferocious lizards and crocodiles that ravaged the shallows. Now this is liable to a double difficulty: it makes the Perfect and Absolute—for such He is, even as the Pantheist's theory, though He be but an aggregate—it makes Him to consist of, alternately, a stone, a fish, and a beast.

It makes *matter* create *God*. Now the pantheistic objection to the theistic argument is that it makes *God* create *matter*. It is impossible, it is said by the pantheists, for the *Intelligent* to create the *Material* out of nothing. But how much more strongly does this apply to the position which modern geological discovery compels the pantheist to take, that the Material out of nothing creates the Intelligent.

CHAPTER V.

DEVELOPMENT.

a. In what the development theory consists.

§ 261. Casting aside the theory of ecclesiastical development, which scarcely falls within our present range, development may be considered as of two classes :—

a.[1] *Cosmical.* *b*[1]. *Organic.*

a[1]. *Cosmical.*

§ 262. An original and universal fire-mist, formed of nebulous vapor, existed, it is assumed, first in a state of intense heat, and then was by cooling condensed in part into a fluid, and in part into a solid. As it cooled, certain nuclei were established which became centres of aggregation to which the neighboring diffused matter was drawn. This very process, it is declared, imparts a rotatory motion. As, however, the nucleus increased to a bulb in whose circumference the centrifugal force exceeded the agglomerating force, rings would fall off which would pursue their own appropriate motion. In this way, first a central sun, and then a planetary system, may be supposed to arise. Even now, it is said, this process of development is going on, and the milky-way is but the fluid out of which future stars are to be churned.

I do not propose to go into the astronomical question

involved. Two views, as is well known, have been taken, one denying, the other affirming, the resolvability of the nebulæ. The *first* was summed up, in 1854, by Sir David Brewster,* who gives us the following conclusions. Nebulæ should be classed as follows: 1, Nebulæ that the telescope has resolved; and 2, Nebulæ that the telescope has not resolved.

§ 263. Now the latter class, as the power of the telescope increases, has gradually been giving way to the former. "As it is now an astronomical fact that nebulæ which Sir William Herschel with his finest telescopes could not resolve, and which had *no appearance* whatever of being resolvable, have been resolved into distinct stars by the magnificent reflectors of Lord Rosse, we are enabled without any hypothetical statements to place the question of the existence of star dust or purely nebulous matter, in its proper aspect; that is, we can assign a satisfactory reason to the reader for considering every nebula in the heavens as a cluster of stars which is likely to be resolved by telescopes superior to those of Lord Rosse. * * * The interesting discovery made by Lord Rosse of what is called *spiral nebulæ*, where the nebulous matter may be considered as having been thrown off by some singular cause from the centre of the nebulæ, may be regarded as hostile to the opinion that such nebulæ are composed of separate stars. * * *

"As the appearance of motion, therefore, in particular nebulæ is no proof that they consist of purely nebulous matter composed of invisible particles, we are entitled to

---

* More Worlds than One, etc., p. 175; New York, R. Carter & Bros.

draw the conclusion that this large class of celestial bodies are clusters of stars at an immense distance from our own system,—that each of the stars of which they are composed is the sun or centre of a system of planets, and that these planets are inhabited, or if we follow a strict analogy, that at least *one planet* in each of these numberless systems is like our earth, the seat of vegetable, animal, and intellectual life.

"Before we quit the subject of nebulæ, and purely nebulous matter, we must notice two points connected with the optical appearance of nebulæ which we think are strong arguments in favor of their being resolvable into stars. If a nebula consisted of phosphorescent or self-luminous atoms of nebulous matter, its light would be immensely inferior in brightness to that of the same nebula composed of suns which are provided with a luminous atmosphere for the very purpose of discharging a brilliant light. When we see, therefore, two nebulæ of the very same brightness, and find by the telescope that one of them only is resolvable into stars, we can scarcely doubt that the other is similarly composed. We cannot conceive that a nebula of phosphorescent stars could be visible at such enormous distances from our system. When a planetary nebula is equally bright in every part of its disc, like that which is a little to the south of *β Ursæ Majoris*, and which resembles a *flat disc*, 'presented to us in a plane precisely perpendicular to the visual ray,' it is impossible to regard it as nebulous matter in a state of aggregation. In like manner, all those nebulæ, which have strange and irregular shapes, indicate the absence of any force of aggregation, and authorize us to regard them as clusters of stars."

§ 264. Sir John Herschel, differing in this respect from his illustrious father, thus speaks: "We have every reason to believe, at least in the generality of cases, that a nebula is nothing more than a cluster of stars."*

§ 265. To the same effect is the language of Dr. Nichol, in his work on the Architecture of the Heavens.† Before the application of Lord Rosse's telescope to the nebula of Orion, Dr. Nichol held to the belief that this and the other masses in the heavens were to be presumed to be, in part at least, a nebulous fluid. In 1851, however, when Lord Rosse's discoveries at Parsonstown were known, Dr. Nichol thus revises his former opinion: "On the ground of a certain characteristic, Herschel felt disposed to divide unresolved nebulæ into two classes; he declined to believe one class to be stellar, because that conclusion would have constrained his acceptance of what seemed opposed by all analogy, viz., the existence of aggregations of stars in a condition of *compression* to which he had found nothing even approximately similar, in the course of his previous examination of the universe. Now, the nebula of Orion being an eminent instance of this latter class, its decisive resolution broke down the force of the characteristic on which Herschel depended as a discriminating one: it showed *that* to be a *fact,* on the presumed *improbability* of which the entire theory depended. Assuredly, it is not impossible that matter may be found somewhere in a rude or chaotic state, not

* Memoir on Nebulæ and Clusters of Stars; Lond. Phil. Trans. 1833.

† Pages 144–5.

having yet put on the organization of stars. To the abstract possibilities of existence no man dare assign any limit; but that which alone is existence or reality for the mind—the domain of its belief, is guarded by strict rules of evidence; and *now* the astronomer can adduce no justification of the assertion, that any nebula, however stubborn, ought to be interpreted contrary to the analogy of all other known objects of its kind, or termed irresolvable, except in relation to the capacity of the telescope with which he had sought to explore it."*

§ 266. I have thus given the views of these eminent writers on this vexed question. I am far, however, from thinking that there is any necessary connection between revelation and the theory on which these views rest. On the contrary, I hold there are many reasons why we should refrain from mixing the question with religion in any way. The theory itself is not capable of absolute proof. Its disproof, which at any time is at least possible, would involve, should it be thus connected with the popular faith, a shock which it is not wise unnecessarily to encounter. Let us see, then, whether there are not grounds, at least enough, to lead us to hold our opinions in this respect in abeyance.

The chief arguments which are relied on to prove the resolvablity of the nebulæ are very lucidly and felicitously stated by the author of "The Plurality of Worlds."† It is there urged that the analogy of the Magellanic Clouds, of

---

* Nichol's Architecture of the Heavens; ninth London edition, p. 145.

† Gould & Lincoln's edition, p. 135.

the Zodiacal light, and of the tails of comets, goes to show that there may be luminous irresolvable matter; that at the best, the dots into which Lord Rosse's telescope has resolved Orion are not necessarily suns, but may themselves be nebulous lumps; that the spiral shape, like "a curled feather, or whirlpool of light," exhibited by many of those nebulæ, is that which would be assumed by a luminous mass if detached from a comet when moving along its orbit; and that their form and character indicate that they are incapable of permanency or system. Hence the conclusion is taken that they are vast masses of incoherent vapor, of immense tenuity, diffused in forms more or less irregular, but all of them destitute of any regular features of solid moving bodies.

§ 267. Now let us observe that no man can risk a dogmatic assertion of either the truth or error of this position. When we reach the limit of Lord Rosse's telescope, we have opened to us, on the hypothesis that the nebulæ in sight are resolvable, a new series of nebulæ as to which we have analogy alone as a guide.

The probability may be, to use the language of Dr. Harris,* "that a still superior telescopic power would resolve other nebulous appearances and bring new ones to light; and so on without end." We then fall back on analogy. On the one side, we have the resolvability of the nebulæ whose masses the telescope has so far penetrated. On the other side, we have the prior condition of our own earth, whose surface bears witness to an almost indefinite succes-

* Pre-Adamite Earth, p. 74.

sion of stages in the process by which it was manufactured for human use.

And observe that if the latter hypothesis affects the theistic argument, it is only to strengthen its proof, in the same way that geology, by proving actual cosmical change produced by physical force, accumulates the testimony of a Divine agency. The proof of contrivance in the watch, which Dr. Paley's inquirer is supposed to pick up in a field, is greatly augmented by a visit to the watch-maker's shop, where the material is seen in the process of preparation. Our conviction of the omnipotence and benevolence of God is in like manner augmented by viewing the majestic care with which, in ages indefinitely remote, the fuel, the soil, and the irrigation of the human era were provided for.* If in the more remote of these stars there be inhabitants provided with instruments of sufficient penetration, such observers may now be viewing our globe in the course of chaotic preparation. If so, they merely see aditional evidence of the creative interposition of God. If we assume the converse to be true, the conclusion is the same.†

---

* See this point more fully discussed, *ante*, § 68, 70, etc.

† The folly of committing the church to the position of the resolvability of the nebulæ, is thus admirably stated: "The real difference between Sir David and the Essayist, with regard to the Nebular Theory, consists in the exercise or neglect of a wise discrimination. Sir David stands at a safe distance and cries out 'Fire,' but does not bring a single cup of water to stop the evil. The other pulls down the sheds which form a road for the flames from the burning out-house to the dwelling, and makes the engines play vigorously to put down

§ 268 *b*[1]. *Organic development.*

a[2]. On this point we are referred, by the author of "Vestiges of Creation," to the experiments of Mr. Crosse and Mr.

---

the conflagration. The idea that brute matter, by its own energy, can exalt itself successively into the fungus, the zoophyte, the insect, the fish, the quadruped, and, even still higher, into human intelligence, is a falsehood not only opposed to all the facts of science, but near of kin to open atheism. But the opinion that it is formed, at first, in a diffused or nebulous condition, and left to condense, by its own laws, into globes and systems, receptive, in due season, of vegetable and animal life—is quite consistent with the most profound religious faith, while it has certainly several analogies in known facts, and some presumptions of science in its favor. It detracts nothing from the wisdom really implied in the act of creation, and only renders it more profound in its own nature, and more gradual in its manifestation. An oak is not the less beautiful or wonderful, as a work of Divine power, because it is developed from a little acorn, in which none of its properties could be seen by the keenest eye, than if it were formed in a moment, with all its gnarled boughs and graceful foliage complete. There may be minds which would regard the work of creation as most worthy of the Almighty, if a vast number of larger and of smaller globes were called into being suddenly in their actual form, and then placed at their several distances, and set in motion around each other and their own axes, by so many distinct and independent impulses of the Creator's hand. But the same principle would seem to involve the consequence that every form of vegetable, animal, and human life would also have been introduced at one and the same moment; and the six days' interval in Genesis, and the long periods of geology, would be alike excluded, as disguising the simple energy of Omnipotence. The view, it seems to us, is equally magnificent, and rather more consistent with the analogies just named; that matter may have been created in a state in which its future harmonies

Weekes, by which, as is alleged, a small insect (*Acarus Crossii* or *Acarus Galvanicus*) was generated through a voltaic battery in a saturated solution of the silicate of potash or the nitrate of copper, or the ferrocyanate of potassium. This supposed discovery was made in 1837, by Mr. Andrew Crosse, and was first published in detail in the Transactions of the London Electrical Society.* Experiments, tending to the same result, were made in 1841–2 by Mr. W. A. Weekes, and published in the same journal.†

Now, it is not for me to go into a technical examination of the experiments by which Mr. Crosse and Mr. Weekes were led to the conclusion stated above. It is sufficient, and it is far more appropriate, to quote the opinion, on this very issue, of men of acknowledged scientific authority. The discovery in question is supposed to have been made in

---

were not conspicuous, though all virtually involved in the conditions first assigned it; and that the wisdom of the Creator may be shown by its gradual development, under the laws He had given, into a state receptive of higher modes of being; while every step in the upward ascent, from mere matter to the vegetable, from the vegetable to the animal, the lower animals to man, from man defectible, and then actually fallen, to man redeemed and glorified, needs the immediate interposition of the great Lord and Master of the universe. Such is the view implied in the Essay, and more plainly advocated in other works of its author; and the attempt to confound it with the virtual atheism of the 'Vestiges' evinces a serious defect either of Christian candor or critical discernment." (*London Christian Observer*, July, 1855, p. 47.)

* Vol. from 1837 to 1840, p. 11.

† Vol. from 1841 to 1843, pp. 240, 391.

1838. Since 1842, no additional facts have been educed, though the subject has received severe and continued scrutiny on the part of a body of observers, many of them by no means prejudiced against the truth of the hypothesis.*

---

* Since the above was written, the alleged discoveries of M. Pouchet, Professor of Zoology at Rouen, have been brought to the author's notice. M. Pouchet claims to have "seen cryptogams and animalcules to be produced in vessels when every organic germ has been previously destroyed, and when the air had been washed in sulphuric acid or had traversed a tube of porcelain heated to a red heat. He has even succeeded in developing organic beings in artificial air and also in pure oxygen." The details of one of his experiments are as follows:—A flask, holding a litre, was filled with boiling water, then hermetically sealed with the greatest precaution, then inverted in a mercury trough; then, when the water is cold, it was opened under the mercury, and half a litre of pure oxygen introduced. Immediately after, was added to it, under the mercury, a small box of hay weighing ten grammes, which had just been raised in a flask, by means of a stove, to a temperature of 100° C., and kept at this temperature for thirty minutes. The flask was then hermetically sealed by the aid of its stopper ground with emery; and to make it sure, when taken from the mercury, a coat of varnish and vermilion was put over the aperture. Eight days afterwards, small globules were found in the liquid and on the hay. On opening the flask at the end of ten days, the oxygen appeared to have remained pure. The whitish globules were due to a fungus in tufts, which Mr. Montagne, the micrographer, called *Aspergillus Pouchetii*.

A plant is thus developed in a medium from which it was endeavored to exclude every species of organic germ; but the conclusion of M. Pouchet is quite too general, as no facts prove that every kind of vitality was destroyed during the exposure of the hay for thirty minutes to 100° C.

In addition to this, it is observed, as is mentioned by the journal

Let us see, then, what, after the lapse of twenty years, is the accepted conclusion with regard to this phenomenon.

§ 269. First, let me cite from Mulder's "Chemistry of Vegetable and Animal Physiology," of which the edition before me is that of Mr. J. F. W. Johnston, published in London in 1849, at a period when the alleged "Acarus Crossii" was fresh before the scientific eye. "What we know," says this author, "of the acarus scabiei, the filaria aracunculus, the echino-cocci, and a great many other entozoa, shows that they may be produced from ordinary organic molecules in the animal body, as every small organic globule of mucus, for instance, or of milk, or of pus, etc. is formed." "The idea of an ovum, therefore, coincides exactly with that of an *organic molecule;* that is, of such a molecule as consists of elements which may exhibit themselves under a change of circumstances in infinite modifications, may form new combinations, attract other elements, incorporate them, unite into definite compounds, and thus separate from other bodies with which they were originally combined." "The idea of an ovum is thus reduced in truth to that of an organic molecule; and the dispute as to equivocal generation and epigenesis is at an end."*

---

last quoted, that it is shown "by the experiments of Schultze and Schwann, as well as by those of Schroeder and Dusch," "that animal substances do not ferment when they are inclosed in air which has previously traversed a red hot tube," "and that these same substances may be preserved indefinitely in air which has previously been made to pass through a tube containing cotton." (*Silliman's Journ.*, March, 1859, p. 253.)

* Mulder's Chemistry, etc. Lond. ed., 1849, p. 77–8.

I have next the third edition of Dr. Carpenter's "Principles of Physiology," issued in London in 1851. "It may be considered," says this authoritative writer, "as a fundamental truth of Physiological Science, that *every living organism has had its origin in a pre-existing organism.* The doctrine of 'spontaneous generation,' or the supposed origination of organized structures *de novo,* out of assemblages of inorganic particles, although at different times sustained with a considerable show of argument, based on a specious array of facts, cannot now be said to have any claim whatever to be received as even a possible hypothesis; all the facts on which it claimed to rest having been either themselves disproved, or having been found satisfactorily explicable on the general principle, *omne vivum ex ovo.*"*

§ 270. Next let us take up a work of great weight and authority on the special topic of Infusorial Animalcules, published in London in 1851, by Mr. Andrew Pritchard. Here, under the title of "the Supposed Method of Manufacturing Infusoria," we have the statement by the author that the "creatures said to have been thus brought into existence, that have come under my observation, were neither the most minute nor the most simple in organization." "That some mistake exists with respect to communicating vitality to matter by this means, there cannot be a doubt."†

§ 271. Take, also, the Micrographic Dictionary,—a work

---

* Carp. Phys., ed. Blanchard & Lea, 1851, p. 866. See also remarks of same author on p. 859, in reply to Vestiges of Creation, on the subject of animal development.

† A History of Infusorial Animalcules, etc., by Andrew Pritchard, M.R.I. London: Whittaker & Co., 1852, p. 27.

of great exactness and beauty,—published in 1856, by Messrs. Griffith and Henfrey.* Here we find all the hypotheses of spontaneous generation successively exploded.†

§ 272. More curt, though not less decisive, is the statement of M. Agassiz, in his late great work, (1858.) "I do not know what physicists may think about them now, (the *Acari Crossii*,) but I know that there is scarcely a zoologist who doubts they only exhibited a mistake."‡

§ 273. Passing, however, these authorities, let us notice the following points as accounting for the existence of these animals without resorting to the hypothesis of non-natural generation:—Life in infusoria of this class can be maintained in strong chemical solutions. We have a striking illustration of this in Dr. Harvey's contribution to the Smithsonian Institute, entitled "Nereis Boreali-Americana," published in 1858. In this elaborate and comprehensive paper occurs the following passage:—"A remarkable instance of the action of a minute alga on a chemical solution was pointed out to me by Prof. Bache, as occurring in the vessels of sulphate of copper kept in the electrotyping department of the Coast Survey Office at Washington. A slender confervoid alga infests the vats containing sulphate of copper, and proves very destructive. It decomposes the salt and assimilates the sulphuric acid, rejecting (as indigestible!) the copper, which is deposited round its threads in a metallic form. * * * * Species of the former

* London: John Van Voorst, 1856.

† *Ibid.*, pp. 20, 288; articles *Air*, *Generation.*

‡ 1 Contrib. to Nat. Hist. U.S., p. 9.

genus (*Oscillatoriæ*) are found even in the boiling waters of the Icelandic Geysers. Of the latter (*Calothrices*) one species at least, *Calothrix nivea*, is very common in hot sulphur springs, and I observed it in great plenty in the streams running from the inflammable springs at Niagara."* Some of the same genus, we are afterwards told, "diffuse life" "in the snows of the Polar regions," and on the "Polar ice."†

The creatures produced by Messrs. Crosse and Weekes, reproduced themselves, in the same chemical solution, by natural generation. If the solution was not strong enough to prevent this in the second generation, why was it too strong to prevent it in the first? Again, if the parents were produced by an electric shock, how is it that the pattern struck by the same mechanism and at the same blow, varied, in one case a male being produced, and in another a female?

The air contains the eggs or germinal molecules of innumerable forms of animal life, capable of entering into activity whenever they meet with the requisite conditions. If the chemical solutions used by Messrs. Crosse and Weekes supplied these conditions, as was proved by life afterwards continued, the germinating of the Acarus depended only upon the question whether the surrounding air was freighted with its eggs. That this was probably so is shown by innumerable productions, without the aid of the voltaic battery, under similar conditions.

Vitality may remain dormant for an indefinite period,

---

* Dr. Harvey's Nereis Boreali-Americana, p. 6. † *Ibid.*, p. 18.

ready to be awaked whenever the proper call arrives. In piercing a well in Maine, forty miles from the sea, sand was dug up which must have been covered thousands and tens of thousands of years. It was scattered on the soil, and in the next season there sprung up the beach-plum, a tree peculiar to the sea-shore, whose seed must have been covered up with the sand. Wheat taken from mummies is well known to form now a distinct species. Flies, or insects which have been for years dormant in bottles, come to life on exposure to the air. Raspberry seed, taken from the stomach of a man who was buried seventeen years before, germinated when planted.*

On the "development" hypothesis, these animalcules should be monads, or the rudimental types. They are the first blows of the "electric force" on matter. But, on the contrary, they are very complicated little creatures, neither "minute" nor "simple." "If," asks Mr. Walker, on this point, with great force, "Mr. Crosse could begin with the Articulata and create an Acarus which had no parent, why may not the Divine Power accomplish as much? If Mr. Crosse can form both germ and insect by the same process, why may not the Divine Power form both germ and mammifer?"†

§ 274. Let us pass, however, to the remaining analogies relied on by the author of the "Vestiges of Creation."

*b*2. The tad-pole "develops," he tells us, into a "frog;" forgetting this change is the growth of each individual of

---

* Carpenter's Physiology, p. 75.

† God Revealed in Creation, p. 105.

the frog species, and not the progressive ascent of the species itself. It would be just as correct to cite the accession of individual beards as a proof of the "development" of the human race.

c^2. To the larva and the butterfly the same remark is applicable.

d^2. The working bee, which may be transformed into the queen bee, on a particular change of diet, is merely an illustration of a bifurcate structure in a particular species. The character of a species, to be complete, must include all its forms; and from this aggregate, in order to be a development, there must be an ascent. Now, in the case of the queen bee, there is but a subordinate modification, not a general ascent.

e^2. Cultivated plants and tame animals. Here there is no development, but merely a modification; and the plant or animal, if excluded from human care, reverts back to its original type.

After considering these points, which are all that the defenders of organic development have adduced, we may well concur in the position of Dr. Carpenter, "that no higher type has ever originated through an advance in developmental powers; for although various instances have been brought forward to justify the assertion that such is possible, yet these instances entirely fail to establish the analogy that is sought to be drawn from them."*

---

* Carpenter's Physiology, p. 869. See also on this point an interesting article by Professor Dana, in Biblioth. Sac. for 1846, p. 100–2.

b. GENERAL PROPOSITIONS BY WHICH THIS THEORY CAN BE MET.

§ 275. a^1. *No progressive cosmical development.*

There is no progressive cosmical development. The transformations of the globe, to which geology bears witness, were not symmetrical and gradual, but exceptional and convulsive, involving a break of continuity, and a new arrangement of the material before existing.*

§ 276. b^1. *Premeditation preceded creation.*

There is evidence of premeditation prior to creation. Every prior type is an anticipation of that which is to succeed; all point back to an original comprehensive design and omnipotent and omniscient designer. "Enough has been already said," is the calm summary of Agassiz, "to show that the leading thought which runs through the successions of all organized beings in past ages is manifested again in new, in the phases of the development of living representatives of these different types. *It exhibits everywhere the working of the same creative mind, through all time and upon the whole surface of the globe.*"†

§ 277. c^1. *New forms of life introduced at distinct periods.*

We have specific proof of the introduction at precise periods not only of new forms of animal life, but of the reapplication of life itself.‡

§ 278. d^1. *Advance sometimes broken by retrogression.*

---

* See *ante,* § 79, 173.

† Essay on Classification, p. 116. See *ante,* § 32–35.

‡ See *ante,* § 78–9. See also Silliman's Journal, 1858, pp. 204–5.

As the terraces of geology ascend, and higher types appear, this superior order is broken in upon by an increased number of abnormal and degraded shapes.*

§ 279. e^1. *The rudimental atoms themselves prove contrivance.*

The rudimental atoms are impressed to an eminent degree with the marks of a Creator. We have fifty-four or fifty-five substances which are indivisible and final, and which form the individual syllables of which the great book of nature is made up. But each one of these syllables shows a contrivance whose exquisiteness appears the more vividly as we contemplate the vast number of combinations to which they are adapted. First we have, as the marshaling agents of these atoms, three primary physical forces—polarization, chemical affinity, and cohesion. Then we find, as the manual by which these marshaling agents are to act, laws prescribing certain proportions, definite as to number and weight, in which alone these atoms unite.† In the august economy and simplicity by which these elements, in the various combinations of which they are capable, are made to serve the almost infinite purposes of cosmical creation, we may find additional reason for concurring in the remarks of Sir John Herschel:—"These discoveries effectually destroy the idea of an external self-existent matter,

---

* See Hugh Miller, Foot-Prints of the Creator, p. 192, etc. See also the theological bearings of these phenomena very strikingly depicted by Dr. Bushnell, Nature and the Supernat., p. 208.

† Thus oxygen and nitrogen are constructed as follows:—14 of oxygen to 8 of hydrogen: 14—24; 14—32; 14—40.

by giving to each of its atoms at once the essential characteristics of a manufactured article and a subordinate agent."*

§ 280. f^1. *This primary care presumes a continuing Providence.*

If we assume, as does the development hypothesis, that each of these atoms contains the generative apparatus for the production of all future forms of life, then not only is the argument from contrivance indefinitely strengthened by the exhibition of so transcendently wonderful an apparatus, but we have increased energy given to the argument for a continuing special Providence. Is it probable that a God with wisdom, forethought, goodness, and power enough to construct such marvelously delicate and beneficent mechanisms, should, after the creative work is done, retire from the work of guiding and guarding that which was thus carefully made?†

§ 281. g^1. *Physical forces involving a director.*

Physical forces, themselves incapable of action unless directed by intelligence, have from time to time operated "to work out a condition of things which evince the presiding agency of the Divine mind, adjusting all the changes from first to last in view of a future definite end."‡

§ 282. h^1. *Creations exhibiting reciprocal adaptations.*

Creations, widely distinct in time, and having no connec-

---

* See God Revealed in Creation, p. 32, by Mr. Walker, a book to which the reader is referred, as containing an able elucidation of this special topic.

† See *ante*, § 234–5. ‡ Walker's God Revealed in Creation, p. 78.

tion as to organic life, so fit in and adapt themselves to each other as to make one the complement of the other. Take, as an illustration of this, the juxtaposition, through the agency of widely separate creations, of coal, lime, and iron, in those neighborhoods and climate, where they would be most needed and most likely to be worked.*

§ 283. i^1. *"Development" makes "matter," create "mind."*

The development hypothesis, like pantheism, involves the absurdity of matter creating mind.†

§ 284. k^1. *A first cause still remains.*

The clock that goes a hundred years, requires winding up as much as one that goes a day. There is this distinction, however. The argument from contrivance increases as we increase the period during which the clock runs without being rewound.

"Nor can any such theory," says the author of the Greyson letters, "really affect the question of *Theism* at all; if, indeed, such rare 'transformations,' and 'transmutations,' and 'developments' of organized beings, as it supposes, (were there but any proof of them,) ought not rather to *enhance* the proof of Divine power and intelligence. Surely such transmutations not less require power and intelligence than the received hypothesis of successive creations; for, even if the elements of the material universe, if matter itself, be supposed eternal, it can never be proved that the properties and laws in virtue of which it has been 'developed' into such wondrous results inherently belong to it;

---

* See *ante*, § 70.

† See *ante*, § 260.

or that if some properties *did* belong to it, a chance medley combination or blindly necessary application of them would make such a symmetrical and harmonious universe. If A, B, and C be all stamped by their respective signatures of design, it were strange to suppose that that inference is invalidated, because C came from B, and B from A."

The "churn" by which the fluid of the milky-way is made up into stars, requires the application of an intelligent motive power, at least as much as if those stars were worked up by hand.

The "monad" that contains the germs of all future existences of the same family, shows a care at least as minute, a prevision at least as searching, a scheme of government at least as comprehensive, as is exhibited in a special continuous providence, giving to each birth its impulse, and each event its particular direction.

The author of the "Vestiges of Creation" himself, is careful—and it is believed sincerely—to disavow the anti-theistic inferences so generally attributed to his scheme. In point of fact, he himself finds an original motive power essential to make "development," more plausible. "*The electric spark*," he tells us, "*struck life* into an elementary and *reproductive* germ; and sea-plants, the food of animals, first decked the rude pavement of the sea."*

---

* Observe on this point, the following passage from the "Westminster Review" for April, 1858, which may be considered as abandoning the whole of the anti-theistic inference from the development hypothesis:—"It remains only to point out that while the genesis of the solar system, and of countless other systems like it, is

thus rendered comprehensible, the ultimate mystery continues as great as ever. The problem of existence is not solved; it is simply removed farther back. The nebular hypothesis throws no light upon the origin of diffused matter; and diffused matter needs as much accounting for as concrete matter. The genesis of an atom is not easier to conceive than the genesis of a planet. Nay, indeed, so far from making the universe less wonderful than before, it makes it more wonderful. Creation by manufacture, is a much lower thing, than creation by evolution. A man can put together a machine, but he cannot make a machine develop itself. The ingenious artisan, able as some have been so far to imitate vitality as to produce a mechanical piano-forte player, may in some sort conceive how, by greater skill, a complete man might be artificially produced; but he is totally unable to conceive how such a complex organism gradually arises out of a minute structureless germ. That our harmonious universe once existed potentially as formless diffused matter, and has slowly grown into its present organized state, is a far more astonishing fact than would have been its formation after the artificial method vulgarly supposed. The nebular hypothesis implies a first cause as much transcending 'the mechanical god of Paley,' as this does the fetish of the savage."

THE END.

www.ingramcontent.com/pod-product-compliance
Lightning Source LLC
LaVergne TN
LVHW020115110826
845151LV00001B/166

* 9 7 8 1 4 2 5 5 4 2 3 7 5 *